I0884142

Social Studies Curriculum and Methods for the Caribbean

Social Studies Curriculum and Methods for the Caribbean

Anthony D. Griffith and James L. Barth

University of the West Indies Press
Jamaica • Barbados • Trinidad and Tobago

University of the West Indies Press
7A Gibraltar Hall Road Mona
Kingston 7 Jamaica
www.uwipress.com

© 2006 by Anthony D. Griffith and James L. Barth

All rights reserved. Published 2006.

10 09 08 07 06 5 4 3 2 1

CATALOGUING IN PUBLICATION DATA

Griffith, Anthony D.
Social studies curriculum and methods for the Caribbean / Anthony D. Griffith and James L. Barth

p. cm.

Includes bibliographical references.

ISBN: 976-640-125-X

1. Social science - Study and teaching (Primary) - Caribbean, English-speaking.
2. Social science - Study and teaching (Secondary) - Caribbean, English-speaking.
3. Curriculum planning - Caribbean, English-speaking. I. Barth, James L. II. Title.

LB1584.5.C3G74 2006 372.83

Book and cover design by Robert Harris.
Set in Book Antiqua 10.5/14 x 29

Printed in the United States of America.

Dedicated to all Caribbean social studies teachers

Contents

8 Practising the Skill of Asking Questions / 173

9 Identifying and Writing Complete Behavioural Objectives / 189

13 Planning to Teach Social Studies / 284

Preface

The authors have been writing this book for several years, knowing full well that the book would be finished in the twenty-first century. This means that a book on curriculum and methods of teaching social studies would need to reflect a twenty-first-century view of how students learn and remember their social studies instruction. This curriculum and methods book is intended to be different from most others. For example, there are over forty illustrations, so that the reader can both read and visualize the ideas expressed in the book. Also, the most common criticism of schools and teachers is that they are offering instruction that is, at best, thirty, perhaps even fifty, years behind what educators already know. Much of the research on teaching and learning, and most of the recommendations based on that research, have not been applied in present-day schools. How can a social studies teacher of the twenty-first century possibly catch up with what the experts have learned in the twentieth century? The question of catching up to what is already known, but not practised, is a central concern for teacher educators, such as the authors and others charged with the preparation of professional teachers.

Just how professional can you be as a social studies teacher if you are fifty years behind times? This book proposes to narrow the gap between what is known and what is practised, by providing both pre-service and practising classroom teachers, with basic information and training that will, hopefully, wipe out the fifty-year gap, and allow teachers to think as twenty-first-century professionals. Clearly, the purpose of the book is to apply what has been learned in the twentieth century to the preparation of professional teachers in the twenty-first century.

For Whom Was the Book Written?

This book was designed for teachers in sixteen distinct Caribbean communities. Those sixteen communities include Anguilla, Antigua and

Barbuda, Bahamas, Barbados, Belize, Dominica, Grenada, Guyana, Jamaica, Montserrat, St Kitts and Nevis, St Lucia, St Vincent and the Grenadines, Tortola, Trinidad and Tobago, and Turks and Caicos. These communities are the focus of the book's illustrations, programmed lessons, examples, and references, such that the reader will be able to identify with the content of the book.

What Are the Major Topics and How Are They Organized?

The content of the book is organized into thirteen chapters, which may be used in sequence, as in a social studies methods course, or could stand alone for use in workshops and seminars. Though the central theme is social studies education, some of the chapters can also be used with almost every subject area, because the basic concepts discussed in each chapter are the same for all subject matter. A brief review of the chapters will demonstrate the sequential development of the book.

Chapter 1 discusses the meaning of social studies as citizenship education in the Caribbean. Chapter 2 discusses what is known about the growth and development of children. Then, based on that understanding, a school social studies programme can be developed. Chapter 3 identifies how students learn and remember best through effective teaching practices. Chapter 4 focuses on the specific methods, techniques and strategies that can be used in a developmental, sequentially planned curriculum, and that are appropriate practices for effective teaching. Chapter 5 discusses the specific application of selected methods, techniques, and strategies, while chapter 6 identifies audio-visual aids and their use and construction as they relate to the methods, techniques, and strategies. Chapter 7 presents the three taxonomies: cognitive, affective, and psychomotor, which offer a system of classification that helps to guide classroom teaching. Also based on the taxonomies, chapter 8 provides a programmed practice to develop the skill of asking questions. Based on the taxonomies, chapter 9 provides a programmed practice to develop the skill of writing complete behavioural objectives which are precise guides to classroom teaching, and chapter 10 encourages the practice of creating knowledge through an understanding of how facts, concepts, and generalizations become knowledge. Chapter 11, based upon chapter 10, demonstrates how knowledge is created through a problem-solving method. Chapter 12 demonstrates how teachers would evaluate growth and development in learning, thinking and performance. Chapter 13, based upon all the previous chapters, demonstrates how annual, unit, and daily lesson plans can be designed.

In summary, if you know how children grow and develop, what the research says about how children learn best, what are alternative teaching strategies, what is the appropriate age and grade level of skills, attitudes, and physical development, how to ask different levels of questions, how to state behavioural objectives for lessons, understand how to create knowledge, how to apply the creation of knowledge, how to evaluate student progress, and finally, how to plan lessons based on all the above, then you are a twenty-first-century professional teacher.

Acknowledgements

No book for teachers should be written without consulting the people who will use the book. The authors wish to express their thanks and appreciation to the following persons and organizations for their support and critical input:

Mrs Elizabeth Cardenas, Belize Teachers' College, Belize

Mrs Donna Allman, St Christopher Primary School, Barbados

Mrs Suzanne Ellis, Parkinson Secondary School, Barbados

Mrs Hyacinth Harris, Bay Primary School, Barbados

Ms Ancillia Louis, Sir Arthur Lewis Community College, St Lucia

Mrs Renee Girard, Sir Arthur Lewis Community College, St Lucia

Dr Henry Hinds, Educational Reform Unit, Organisation of Eastern Caribbean States, St Lucia

Mrs Marjorie Brathwaite, Educational Reform Unit, Organisation of Eastern Caribbean States, St Lucia

Ms Gweneth Hanley, Curriculum Development Unit, Ministry of Education, St Kitts

Ms Jacquelin Chiverton, St Kitts

Ms Delyth Christmas, St Kitts

Ms Valerie Richardson, St Kitts

Mrs Merlyn Jno-Baptiste, Roseau, Dominica

Ms Maxine Moore, Erdiston Teachers' College, Barbados

Mr Frank Forde, Bay Primary School, Barbados

The Audio/Visual Resource Centre of the Ministry of Education, Barbados

The authors also wish to recognize the invaluable contribution of Mrs Barbara Barth, who typed and prepared the original manuscripts and worked on many of the illustrations; Mr Carl Branch of the Educational Media Services, University of the West Indies, Cave Hill, Barbados, who worked to provide the several photographs; and a very special word of appreciation for Mrs Beverley Marshall, for her patience and dedication in putting together the final edition of the manuscript. Without the input and dedication of these persons, the text would never have become a reality.

A very special word of appreciation also for the assistance of Mrs Donna Allman, senior teacher at St Christopher Primary School, and for the staff and students who are featured, with permission, in the photographs.

Finally, the authors wish to acknowledge the support received, towards secretarial assistance, fieldwork and materials, from the Campus Research Awards Fund of the Cave Hill campus of the University of the West Indies.

1

Social Studies Is Citizenship Education

A country's heritage and aspirations are the real basis for teaching social studies.

Introduction

The national pledge of Grenada speaks of "justice and equality for all" and of upholding the laws and institutions of the country. While in Dominica, the pledge commits citizens to working in the service of the country and of fellow citizens, and to building a prosperous and peaceful nation.

These national aspirations are all noble and important, and their fulfilment depends on citizens who are well informed about the local and national society and issues, and who are committed to achieving the national goals. All these aspirations are addressed through the school subject that has, as its major goal, to prepare our young people for citizenship. This subject is social studies.

The aims of the social studies programme in St Lucia is "improved behaviour through the acquisition of knowledge, skills and attitudes which are pertinent in the lives of children, both now and in the future"; and most curricula or syllabuses in Caribbean schools include, in their aims and major objectives, some reference to knowledge of local social institutions, social skills, and the development of pro-social behaviours and civic responsibilities.

Social studies, from its early beginnings, was intended as a nation-building subject, as distinct from other fields of study, because each country that adopts social studies as its citizenship education programme uniquely develops the subject based upon that country's history, experience, and social realities. Even though social studies content uniquely reflects the image of a particular country, the field itself has evolved certain basic foundational beliefs. We need, however, to first identify what exactly is social studies.

The Goal of Social Studies Is Citizenship Education

The term "social studies" was first used to identify a particular area of the school curriculum that was devoted to social concerns and citizenship. The school was created by the society to transmit portions of cultural heritage and to prepare the country's youth for life in society. Since primary education reaches most students, its curriculum is a general one to which all citizens are expected to be exposed if they are to be productive citizens in a democracy. Thus, while the total school programme contributes to citizen education, social studies, by nature of its curriculum, is expected to provide the formal instruction for effective citizenship.

Another major focus of the subject, from its inception, was the provision of a framework for citizenship and for cultivating "civic competence". This, in the American tradition, involves a conscious effort to critically examine the workings of democracy with a view to producing informed citizens who are competent to make reasoned decisions for the public good and to strengthen their democratic institutions. Some of the indicators of this civic competence are seen as (1) knowledge of the institutions, structures and processes of government, (2) familiarity with one's rights and responsibilities, (3) an understanding of current conditions and problems, (4) loyalty to one's country and principles of government, (5) monitoring public policy and engaging in action to influence it, and (6) tolerance of diversity. Clearly inherent in all of these competencies is an intention to empower individuals to share in the governing of their society and of any groups to which they belong, and to develop virtues of thoughtful, reasoned citizenship.

What do we understand by the term "citizenship"? This term is often limited to mean being a native or naturalized member of a country with accompanying rights and responsibilities. The rights are those granted by the country, while the responsibilities are duties required of citizens. However, social studies includes a broader definition of citizenship to mean the enhancement of human dignity and worth through membership in various social, political and economic groups at various levels, from the family, to the nation, and even the world. As human beings with dignity and worth, we share citizenship with our community, our nation, and all people throughout the world. All of these shared citizenships carry with them rights and responsibilities. Social studies, as citizenship education, is intended to prepare pupils to assume these shared rights and responsibilities as their world of knowledge and experience expands.

Every country is concerned with citizenship education, and those countries that have adopted social studies as a school subject have, in reality, committed themselves to an integration of the social sciences and humanities for the purpose of citizenship education. But why this emphasis on integration? The assumption is that citizens do not think about problems and issues in narrow specific terms, such as in only economic terms, or only political, psychological, sociological, anthropological, geographic, or historical terms. Scholars in the social sciences and the humanities (literature, philosophy, art, and so on) tend to devote their study to particular disciplines, and they often attempt to isolate information into specific fields of study – for example, history, government, and geography. The point is, however, that life is not at all like the separate social science disciplines, because citizens face the issues of life as complex, interrelated happenings. Social studies, in imitating real-life situations, deals essentially with integrating life experiences into a meaningful pattern for the individual citizen.

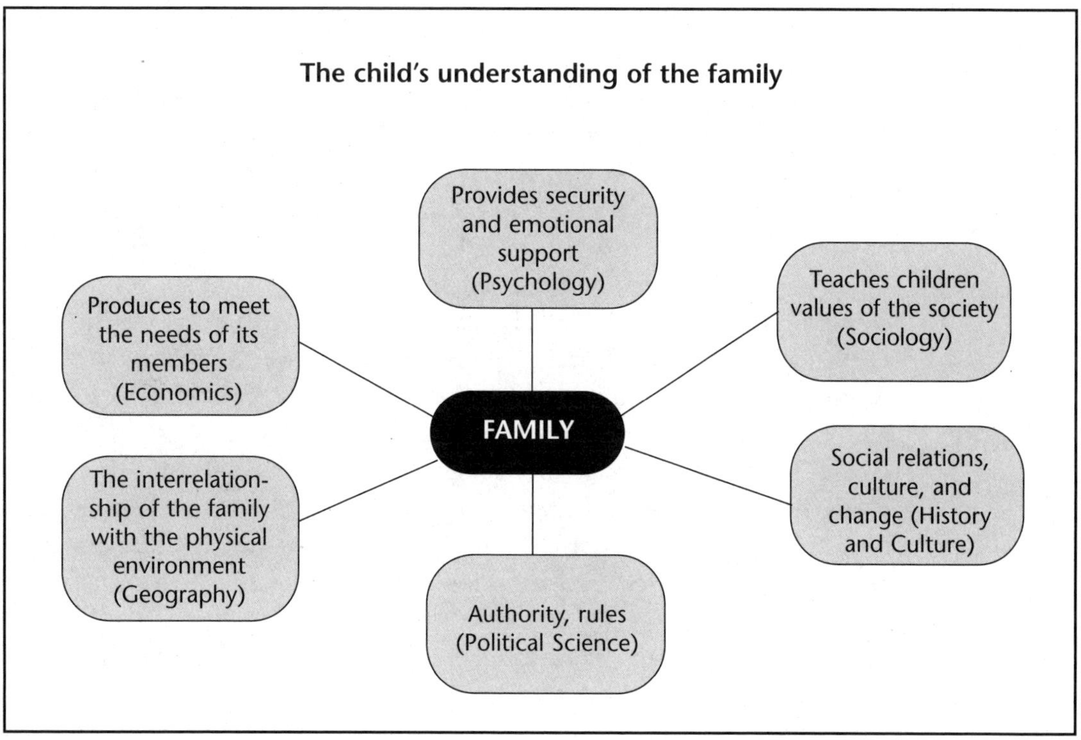

Figure 1.1: The Family

Social studies educators believe that citizens understand problems and issues of personal concern as integrated wholes. Children start school with a sense of how things are integrated, such as family or the village. As one experiences formal education, intellectual walls are built between the subject matter. The more one becomes schooled, the more walls are built between the subjects studied, and the more specialized one becomes. Thus, education, which really starts with integration of knowledge, often ends, after many years of study, with highly specialized areas of knowledge. However, citizenship responsibilities demand that citizens be able to integrate knowledge in order to adequately investigate issues, to solve problems, and to be able to make decisions. A social studies curriculum promotes the integration of human experience for the purpose of making effective decisions about persistent and continuing problems and issues that face a person, a community, or even the world and the universe.

Citizenship in a Changing World

We live in a rapidly changing world, which has made us quite different from earlier generations, and it would be difficult, if not impossible, to impede change and progress as we move into the twenty-first century. In fact, it is rapid change that has caused social studies to be created as an important field of study. In no area has change occurred more than in the individual's duties and responsibilities associated with being a citizen. Earlier generations were citizens of their family, their group, their village, perhaps their local region. But with independence and development, rights, duties, and responsibilities have changed. Development has often meant the growth of urban areas, industry, and population, together with environmental problems and the demand for more social services. Although we may still plough the field with oxen, we can also, through space programmes, reach for the moon and stars beyond. Besides the local community, we are now citizens of nations, citizens of a region, and citizens of the world and the universe. Living in a complex world requires citizens to be better educated and more flexible than their predecessors. Through change and development, we have learned that we are not alone; we are interrelated and interdependent, and have thus acquired an expanded, broader view of being a citizen. The social studies curriculum is intended to reflect the changes brought about by development and by the expanding sense of wider responsibilities of citizenship.

Essential Beliefs about Social Studies

The fact that social studies is applied in unique and different ways in each country often means that the beliefs supporting a social studies programme are not always clearly understood. Many independent countries have adopted a social studies approach to citizenship education as one way of ridding that country of an earlier colonial influence. The colonial system emphasized the values and beliefs of the colonial power through a separate-subject approach, and with a rather heavy emphasis in knowledge and factual information. Social studies, however, emphasizes nation building through stressing the history, traditions, values, and beliefs of a particular country as well as a sense of a broader view of citizenship.

There are differing definitions of social studies reflecting the varied cultural contexts in which the subject area is applied to citizenship education in the various countries. But are there any essential beliefs that are basic to a social studies programme?

There are, according to the literature, at least four essential beliefs that have guided the development and adoption of social studies during the twentieth century:

1. The goal of social studies is citizenship education.
2. The social sciences and humanities should be integrated for the purpose of achieving the goal of citizenship education.
3. The proper content of social studies is persistent and contemporary social/personal conflicts, issues, and problems expressed as concepts, topics, and themes.
4. Effective citizenship education requires the active practice of enquiry, problem solving, and decision making throughout the social studies curriculum.

If these are the essential beliefs, then a definition of social studies might be that social studies is the integration of social science and humanities concepts for the purpose of practising problem-solving/decision-making citizenship skills on issues of personal and social concern.

The Four Citizenship Skills

The definition of social studies mentions citizenship skills and the practice of these on social and personal issues. A social studies programme, which has the development of responsible citizenship as its goal, must therefore provide students with the skills that allow them to (1) gain knowledge, (2) process information, (3) examine values and beliefs, and (4) actively participate as citizens in society. Often these skills are expressed as cognitive skills, affective skills, psychomotor skills, and social/interpersonal skills. Although these sets of terms are essentially compatible, it is our judgement that gaining knowledge, processing, valuing, and participating are words that better describe the skills assigned to citizenship and the skills that should be taught in a social studies curriculum.

Most schooling centres on *gaining knowledge* through reading textbooks, writing reports, researching, and the things done in order to pass tests. But the skill of *processing information* is both more important and more difficult, and is related to the democratic way of life.

Processing is a form of reasoning and has to do with how knowledge is used. Some examples of rational processing systems are as follows: enquiry, problem solving, reflective thinking, critical thinking, and discovery, all of which are logical ways of deciding what is the truth. All of these reasoning systems are designed to establish proof, which simply means a system to establish what is accurate and true, an absolute necessity for effective, democratic decision making.

The third skill is the *examination of values and beliefs.* The assumption here is that pupils ought to have the skill to identify what they believe and value, and to think about why they believe it. A democracy requires citizens to be able to examine the consequences of holding their beliefs and values. What this skill is suggesting is that values drive behaviour (how we act), and because citizens make choices by supporting and voting on issues, they should be clear about what they value. In short, learn to "know thyself".

The fourth skill is *participation.* What should be the end product of gaining knowledge, processing information, and examining values? The answer would appear to be using these skills to participate in decisions and actions about the things that affect the quality of one's life.

The Nature of Social Participation

Most writers in social studies view the subject as being underpinned by a commitment to social and individual development and improvement, and this goal, it is argued, can perhaps best be achieved through preparing our young people to examine real and existing social problems, issues and events, with a view to understanding them and examining possible solutions to real problems and issues. Social participation may be defined as engagement in active roles, in performing social tasks and activities, both in and outside of school, which strengthen one's knowledge, skills, and values and which involve the real-life application of what one is learning. Social participation thus becomes, in effect, the second major goal of social studies instruction, and a vehicle for engaging students in social criticism on issues of public concern and for bringing these into the classroom in the form of real-life situations.

In summary, the democratic way of life can be developed by learning to practise the four skills of (1) gaining information, (2) thinking rationally through a systematic process such as reflective enquiry, (3) examining values and beliefs, and (4) learning to participate as a thoughtful member of society.

The Development of Social Studies in the Caribbean

The origins of social studies in the Caribbean lie in our colonial past. Although the title "social studies" is relatively new to the Caribbean, the purpose and content of it, as a formal school subject, originated with the colonial settlement of the Caribbean islands by European countries in the fifteenth and sixteenth centuries. Since that time, citizenship education in the Caribbean may be seen as evolving through three phases: (1) the colonial period, (2) the post-colonial period, and (3) the period of the modern development of social studies.

The Colonial Period

Phase one marks the settlement of the Caribbean by European colonists, and later by Africans who were brought in as slaves. The formal education system introduced by the Europeans was intended to produce students and citizens with a good knowledge of, and appreciation for, the society and aspirations of the colonial power, and with a commitment to defend it and to participate in its development. This was essentially an elite system based on European models and designed to confer prestige on future colonial leaders. Knowledge of the empire was seen as the critical factor in educating citizens; and this knowledge in the hands of the rulers gave them the requisite power of control over the enslaved black workers. In fact, within the prevailing philosophical framework, it was considered undesirable, even dangerous, to educate the black workers, since it was felt that this would make them dissatisfied with their station in life. By the early part of the eighteenth century, however, educational facilities and opportunities were being extended to the black population, largely under the influence of the churches.

Citizenship, under this colonial regime, was therefore more for empire building than for nation building. This was accomplished through an educational system that focused on the geography, history, culture, and values of the colonial empire through the formal study of the separate subjects: history, geography, and civics. Under this system, textbook content that promoted the colonizer and empire was to be honoured. The fact that the content did not reflect the experience or the realities of Caribbean slave society and their traditional African customs was essentially ignored. Caribbean issues and matters were seen as significant only to the extent that they contributed to the wealth and dominance of the metropolitan power. The emphasis in schools was therefore on what existed (structure and function) which meant the learning of factual information on the political, social, and economic institutions of the empire. This approach represented what was perceived, at the time, as the essence of citizenship education.

The Post-Colonial Period

After gaining independence, most of the new Caribbean nations assumed control over their education system, and rewrote the syllabus they had inherited from the colonial period. In most cases, the new content more accurately reflected Caribbean history, culture, and aspirations; however, it was still organized in terms of the colonial model and still focused on structure and function, and on essentially factual information delivered mainly through history, geography, and civics/general knowledge. Nevertheless, the essential goal of citizenship education remained, though now more closely related to experiences with nation building. Some would still argue, however, that Caribbean governments and educators, despite assuming technical and political control, still do not appear to have conceptually envisaged or articulated a role for social studies in the enterprise of dealing with the problems and issues that come with independence and democratic decision making.

Modern Development of Social Studies

During the third phase, social studies was formally adopted into the curriculum of Caribbean schools; this adoption marks the beginning of the current period of social studies development in Caribbean countries. In theory, the new approach to social studies emphasized the holistic integration of nation-building content around relevant issues and topics that included environmental concerns, population, attention to attitudes, values, beliefs, and the skills of problem solving – in short, a curriculum that could impart the four skills discussed above. Each territory has, however, developed its own social studies syllabus, emphasizing what they perceive to be the major and necessary areas of study for their students. Social studies has thus become, for Caribbean schools, the study of the family, community, and nation in the context of the social, legal, political, and economic subsystems. This study has, however, tended to focus mainly on the cognitive aspects of learning, and rather less on the functional and affective.

Given the effects of development and change, educators and social critics believe that formal instruction in citizenship education should not be left to an unorganized programme for students based on the separate-subjects approach adopted during the colonial period, since that approach did not necessarily prepare citizens for self-development and a democratic way of life. Social studies educators believe that for the purpose of developing the four citizenship skills, the integration of concepts from the social sciences and humanities is necessary if citizens are to thoughtfully participate in the development of their country. Thus, social studies as a school subject has evolved as one means by which a country prepares its citizens for thoughtful participation in its development by being engaged in the study of its traditional history, values and customs, and the current issues and problems which the country faces. Given its overarching goal of citizenship education, it is important that a strong social studies programme be an essential part of primary education, particularly since, for most Caribbean children, this will be their only formal opportunity to develop lifelong citizenship skills and to practise democratic attitudes and ways of life.

Social Studies in the Caribbean

At the end of the Second World War, social studies as a subject area in the school curriculum was unheard of in the Caribbean. But education officials and planners in the region became increasingly aware of the critical role of all citizens in a rapidly changing society, and by the 1960s, they were recommending the inclusion of social studies in the school programme.

The subject was seen as an interdisciplinary one, with a specific emphasis on the development of democratic citizens who are knowledgeable, competent, and skilled in decision making, and committed to active participation in the affairs of their community and in national development. This goal reflects the concept of democratic citizenship education, and most curricula and syllabuses in social studies in Caribbean schools include, in their aims or major objectives, some reference to knowledge of social institutions and processes, social skills, and development of pro-social behaviours and civic responsibilities. We can conclude, therefore, that, in theory at least, the social studies programmes in the Caribbean were conceptualized on the same philosophical premises and with similar goals as in the democratic former colonial nations. These nations had also sought freedom by providing the youth with the knowledge, skills, and dispositions which would empower them to be effective, participating citizens and to share in the governance of their society.

Although having common ancestry in a number of ways, social studies as a formal school subject was introduced into the curriculum of Caribbean territories at different times and under different conditions. The subject was introduced in Jamaica as a course in the teacher-training programme at the teachers' colleges in 1958, and as an adjustment on the school curriculum in Trinidad and Tobago in 1959. By the mid-1960s, sustained activities in social studies curriculum development occurred in several Caribbean countries focusing on the major concerns of developing curriculum guides, resource booklets, and teaching materials, and on providing teachers with a repertoire of teaching skills in social studies. Some of these activities were funded by the World Bank, by other donor and aid agencies such as the US Agency for International Development and the Peace Corps, and some were funded by the local ministries of education. The University of the West Indies either spearheaded these undertakings or initiatives, or was invited to take an active role in them.

By the early 1970s, the Faculty of Education on all three campuses of the university, as well as at the University of Guyana, had instituted programmes aimed at enhancing the competence of practising teachers and providing professional training for untrained graduate teachers. The teachers' colleges in the region, which were now increasing in number as most territories established their own facilities, also became involved in preparing teachers for social studies at the primary and junior secondary levels.

The increasing number of graduates of the University of the West Indies with training in history, geography, and social studies, and the return of graduates with North American degrees in these areas, together with the upgrading of teacher education programmes, all helped to provide a corps of leaders with competence in teacher education, curriculum development, and the production of resource materials. However, the presence of these separate-subject specialists tended to colour the selection and treatment of the content in the classroom. This inevitably had an impact on curriculum development activities, on the quality of teaching in the subject, and on the attention to concepts and skills in social studies.

Intensive workshop activities in the Caribbean in the late 1960s and early 1970s produced a number of notable publications in social studies education. These included the following:

- 1974 *Bulletin of Concept Learning,* published by the Faculty of Education at the St Augustine campus

- 1974 *Social Studies Education,* a journal published by the Faculty of Education, St Augustine campus
- 1978 *Teaching Social Studies the Inquiry Way,* published by the Faculty of Education at the Mona campus.
- 1983 *Social Studies through Discovery,* a textbook by R. King, P. Morris, M. Morrissey, and P. Robinson, published by Longman.

The journal *Social Studies Education* featured articles and papers on social studies methodology, and it was "intended to provide a forum for student-teachers, teachers, educators, researchers, and supervisors engaged in social studies education [and to encourage] a greater awareness of the possibilities, practice, and problems of social studies as an interdisciplinary field" (*Social Studies Education* [1974]: 2). The journal was also the first attempt to link Caribbean social studies educators across the region in providing an exchange of ideas among practising colleagues. The journal remained active for the next fifteen years, but since 1989, it has appeared infrequently and its future now seems uncertain.

The 1970s and 1980s also witnessed a number of other notable initiatives and proposals, which unfortunately have not borne fruit. Among these are the following:

- Commonwealth Caribbean Inventory of Social Studies Educators (1974)
- Regional Conference of Social Studies Educators (three conferences were held in 1976, 1978, and 1980)
- Commonwealth Caribbean Social Studies Council (1974)
- Caribbean Association of Social Studies Educators (1980)

At the Second International Social Studies Conference, which was held in Miami in 1991, another attempt was made to revive the idea of a Caribbean association, but this has apparently failed to get off the ground.

One initiative which has, however, been tremendously successful is the development of a secondary school-leaving examination in social studies by the regional examining body, the Caribbean Examinations Council. The syllabus for this examination was put together by a panel of social studies teachers and educators across the region. It represents a truly innovative undertaking, since the British examining board, which the Caribbean Examinations Council replaced, had never offered this subject, and therefore, unlike for the other subjects, provided no model for its development. Thus, the design and methodologies adopted were largely influenced by the literature and approaches coming out of the United States. This initiative effectively places social studies on the secondary-school curriculum with the same footing as the other "established" subjects. The first cohort of candidates sat the examination in 1981, at both the general and the basic proficiency levels. The number of candidates increased steadily from 4,788 in 1981 to over 14,000 in 1989. Since then, the figure has averaged about 15,000, higher than for either history or geography.

Another major social studies project in the region was the Primary Education Project (1979–84). This project, which was based at the Cave Hill campus of the University of the West Indies, was funded by the US Agency for International Development and was intended to develop a four-year upper-primary school curriculum for ages seven to eleven for the Caribbean. Units, teachers guides, and resource materials were prepared for each year level. This project has had a tremendous impact on social studies in the primary schools in the Caribbean. There is now a common curriculum document available to all territories; and although some territories have adopted and implemented the curriculum document without modification, many others have modified it in order to develop their own individual syllabus. Thus, although there is no common syllabus across territories, the existing ones all have common ancestry.

The higher profile of social studies resulting from all these activities has stimulated the interest and attention of commercial publishers with respect to providing textbooks for both primary and secondary grades, and a number of these texts are currently available on the market. With a few exceptions, these texts were all written by Caribbean authors.

It is safe to say that social studies is now firmly established on the curriculum of Caribbean schools, in spite of the setbacks experienced over the years. The subject area, however, appears to have lost some of its initial focus and some of the enthusiasm and active official support which it once enjoyed. Further, the subject faces certain persistent weaknesses that detract from the achievement of its major goals and from the effective teaching and learning of the subject. Among the major weaknesses are the following:

1. A persistent emphasis on content and academic knowledge by both teachers and tutors (and in examinations), rather than on concepts and higher-order cognitive processes. In short, the exclusive emphasis is on gaining knowledge while ignoring the three other skills of democratic citizenship: processing, valuing, and participation.
2. A continuing reliance on standard textbooks (which are themselves heavily content-oriented), rather than taking advantage of available and accessible local resources to engage students in concept development and in higher-order thinking processes.
3. A tendency by teachers to pay rather limited attention to using out-of-class activities as important instructional techniques.

4. A limited emphasis on concepts generally, but particularly on those with the potential to develop national and regional consciousness and commitment, and to promote Caribbean identity and integration.

As we face the growing problems of living in increasingly complex national and global societies, we need to recapture some of the enthusiasm and revision that guided the development of social studies in the 1960s and 1970s. Caribbean educators and social studies professionals need to redirect attention to the creation of innovative learning resources, and to a focus, in our teacher-training programmes, on the practice of teaching and on equipping teachers with an adequate repertoire of up-to-date teaching and classroom management skills. Greater attention needs to be paid to all four of the citizenship skills by emphasizing enquiry and problem-solving and decision-making processes. These require that greater attention be paid to concept development and higher-order thinking, and rather less attention to academic knowledge and factual information. The teaching and learning of social studies in the Caribbean needs to move away from a concern for mainly academic knowledge and academic skills, and focus more on the other important skills of processing information, examining beliefs and values, and social participation. Our teacher-education programmes should also aim to produce teachers who have skills and a set of attitudes that foster learning (pedagogical content knowledge), and who will function as skilled and competent practitioners.

Summary and Conclusion

Social studies education was adopted into the curriculum of Caribbean schools as citizenship education, and was initially intended to provide a formal course in this area. Considerable progress has been made in establishing the subject in the school curriculum.

There are certain common, essential beliefs about social studies such as: (1) social studies is citizenship education, (2) social studies is integration of the social sciences and humanities, (3) the content of social studies is persistent and contemporary social problems, issues, concepts, and themes; and (4) social studies requires practising a problem-solving process of thinking. One other common belief is that a democratic way of life requires practising the following citizenship skills:

- gaining knowledge
- processing information
- examining values and beliefs
- social participation

These skills are to be practised in every social studies course with the purpose of preparing pupils for their role as effective citizens. The mere existence of essential beliefs about what social studies means and what skills should be practised does not point to a particular curriculum. However, the beliefs do form the basis for developing curriculum materials. The next chapter will examine how curriculum organization and materials emerge out of the essential beliefs about social studies.

2

The Social Studies Curriculum According to Theories of Growth and Development

Introduction

This is an important chapter. Why? Because the child's growth and development is related to the topics, themes, concepts, techniques, and strategies for teaching the social studies curriculum. Understanding how social studies should be practised throughout the school curriculum depends on the teacher identifying how a developmental social studies programme meets the needs of a country's citizenship education on the one hand, and the growth and development of its children on the other hand. The social studies curriculum may be the key to children becoming active citizens and knowledgeable participants in their society. Childhood and the early adolescent years (ages six to thirteen) represent the period when children's attitudes and beliefs are developed. How children view themselves in relation to other people will affect their attitude towards others. A democratic society requires from us a concern about others and an open-mindedness towards the ideas of others, and these attitudes are to be encouraged from an early age. Studies on attitude have concluded that after about the age of thirteen (third form) perceptions and attitudes become extraordinarily difficult to change, and that middle childhood is therefore a "critical period" for developing children's attitudes about themselves and their world (Buergenthal and Torney 1976).

What we do know is that schooling practices and the society's other broader efforts at the education of its citizens do have a profound effect on the perspectives of children and youth. A successful citizenship education programme will educate children with the knowledge, skills, and attitudes to undertake their role as effective citizens in a national, international, interdependent, and rapidly changing society.

The Four Stages of Growth and Development of Children and Youth

Unquestionably, the developmental stage of children's perception of their world is an important component of an effective citizenship education curriculum. "Developmental" refers to how a child progresses from an early stage to a later stage of maturation. As a generalization, children develop from the stage of being self-centred and learning from concrete experiences, to a more abstract, sophisticated stage of understanding that they are part of ever-expanding groups, such as the family, community, world, and universe. In short, the stages of growth and development follow a definable pattern. Research indicates that children go through four stages in learning about the world.

In the *first stage,* up to about three years of age, children touch, look, and listen. Thus their world is experienced through concrete sensory contact.

In the *second stage,* which continues up to age seven, children develop strong attachments to their own country. They are very egocentric and continue to learn through concrete experiences, finding abstract ideas difficult to comprehend.

The *third stage* continues in the primary years through ages eight to ten. Here, children begin to use logic to understand objects and events, and they begin to see other points of view. In this third stage, children's ideas about their country rapidly become more sophisticated, and they develop the ability to think at higher levels: abstractly (meaning to have a mental image that summarizes experience), and ideologically (meaning an imagined state of perfection). By age ten, positive feelings towards the country, generated through acceptance of national ideals and the internalization of symbols of national identity, such as the flag, create a patriotic filter through which children view their world. They screen out negative images of their country. They have an idealized image of their country and tend to fear any change that might disturb their home and security.

In the *fourth stage* of development, students between the ages of eleven and thirteen are capable of abstract thought and have the ability to imagine alternatives to reality. Commencing in the intermediate grades, students begin to view themselves and their nation as part of a larger organized system. Their typically positive attitudes towards their country stabilize; their perceptions and attitudes towards foreign nations, peoples, and ideas become fairly firmly established; and after age thirteen, these are difficult to change. If the researchers are right about the four stages of children's and youths' developmental perceptions about the world, then it is absolutely important that primary teachers be sensitive to the key role they are called on to play in preparing youth for citizenship participation in their country's future.

Windows of Opportunity

"Windows of opportunity" refers to the four levels of growth and development. Each level is a limited time frame, an open window when it is the best time to introduce and practise a subject, an attitude, or a skill such as a foreign language, a constructive attitude, or certain sport skills. What could easily be learned while the window is open might be difficult to learn once that window of opportunity closes.

The Four Stages of Cognitive (Knowledge) and Affective (Attitude) Development

1. Up to three years of age, the child's world is explored through sensory contact of touch, look, and listen.
2. From ages three through seven, the child's world is explored through concrete experiences, and the child often develops a strong attachment to the country.
3. From ages eight through ten, the child starts to think abstractly, begins the internalization of symbols of national identity and the acceptance of positive national ideals.
4. At ages eleven through thirteen (first to third forms in the secondary school) children are capable of abstract thought and an ability to imagine alternatives to reality, and their attitudes and perceptions stabilize.

After about age thirteen, perceptions and attitudes are difficult to change, thus the importance of having a citizenship education programme in primary education.

▶ **Chart 2.1:** Summary of Developmental Perspective of Children and Youth

Patterns of Growth and Development Guide the Social Studies Curriculum

Taking into consideration the growth and development of children, the following developmental (meaning sequentially structured) curriculum in social studies for each age level is intended as a guide when teaching citizenship education. The discussion at each age level in this chapter will suggest knowledge, skills, and attitudes that are appropriate to growth and development at that age level. A citizenship education programme would normally be delivered in a curriculum organized as a scope and sequence. "Scope" refers to the depth of knowledge, skills, and attitudes studied at each level, and "sequence" refers to the pattern or order in which topics are to be taught and instructional materials are to be used from preschool through the primary and secondary levels.

Scope and Sequence

How is the social studies curriculum organized? It is normally organized through a scope which identifies what is to be taught at each age level, and a sequence which refers to how what is taught is related to the other levels throughout the social studies curriculum. For example, suppose that children, at age six, study the change in family life over the past two generations. Because children study "change" as part of the scope of study at this age level, it does not mean that the teacher would drop the study of change at the next age level. Rather, the concept of change would be sequenced in each succeeding age level at an ever-increasing level of depth and complexity. The curriculum, organized as a scope and sequence, is of course based on a theory that as the child grows through the four stages, the capabilities of that child also grow. Thus, children are able to consider more complex and demanding tasks as they grow older and as they proceed, by year, through a citizenship education programme (see Figure 2.1).

Under the concept of the "expanding environment", sequencing involves moving from topics that are near at hand to those that are far away. For example, at the six to seven age level, one topic may be the family (that is, something near at hand). At the next level, the topic may be the school and the neighbourhood. In brief, the child's environment has expanded from the family to include the school and neighbourhood. This does not mean the family has been forgotten, but that two additional topics have been added. "Spiralling" indicates expanding the topics in such a way, from ages five to eleven, that each topic still appears at each succeeding level where it is studied in greater depth and detail.

"Scope" refers to the depth of study undertaken on each topic at a particular grade level. For example, how deep or extensively you are going to study the topic "The Family" or "The School" or "The Neighbourhood". Look at the illustration below of the spiralling social studies curriculum. Note the sequence and the scope.

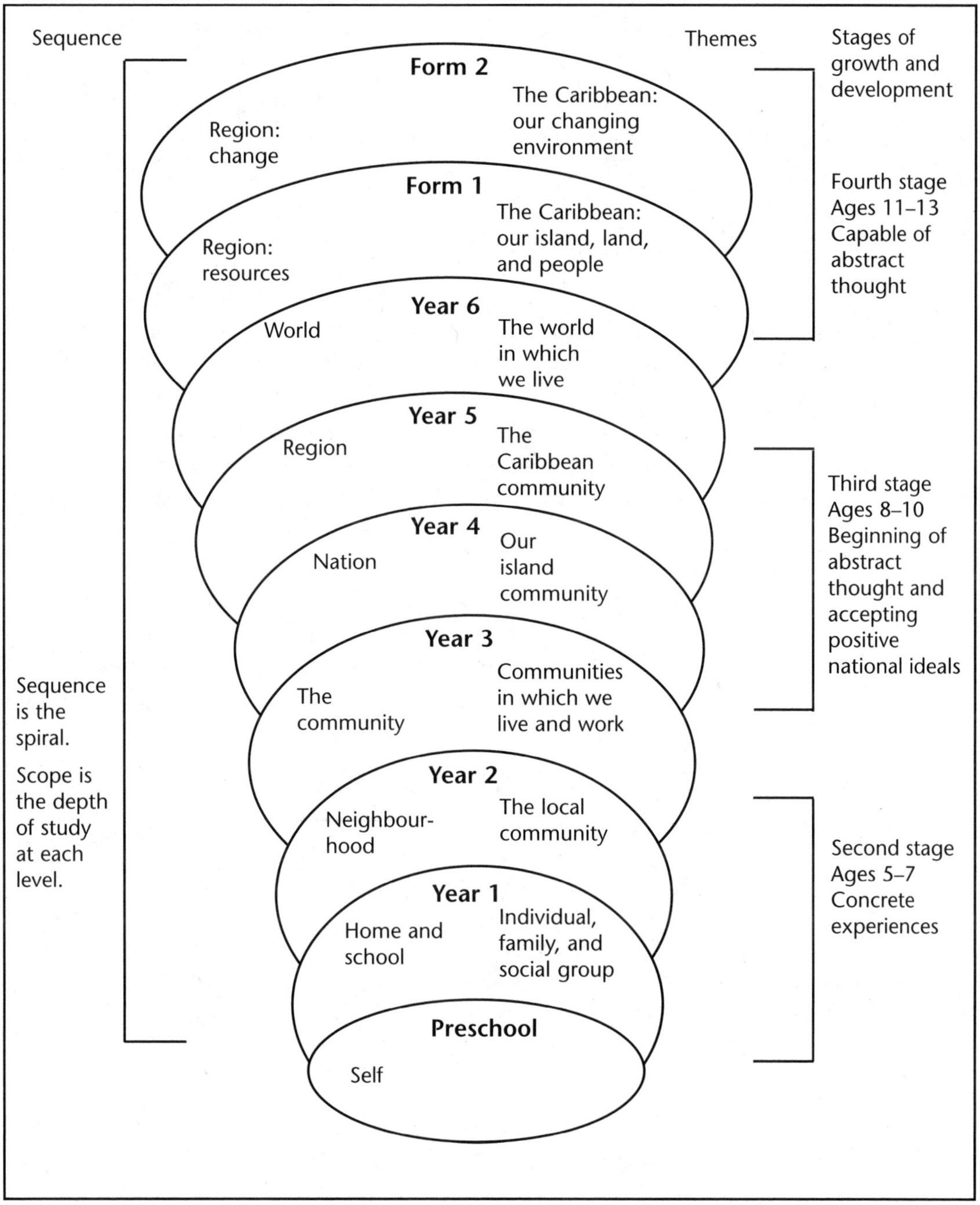

▶ **Figure 2.1:** Social Studies Programme for Preschool, Ages Five to Thirteen

A final note: The citizenship education programme should reflect pre-primary school experiences that should be part of any preschool programme. Remember that the second stage, ages three to seven, posited that the child's world is explored through concrete experience; but that also during this age period, children develop a strong attachment to their country. At times, preschool teachers do not understand their important role in developing a foundation for a citizenship education programme and thus neglect this responsibility. Because of the importance of a consistent scope and sequence throughout the early years of a child's development, the citizenship programme that follows will start at the preschool level (ages three to five).

Preschool Programme Guidelines

The Child: Growth and Development

Preschool children (ages three to five), at stage two of their growth and development, are concerned about themselves and need to understand that, while they are unique, they have many of the same feelings and problems as other children. Being egocentric, preschool children have to learn to get along with other children, to understand that they should share materials, and to cooperate to complete tasks. They also need to feel good about themselves and to experience success as well as failure in their activities. They should have experiences that enable them to move about, exploring and manipulating the school environment and satisfying their intense curiosity. They need experiences where they can learn to express their ideas and feelings to others rather than spilling them out in a jumbled fashion. Their world is limited, and their cognitive developmental level requires that most learning experiences be concrete and related to their immediate environment.

The Preschool Social Studies Programme

Content in the preschool classroom should focus on children's egocentric concerns and are largely related to self. Important questions are, "Who am I?" "How am I like other children?" "How am I different?" The skills and attitudes to be learned include the following:

- working with groups (attitude)
- using classroom tools such as scissors and crayons (skill)
- sharing materials (attitude)
- developing such skills as observing, comparing, grouping, classifying, interpreting, and inferring (skill)

- expressing ideas and feelings verbally and visually (skill)
- representing real things and real people with symbols (skill)
- perceiving simple placement relationships of objects in the classroom, house, school, and places in the community (skill)
- developing a sense of social participation by helping those in need (attitude)

The following two illustrations of classroom teaching activities will include both the *concepts* to be introduced and the *objective* for the lesson.

Teaching Activities for Preschool (Kindergarten or Reception)

▸ Example 1

Concepts: Self-esteem, and attitudes towards self and others

Objective: Children identify themselves as unique individuals who interact with other individuals and with many groups including the family, school and community.

Activity: Making "ME maps"

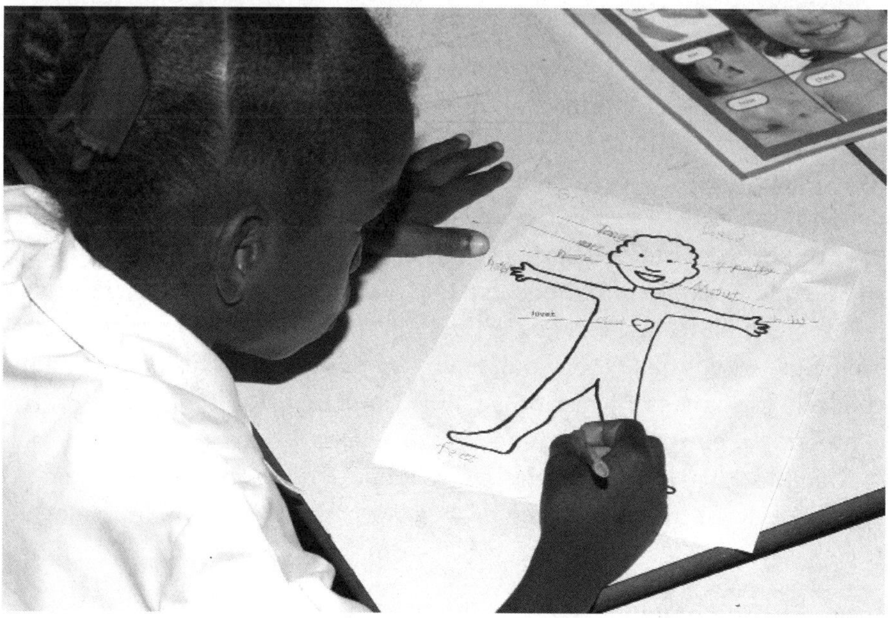

Making "ME" maps helps children explore their self-image. Use large sheets of paper, such as newsprint, on which children can draw outlines of one another. Each child colours in his or her features and clothes. Display the "ME" map in sections around the room, and give children the

opportunity to discuss likes and differences according to size, shape, hair, eyes, and so on. Through this activity, the teacher can help children develop such skills as *observing* and *describing* by asking children to describe themselves or guess who other "ME" maps represent. Another important skill is *comparing* through such questions as, "How does William look like Thomas and how does he look different?" *Classifying and grouping* are learned by asking children to form groups by size or height. Children should also be taught to identify pictures and maps as symbols that represent the physical features of real people and places. A simple activity such as this develops many important sensory motor skills, encourages cooperation, and provides an opportunity for verbalizing. This activity not only develops learning, it also helps children feel good about themselves.

▸ Example 2

Concepts: Social behaviour, including sharing, expressing feelings

Objective: Children demonstrate through participation that they recognize the feelings and needs of others.

Activity: Expressing feelings

Make finger puppets of peanut shells or paper with different expressions on the faces, such as smiling, frowning, crying, looking angry, frightened, or thoughtful. An alternative is to find these expressions in magazine pictures of children and paste them on puppets. Ask children to place a puppet with a certain expression on their hand and discuss how that child or the puppet would feel. Ask them, "When have you felt this way before?"

Role-play simple situations on the playground or in the classroom involving such feelings as anger over sharing toys or happiness in winning a game. Discuss when such feelings might occur. This activity helps children to express ideas and feelings and to listen to other children expressing their feelings and ideas.

If children have not attended preschool, then the two previous activities are also appropriate for the first year of primary school (age five).

Learning Outcomes

Ideally, by the end of preschool, children should have practised and be developing the following social studies citizenship skills that will be built upon in the first year of primary school.

What Children Should Be Able to Perform at the Completion of the Preschool Programme and at the Beginning of the First Year of Primary School (by Age Five)

Focus on Self

1. Tell stories about trips to visit relatives.
2. Describe trip to and from school or in the neighbourhood.
3. List things that cause danger and noise in the environment.
4. Share and cooperate with other children.
5. Describe how people adjust to seasonal changes.
6. Use terms for relative size and shape, such as big/little, round/square, large/small.
7. Work effectively in groups.
8. Clearly express ideas and feelings.

Chart 2.2: Learning Outcomes, Ages Three to Five

First-Year Social Studies Programme Guidelines (Ages Five to Six)

The Child: Growth and Development

The basic goal of the social studies curriculum in the first three years of school is to help children recognize that they live in a neighbourhood that demands that they must learn to make wise choices and worthy decisions about the resources of their neighbourhood. To this end, the curriculum for the first year (ages five to six) introduces children to the role of an effective citizen in an international, interdependent, and rapidly changing society. For the child who has not attended preschool, the characteristics and programme stated for preschool earlier would generally apply. Children who are entering the first year (age five) are still in stage two of their growth and development, where they need to explore their world through concrete experiences. They have great desire to learn to read and are inquisitive about extraordinary and different places. They are still concerned about themselves, but they do want to learn about other people. Their attention span remains limited, so activities should change frequently, and opportunity for moving about needs to be provided. The child in the first year of primary school is better able to work with small groups to complete tasks.

The First-Year Social Studies Programme

Many of the learning experiences should be related to groups in which children belong, using topics such as starting school, democratic life in class, me and my family, national holiday. Questions should be asked such as:

- How do I behave in groups?
- What are my responsibilities?
- How do other people behave in groups?
- Why are groups formed?
- What are the groups in my community?
- What about groups in other parts of the world?

Skills to be introduced or extended should include: cooperation and problem solving, now extended to include hypothesizing and predicting. Children can also begin to develop such location skills as using directions and interpreting a map legend or key. They can also begin to identify and acquire information and data from field trips. Reading skills are emphasized at this level.

Teaching Activities for the First Year, Five to Six Age Group

▸ Example 1

Concepts: Cooperation (attitude), leader, and group

Objective: Children practise citizenship skills through participation in group activities.

Activity: Determining what is a group

Have children divide into groups of four. Give each group a task to complete without giving them any assistance in organizing their group or indicating how they should proceed. Permit them to work for a short period of time and then discuss how they proceeded. Find out if they are satisfied with their group. If so, why? If not, why not? Talk about leaders and members.

- What is a leader?
- What should the leader do?
- Why do we need leaders?
- What happens if we don't have a leader of the group?
- What is a member's responsibility?
- How does a member help the total group?
- What happens if a member does not do his share of the work?

Then help children organize their groups and complete the task assigned.

▸ Example 2

Concepts: Location, and natural resources

Objective: Children explore the geographical relationships of home, school, and community.

Activity: Learning about maps – Where do you live?

Children begin with a map of the school and extend it to include their homes and neighbourhoods. The map should be done on the floor using large sheets of paper, such as newsprint. Be sure to provide compass directions. Small blocks or empty boxes can be used to represent buildings, or a map legend may be introduced. Children should have an opportunity to place their own houses on the map. Take a walking tour around the neighbourhood if children cannot remember street names. Children who ride to school should add the roads they take to arrive at school.

Learning Outcomes

Ideally, by the end of this first year (age six), children should have practised and be developing the following social studies citizenship skills.

What Children Should be able to Perform at the Completion of the First Year of Social Studies (by Age Six)

Focus on Home and School

1. Know and use terms for location such as near/far, here/there, up/down.
2. Draw pictures of the classroom and locate objects in terms of near and far.
3. Use pictures to record changes in the school or neighbourhood.
4. Make a model of the neighbourhood using blocks or boxes.
5. Draw map of school and label its parts.
6. Describe how seasons affect people at work, at home, at play.
7. Name directions, north, south, east, and west in the classroom.
8. Describe the location of their home and its relation to school.
9. Make a chart to identify the various ways students travel to school.
10. Name their home community and locate it on a map.
11. Point out continents and oceans on a globe.
12. Identify some common activities of children in the Caribbean.
13. Record changes in a tree, plant, or animal over time.
14. Use map to identify symbols for highways and airports.

▶ **Chart 2.3:** Learning Outcomes, Ages Five to Six

Second-Year Social Studies Programme Guidelines (Ages Six to Seven)

The Child: Growth and Development

Children in the second year of primary school (age seven), still in stage two of their growth and development where concrete experiences are most meaningful, are generally outgoing and interested in new and different experiences. Newspapers, radio, and television have introduced them to people and cultures beyond their own communities, but they often do not have an adequate understanding of these cultures. Time and space relationships are difficult concepts for them to perceive. Depending upon their community, far distant places are not quite realistic to them. In addition, even though they have some general knowledge of their own community, it is often superficial. Having acquired some ability to read and limited research skills, which were introduced in the first year, they can begin to search out information on their own. They enjoy working together as partners. Role-playing also offers an outlet for their expressive abilities.

The Second-Year Social Studies Programme

Many of the activities in this second year may focus on return to school, democracy, decision making and change in the community, identifying historic events, and the community's interdependence with other communities. Some of the questions could be:

- Where is our community located and how did our community begin?
- How does the community respond to basic needs?
- How would you improve the local environment?
- What are the cultural and natural characteristics of the neighbourhood?
- What are the healthy sources of food and water?
- What changes are happening in the local environment due to technological progress?
- How does transportation connect communities?

At this stage, children can begin to develop the skill of acquiring information through listening and observing with a purpose and of evaluating information. Map skills may now include reading from flat wall maps, determining distance using scale, and the relation of the community's location to the country, the Caribbean, and the world.

Teaching Activities for the Second Year, Six to Seven Age Group

▸ Example 1

Concepts: Population, customs, social change, cultural change

Objective: Children examine changes in the community.

Activity: Examining how your community developed

Several children should interview some of the older residents of the community to learn how the community developed.

Draw a timeline of the community using the life spans of the children (approximately seven to eight years of age), their parents (approximately thirty years of age), grandparents (approximately fifty years of age), and the oldest community residents (approximately eighty years of age). How has the community changed? Indicate population, industries, recreation, schools, and customs at each point on the timeline. Try to find pictures of the community during different historical periods. Have children research and role-play some of the early customs of the community.

▶ Example 2

Concepts: Political behaviour, citizenship, democracy, political institutions, government, rights, responsibilities, and rules

Objective: Demonstrate why groups and communities have rules and laws.

Activity: Finding out what the rules are in our community

Have children play a game ignoring any rules for the game. Discuss what happens when you ignore rules. Arguing, fighting, the game may not be any fun, how do you know who wins, and so on, these are possible responses. Children should then generalize about "Why do we have rules? "Who makes the rules?"

Children should then investigate rules (laws) in the home and the community. To accomplish this, you may want to ask parents or have community officials visit the class to discuss their thoughts on rule making.

Find out how rules help people. Are there rules that people do not like, that you do not like? How is our community governed? Who enforces rules?

After children learn about the community government, organize the classroom in the same manner as the community. Continue to run the classroom with this form of organization until children have some basic understanding of the roles of community officials. Perhaps compose, with the children, a set of classroom rules that are voted on by the class as an example of democratic decision making.

Learning Outcomes

Ideally, by the end of the second year (age seven), children should have practised and be developing the following social studies citizenship skills.

What Children Should be Able to Perform at the Completion of the Second Year of Social Studies (by Age Seven)

Focus on the Neighbourhood

1. Use directions, north, south, east, and west.
2. Make a directory of classmates' home addresses.
3. Identify continents and oceans on globes and world maps.
4. Describe landforms and water bodies in local area and in the Caribbean.
5. Observe and record the number of daylight hours during different seasons.
6. Describe ways the neighbourhood has changed over time using maps and photos.
7. Use simple symbols and colour to make a map of neighbourhood. Make key for map.
8. Identify common needs of people everywhere and how they are met.
9. Compare tools used to change the environment long ago and now.
10. Use maps to compare ways that people use the physical environment to meet their needs.
11. Tell about celebrations in their country.
12. Describe and define what a neighbourhood is.

▶ **Chart 2.4:** Learning Outcomes, Ages Six to Seven

Third-Year Social Studies Programme Guidelines (Ages Seven to Eight)

The Child: Growth and Development

Children in the third year of primary school (age eight) are experiencing many changes in physical, mental, and emotional characteristics. They have matured from the second developmental stage (ages three to seven) to stage three of their growth and development (ages eight to ten) where they begin to think abstractly and internalize symbols. Small muscles are developing more rapidly than at the two previous stages, resulting in such changes as improved eye-hand coordination. Reading ability increases. Children can now comprehend more completely. The child usually wishes to win approval from authority figures. Children have longer attention spans, can discuss more aspects of topics and can manipulate different types of materials more easily. Individual differences and interests increase.

The Third-Year Social Studies Programme

The major focus of the third-year curriculum could be related to various types of communities in which people live and work: school has started; economic concepts, consumption and productivity; our social life. The diversity of types of communities found provides content for developing and extending individual interests.

Through group work and projects, children should improve their communication and decision-making skills and build a concept of responsible community citizenship. Skills to receive special emphasis include the following:

- using common map symbols
- locating their community, major land and water forms, and reference points on maps and globes
- making simple generalizations about change (past and future) and the influence of geographic location
- giving examples of the role of work and how people make choices about economic wants and needs
- giving examples of the diversity of goods and services
- exploring the heritage of their own and selected communities
- demonstrating responsible decision-making and citizenship skills

Teaching Activities for the Third Year, Seven to Eight Age Group

▶ Example 1

Concepts: Climate, culture, ecology, environment, basic needs, community, economic institutions, economic resources, employment, industrialization, population, and production

Objective: Explain how people make choices about using their environment and resources to satisfy their different needs and wants.

Activity: Exploring where people live

Some suggested questions for this activity are:

- What types of communities are there?
- Where do people live?
- How does living in other communities contribute to the differences among people? To their similarities?
- How do people adapt to differences?
- What factors hinder adaptation?
- What happens when people do not protect their environment?
- What can I do to protect the environment?

Various types of maps can be used to acquaint children with landforms. Have a discussion on how people use land differently. Pictures can be shown of land utilization in different areas.

Children can work in small groups to construct different types of communities after doing some research by reading and observing pictures. Pictures from magazines and other sources as well as various sized boxes, cardboard, toys, and other materials can be used in the construction. Groups can construct large and small communities, industrial, agricultural, tourist, and many other types of communities. Parts from the different communities can be interchanged to answer some of the suggested questions.

Sharing and other group skills, construction and manipulative skills, as well as many other skills are developed in this activity.

▶ Example 2

Concepts: Climate, culture, environment, land, location, population, region, and natural resources

Objective: Show how the geographical location of the community relates to the region and the country.

Activity: A map activity

Use a large bulletin board. Place a map of the Caribbean region in the centre. Indicate where the children are located on the map. As the children study different communities in other places, have them locate them on the map. Pin a piece of yarn or string on the location of the community, and extend it out to the side where pictures of the activities, landforms, or products of the culture can be displayed. Be sure to do the same for the children's own community. Make the displays of each culture studied as extensive as possible. This helps children relate their location to the location of the other communities and also to identify the physical and cultural characteristics of the different communities.

Learning Outcomes

Ideally, by the end of the third year of primary school (age eight), children should have practised and be developing the following social studies citizenship skills.

What Children Should Be Able to Perform at the Completion of the Third Year of Social Studies (by Age Eight)

Focus on the Community

1. Use map to point out the location of their community relative to the parish/district, region, nation, and world.
2. Locate places on a map grid system on a globe.
3. Draw a map with symbols to show the physical features of the community.
4. Interpret a diagram that shows the rotation of the earth to explain day and night.
5. Show pictures of how people use the environment to meet their needs.
6. Explain how climate influences economic activities.
7. Use scale and mileage figures on a road map to compare distances.
8. Compare local community with communities nearby.

▶ **Chart 2.5:** Learning Outcomes, Ages Seven to Eight

Fourth-Year Social Studies Programme Guidelines (Ages Eight to Nine)

The Child: Growth and Development

Children in the fourth year of primary school (age nine) are in stage three of their growth and development where children start to think abstractly.

They want to remain as children, yet want to be grown up, too. Often, they are self-conscious and prefer group activity rather than working alone. These children are beginning to develop a more definite concept of time and can begin to deal with cause and effect relationships and with decision-making processes, such as identifying problems and considering alternative solutions and their consequences. They should be able to draw conclusions about past and present life in the Caribbean region, and in particular about their own country, based on relevant data derived from a variety of historical sources.

The Fourth-Year Social Studies Programme

Skills and concepts should be related to children's lives and should be presented through a wide variety of resources and hands-on activities that include the following:

- collecting and examining primary documents and artefacts
- making models and maps
- talking with community resource persons
- visiting historical sites and buildings

They need to understand their present life with all its geographic, environmental, cultural, and social dimensions. This understanding of their environment can be achieved through a study of the geography and history of the Caribbean. These students should be able to identify key historical events, geographic places, and people that have shaped the region and their country. They should be able to explain how changes have affected people and their nations in the past. They should be given opportunities to actively explore and appreciate the diverse cultures which have contributed to Caribbean heritage. Children, at this stage, should also develop a proficiency in working cooperatively in groups to collect data from a variety of sources, to draw simple conclusions, and to organize data using graphs, charts, maps, and simple timelines. Reading skills should have developed to the point where the children can begin to consider what are acceptable sources of information and to read materials with discrimination.

Teaching Activities for the Fourth Year, Eight to Nine Age Group

▶ Example 1

Concepts: Change, identity

Objective: Trace the historical movements which have led to the development of the country.

Activity: Constructing personal and country timelines

Ask children to list their own personal experiences in chronological order from birth to present age. Some suggestions for the list include birth date, date they learned to walk, date they started school, date they learned to accomplish some specific school activity such as reading or writing, date they learned to play some particular game, date of any important family events such as weddings or a death. Explain that this list is the child's timeline.

Using large sheets of paper or newsprint, make a long timeline on the wall for political, social, and economic events in the nation's history. Discuss with children what major event should be put on the timeline to start with. As historical events are studied during the year they should be added to the timeline. Eventually all the children will place themselves on this big timeline so that they can see for themselves where they fit into their nation's history. This activity is intended to help students identify that they are involved in the development of their country.

▸ Example 2

Concepts: Economic behaviour, social behaviour, culture, custom, family, group, heredity, industrialization, urbanization, norms, responsibilities, role, socialization, society, and values

Objective: Compare similarities and differences of cultures in the Caribbean region in prehistoric and historic times.

Activity: Examining what changes have occurred in the student's family life

How has life changed over the last three generations? How has family life changed? Are the roles and responsibilities of the family members the same as they were twenty years ago, fifty years ago, and two hundred years ago? This activity will encourage the exploration of various cultural and ethnic groups throughout the rich and varied history of the Caribbean. To research these changes, establish committees to investigate family life during early periods in the nation's history and family life today. This study will introduce the problems that families presently face in today's rural, urban, and commercialized society. These contemporary problems should then be compared with problems faced by the early founders of selected Caribbean cultures. The committees can report to the total group through role-playing or panel discussions.

Learning Outcomes

Ideally by the end of fourth year of primary school (age nine) children should have practised and be developing the following social studies citizenship skills.

What Children Should Be Able to Perform at the Completion of the Fourth Year of Social Studies (by Age Nine)

Focus on the Country's History and Geography

1. Use latitude and longitude on a map to locate places.
2. Describe the location of early civilizations in the Caribbean.
3. Locate on a map places where classmates have travelled.
4. Interpret a diagram to describe the earth's revolution around the sun and to explain the changes in seasons.

Chart 2.6 continues on next page

▸ **Chart 2.6:** Learning Outcomes, Ages Eight to Nine

What Children Should Be Able to Perform at the Completion of the Fourth Year of Social Studies (by Age Nine) *(cont'd)*

5. Evaluate the effects of climate on the economic activities in the Caribbean.
6. Locate the major cities or villages on maps of their country.
7. List ways in which people in their country depend on the local resources.
8. Identify areas of high population density and give reasons for the concentration.
9. Identify animal and plant life common to their country and to the Caribbean.
10. Analyse reasons for the locations of major economic activity in their country and in Caribbean countries.

Chart 2.6: Learning Outcomes, Ages Eight to Nine *(cont'd)*

Fifth-Year Social Studies Programme Guidelines (Ages Nine to Ten)

The Child: Growth and Development

In the fifth-year level, stage three of their growth and development, children (age ten) begin to think more abstractly. Historic topics such as the Commonwealth, cultural heritage, Western cultural influence, becoming a nation, and self-reliance can offer a framework for thinking about the past while observing the present. Their increased interest in and ability to gather and organize data should enable them to explore the physical and cultural characteristics of the Caribbean region and its neighbours. This age group of children learn best when flexibly grouped for work and sharing, so that they can express their opinions and become actively involved in "how to" demonstrations. Their natural interest is in science, maps, their personal collections, simulations, educational games, group-planned projects, first-person presentations, and school/community experiences. These children's interest in collecting and demonstrating the uses of old objects provides avenues for extending time concepts.

The Fifth-Year Social Studies Programme

For this age group, the focus should be on developing the children's understanding of the historical and physical/cultural geography of the Caribbean, including the relationship between geographical factors and the historical development of the Caribbean region. Attention should be given to the physical features and climates, natural resources, ways of making a living in the region, cities, and places of special interest. Activities should emphasize the following problem-solving skills:

- questioning
- examining facts and opinions
- analysing and evaluating historical sources of information
- contrasting and comparing
- using primary and secondary sources
- conducting research using a variety of sources on historical topics: colonialism, our region, homeland, and neighbours

Additional skills to be taught include the following:

- analysing maps, globes, and charts
- creating and interpreting graphs
- identifying relationships
- debating issues
- posing alternative actions
- developing critical-thinking and independent study skills using geographical and historical content

Teaching Activities for the Fifth Year, Nine to Ten Age Group

▸ Example 1

Concepts: Environment, culture, climate, land, government, natural resources, human resources, technology, and economic distribution

Objective: Identify the physical and cultural characteristics of the West Indies and describe the relationship of the different areas of the region.

Activity: Exploring how the environment has affected the development of different cultures

Divide the class into committees to study how the environment has affected the development of culture. Select different regions for comparison. Find out about the following: (1) climate, (2) topography, (3) natural resources, (4) human resources. Determine how these factors have affected the economic development of the regions and the various aspects of their culture: (1) clothing, (2) art and music, (3) family life, (4) government.

▸ Example 2

Concepts: Conflict, culture, maps and globes, and geographic regions

Objective: Demonstrate the influence of physical and cultural factors upon countries of the Caribbean.

Activity: Examining where and what is the Caribbean, and why should this region be studied

Because of the region's contemporary significance, it is an excellent topic to emphasize the relation of geography to the historical development of the Caribbean and its interrelated countries.

Ask children to bring current news magazines, newspapers, and other materials and to cut out articles and pictures relating to the Caribbean. Divide the class into small groups of four or five; distribute clippings and pictures. As a group assignment, see if they can answer questions from the clippings. Suggested questions might include the following: "What is the Caribbean?" "Where is it?" "Why is it important?" "Why is your country important?"

One group might assume the responsibility of preparing a bulletin board from the collected clippings and pictures. Each of the other groups may prepare something on a different country.

Children will list the countries that are usually considered to be part of the Caribbean and the Eastern Caribbean (as a separate category) and locate them on maps and a globe. They will form a hypothesis as to why this area is called the Eastern Caribbean and seek information to verify or refute it. They will identify, from the articles and pictures, aspects of life and culture in the Caribbean as a unique geographical region.

Learning Outcomes

Ideally, by the end of the fifth year of primary school (age ten), children should have practised and be developing the following social studies citizenship skills.

What Children Should Be Able to Perform at the Completion of the Fifth Year of Social Studies (by Age Ten)

Focus on Country's History and Geography

1. Use latitude and longitude to locate countries in the Caribbean.
2. Identify specific reasons for the location of selected places in the Caribbean.
3. Recognize the significance of physical environment on settlement patterns and economic activity.
4. Use historical maps to identify changes over three hundred years in the Caribbean.
5. Define resources.
6. Locate major resources found in the Caribbean and in their own country.
7. Use maps, charts, and graphs to determine how a community, city, or village has changed over time.
8. List advantages and disadvantages of technology as an agent of change in the environment.
9. Compute distance between cities in the Caribbean.
10. Identify ways that cities are linked to other countries.
11. Explain the purpose of the British Commonwealth.

▶ **Chart 2.7:** Learning Outcomes, Ages Nine to Ten

Sixth-Year Social Studies Programme Guidelines (Ages Ten to Eleven)

The Student: Growth and Development

This age level is generally a transition period for students (age eleven). They have now reached stage four of their growth and development where they are capable of abstract thought and they have the ability to imagine alternatives to reality. Students are acquiring more of the responsibilities of an adult, but have not lost their enthusiasm for the fun and games of childhood. More decision making will be required of the student. Children at this age are usually very sociable individuals who want to participate in activities with their peers. Frequent opportunities for expression of their feelings and opinions should therefore be provided.

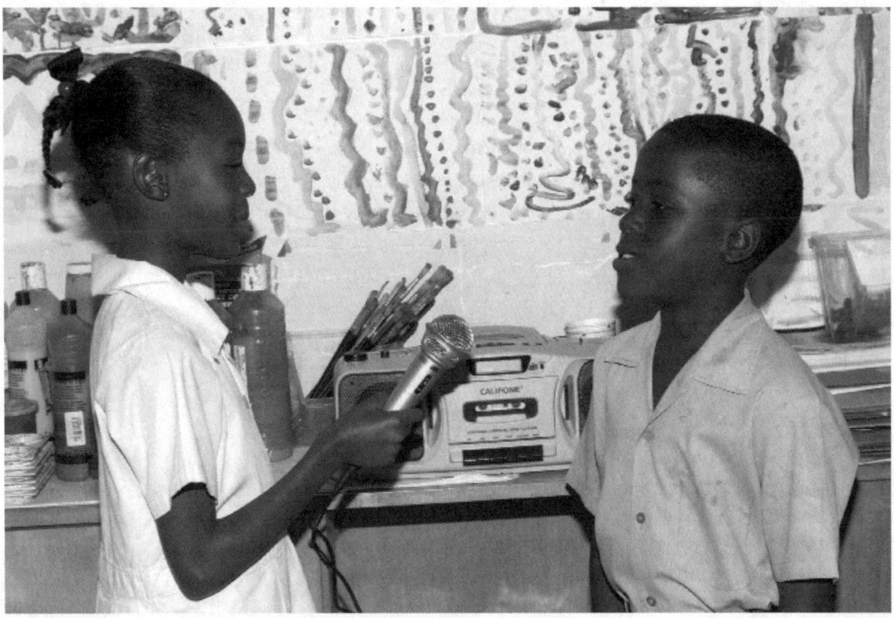

The Sixth-Year Social Studies Programme

The general objectives for this age group should be developing the students' world view on such topics as the Caribbean's position in world conflicts; reinforcing and expanding their understanding of geographic concepts and skills through studying the islands of the Caribbean. After an introduction to physical and economic geography, selected countries are studied with attention to physical features, climate, resources, industries and products, and the way of life of the people. The following topics are typical: our world and the Caribbean, economic features of the Caribbean.

Teaching Activities for the Sixth Year, Ten to Eleven Age Group

▶ Example 1

Concepts: Climate, ecology, environment, location, region, natural resources, human resources

Objective: Explain the relationship between physical and cultural features on the Earth's surface.

Activity: Looking at neighbouring islands in the Caribbean

To help students better understand the geography of neighbouring islands, divide the class into committees or groups. The first committee should draw on heavy paper a large map of the islands of the Caribbean. Using this outline map made by the first committee, the other committees make maps the same size, each committee inserting on their map one of the following features:

- mountainous regions
- river and lake regions
- coastal regions
- desert regions
- latitude and longitude
- populations
- natural resources

These maps will be important aids when discussing such things as environmental problems and cultures.

▶ Example 2

Concepts: Conflict, culture, maps and globes, geographic regions

Objective: Determine those factors from past and current events that may influence future conditions in various cultures of the Caribbean.

Activity: Examining how worldwide news affects the Caribbean islands

Each student must bring in a news story from a magazine, newspaper, radio report, or television. Students tell what their news story concerns and the date it took place. A small piece of paper with the date of the story is tacked to a large map where the story took place. After all the students have reported on their news stories, make a list of story locations. This activity can be limited to new stories about their island or the Caribbean, or may include worldwide news. Some possible headlines might be on topics such as national disasters, political events, scientific discoveries, economic production, and sports or cultural events.

Learning Outcomes

Ideally, by age eleven, students should have practised and be developing the following social studies citizenship skills.

What Students Should be able to Perform at the Completion of the Sixth Year of Social Studies (by Age Eleven)

Focus on Regions of the World

1. Compare climate, landforms, natural resources, and ecosystems within and between regions.
2. Examine time zone relationships.
3. List ways people depend on the government: local, provincial, national.
4. Describe population distribution patterns in various regions.
5. List ways people adapt and change the environment in selected regions.
6. Interpret flow charts illustrating trade and migration patterns with other island countries.
7. Trace movement of raw materials and manufactured products.
8. Evaluate migration patterns within the Caribbean islands.
9. Determine common characteristics of regions.
10. Categorize regions as "developing" or "developed".
11. Define the term "hemisphere".
12. Design map symbols and use them as a legend on a map.
13. Note changes over time in the use of natural resources.

▶ **Chart 2.8:** Learning Outcomes, Ages Ten to Eleven

At the first- and second-form levels, the social studies curriculum course content varies considerably across the Caribbean. However, the stages of growth and development do apply as a standard by which curriculum materials should be developed for those form levels. The following are examples of learning outcomes for forms one and two.

First-Form Social Studies Programme Guidelines (Ages Eleven to Twelve)

The Student: Growth and Development

First-form students (age twelve), in stage four of their growth and development, are adolescents who are not always certain who they are. They are usually open and responsive in classroom situations. Sometimes they welcome the stimulus and challenge of school, but they are subject to peer group leadership and pressure. Emotions run the gamut from high to low - often without much middle. At this fourth stage of development, students' attitudes are now beginning to stabilize about their values and beliefs.

Learning Outcomes

Ideally, by the end of the first form, students should have practised and be developing the following social studies citizenship skills.

What Students Should Be Able to Perform at the Completion of the First Form of Social Studies (by Age Twelve)

Focus on Culture and People

1. Identify countries and trace routes on map and globe of immigration to the Caribbean.
2. Locate on map or globe countries from which settlers arrived.
3. Compare and contrast characteristics and culture of the major settlers.
4. Use maps to show population and patterns in the Caribbean.
5. Describe change brought about by independence.
6. Interpret the difference between the colonial period and the modern period.

▶ **Chart 2.9:** Learning Outcomes, Ages Eleven to Twelve

Second-Form Social Studies Programme Guidelines (Age Thirteen)

The Student: Growth and Development

At the second-form level, students, in stage four of their growth and development (age thirteen) where their attitudes and perceptions stabilize, are ready to cope with the value issues, dilemmas, and problems that underlie most political decisions, such as "What is democracy?" They should be able to employ data drawn from statistical tables, make inferences, recognize limitations, and reach tentative conclusions on such topics as understanding present-day democracy and human rights. Students should also be able to apply an abstract concept to explain a particular instance and relate a theoretical position to a concrete operation by (1) identifying a principle, (2) explaining the reasoning behind the principle, and (3) describing the principle in action, for example, studying basic human rights and responsibilities. At this stage, students should be prepared to become active, effective citizens in a democracy by learning how to protect and develop human rights.

Ideally, by the end of the second form, students should have practised and be developing the following social studies citizenship skills.

What Students Should Be Able to Perform at the Completion of the Second Form of Social Studies (by Age Thirteen)

Focus on Citizenship

1. Compare and contrast judicial, executive and legislative powers of the national government.
2. List basic human rights and responsibilities.
3. Define democracy.
4. Examine rules for maintaining democratic life in the family and expand to the rules for maintaining democracy in the school.
5. Identify world institutions that deal with human rights.
6. Examine the constitution as it compares with the definition of democracy.
7. Summarize the international protections that now exist for human rights.
8. Differentiate between democratic and totalitarian regimes.
9. Describe how the constitution relates to human rights.

▶ **Chart 2.10:** Learning Outcomes, Ages Twelve to Thirteen

Summarizing the Abilities and Skills Needed for Effective Citizenship Behaviour

Ideally, by the end of eight years of the social studies curriculum, students should have practised and be developing the following social studies citizenship skills:

1. *Psychomotor domain skills* centring on ways and means of handling social studies materials, such as
   a. locating and gathering information from a variety of sources (books, listening, interviewing);
   b. interpreting graphic materials (maps, globes, and charts);
   c. developing a sense of time and chronology (sequence of events, time systems); and
   d. presenting social studies materials (outlining, speaking).
2. *Cognitive domain skills* of thinking as applied to problem solving, such as
   a. comprehension (identifying central issues);
   b. analysis and evaluation (judging social studies materials and choosing alternative courses of action); and
   c. synthesis and application (formulating hypotheses and generalizations, identifying possible courses of action).
3. *Affective domain skills* of effective group participation, such as
   a. assessing different roles in the group as these roles are needed for the group to progress;
   b. using parliamentary procedures;
   c. helping resolve differences within the group; and
   d. suggesting and using means of evaluating group progress.

Summary and Conclusion

The characteristics of the four developmental stages which were originally suggested by Piaget do offer common guidelines for teachers working with children and youth. Qualities which teachers need in order to support growth and movement within or between the four stages are as follows:

1. To be open and ready for change.
2. To be active in having children explore their environment.
3. To help children towards self-direction through seeking new patterns of thought and changing old patterns of understanding.

Just by knowing the existence of the four stages of growth and development does not suggest that teachers should try to accelerate children through the stages. It is true that the four-stage classification can help a teacher understand children's behaviour and level of thinking. However, these stages should not be assumed for all children's social, intellectual, and skill development progress. Consider these stages as a context for supporting the potential development of children and youth.

Looking Ahead: How Children Learn Best

Hopefully, this chapter has helped you to think more clearly about what we know to exist, the distinct stages of growth and development for our children and youth.

The following chapter also deals with a fundamental question: How do children learn best? Is there really an answer to this? The answer is definitely, yes. Research from the past twentieth century on how we learn best does reveal what we should be doing to help children learn.

3

How Students Learn Best

Effective Teaching Practices to Promote Learning and Remembering

Let those who know explain to those who don't.
– Nasreddin Hodja

The Application of Research to Teaching

Teaching in the classroom ought to start with a foundational knowledge on what research tells us about (1) stages of growth and development and (2) how people learn best. You may have read in a previous chapter about the four stages of growth and development of children and youth, and those stages do correlate with what is known about learning and remembering. Of course, the question should be asked: Do we really know how people learn best? What we do know is that people learn in many different ways – that is, people have different styles of learning. These styles include listening through hearing, seeing, reading, discussing, and participating.

It appears that we all seem to respond to some stimulus, and we also seem to respond differently to different stimuli. Some students can listen to a lecture and learn and remember a great deal. Others seem to learn more from reading, while still others need direct experience and participation. Some remember best by seeing, while others get the most learning and remembering from discussion. When teachers talk about a style of learning, in reality, they are talking about what catches the students' attention, what students respond to. The key is, students must focus attention on a specific task in order to learn and remember. The job of teaching, therefore, is to help students focus their attention on that task.

In summary, research studies on learning and remembering over the past fifty years suggest that the "average" students, under normal conditions, learn and retain (remember what they learn) at differing rates, according to the degree that they are involved in the lesson. The more students actively participate, that is, cooperate and share in the lesson, the more they will learn and remember because they are focusing their attention on a specific task. Knowing what styles of learning are most effective might be helpful in planning lessons and also in writing curriculum materials. The following approximate percentages on learning and remembering are based upon a summary of studies (a composite of many studies) and responses from thousands of students. The percentages cited below represent general averages, and may not exactly fit any one individual or group of persons. No one person is likely to be exactly represented by any one of the percentages cited here. Keeping in mind the variability among individuals, let us examine how students are likely to learn and remember.[1]

We learn and remember

10% of what we hear

15% of what we see

20% of what we both see and hear

40% of what we discuss with others

80% of what we experience directly or practise

90% of what we attempt to teach others

▶ **Figure 3.1:** We Learn and Remember

Would it be accurate then to generalize that the more actively the student focuses attention and experiences quality "time on task", the more likely the student is working at the higher percentage level (80 or 90 per cent) of learning and remembering?

1. The authors have seen at least three different sets or percentages which suggest that the percentages stated here are merely approximations and are not to be taken literally. The percentages cited here were presented in an occasional paper, "What We Know About How Adults Learn and Effective Training", by the Indiana Department of Education Gifted and Talented Cadre Training Workshop, 18 August 1984.

The Task of Active Learning

The research on learning and remembering, and the four stages of growth and development, confirms what most of you already know from your own experience. You do not need to be a trained research specialist to know that most people would learn and remember more if they were required to teach the content rather than just required to hear the content taught in a lecture. Why is this true? The explanation is clear: the person teaching must focus more attention on the task of transmitting the content than the student does in receiving the content.

The key is concentrating on the task, which is called spending *quality time on task.* All results from research studies on learning and effective teaching agree that students learn better - learn faster, remember more, retain longer, and derive greater enjoyment - when they are actively involved in the learning activity. It follows that passive students (that is students who are inactive, non-participating, and indifferent) quickly forget what they learn, become bored, and resist retaining what is to be learned. Then, what one conclusion can you draw? Activities which focus and prolong attention on the task at hand are more effective in facilitating learning and remembering. The least effective in doing this are activities that encourage a short attention span where minds tend to wander from the task.

We learn and remember 10 per cent of what we hear during any given period of time. This means that, on an average at any given time during a lecture or just listening to the radio, students are actually mentally recording only 10 per cent of what they hear. Consequently, at the end of the lecture, the radio programme, or a normal conversation with others, only 10 per cent of the lesson or conversation will be remembered or retained. You must also keep in mind the importance of learning styles and of the stages of growth and development. Lecturing is perhaps the most abstract of all teaching techniques because the listener must translate the spoken word into a mental image. This mental image is an abstraction. Not until the third stage of growth and development, ages eight to ten (class two to four), do children start to think abstractly and begin the internalization of symbols. Thus the warning that lecturing to early primary students is unlikely to result in effective learning and remembering because they have not yet begun to think abstractly.

However, it is true that some students listen better than others - which is called "paying attention". Therefore, the percentage of learning and remembering what they hear may be greater than that of the average student. Also, the percentage of learning by hearing may be greater in those societies with a strong oral tradition, where hearing is more important

than reading. Apart from these conceptions, studies do show that students in the average classroom tune in and out when they are listening to a lecture, meaning that they listen for a few seconds to the teacher, and then their thoughts stray to something else, and then back to the teacher. They repeat this process of tuning in and out to what the teacher is saying during the whole lecture. This is a process that you know well from your own experience.

It is difficult to hold students' attention to a task if they are just required to hear. But this process of tuning in and out does not just apply to lectures. It also applies to listening to audio cassettes, to conversations with friends, to anything that is just heard. In short, lecturing can be an effective teaching technique only if it is used when the students can concentrate their attention, as they are more likely to do at stage four in their growth and development (ages eleven to thirteen, class six and forms one to two). However, research also suggests that effective teaching through lecturing is an extremely difficult task given the large classes in many primary schools, and given that students constantly tune in and out and, on the average, learn and remember only 10 per cent of what they hear. While it is true that lecturing is often the most efficient means of transmitting specific information or instruction, the information is also least likely to be remembered or retained.

We learn and remember 15 per cent of what we see. It is true that we learn and remember more of what we see than of what we hear. For the teacher, the problem of having students just see – including reading, looking at pictures, witnessing an event – is that, as we know, people tend to see different things, which is another way of saying that we all have selective memories of what we hear and see. Thus, seeing, like hearing, does not necessarily lead to accuracy or understanding. The point is that asking students just to read an assignment will result in only 15 per cent learning and remembering. As in the case of hearing, seeing by itself does not encourage quality time on task and often leads to rather passive learning. Keep in mind that seeing and hearing, by themselves, are mostly inappropriate for the first two stages of growth and development. However, as you are about to learn, hearing and seeing together may enable the students to concentrate more of their attention on the task.

We learn and remember 20 per cent of what we both see and hear. Common sense would tell us that combining hearing and seeing is more effective than either just hearing or just seeing alone. When we both see and hear, abstractions tend to be explained, and thus the combination of seeing and hearing, when used as classroom instruction, is more useful in the third and fourth stages of growth and development. Watching television, seeing a movie, and taking notes on a lecture all fall into the category of 20 per cent learning and remembering. Try this experiment: listen to the radio, then turn off the radio and watch television. Which had the greater effect on focusing your attention? And which held your attention for a longer period of time? Usually television has proven to be a powerful means of communication because it does encourage both hearing and seeing. However, when a substantial amount of time is spent in watching television, it may become passive because learners may not be actively integrating the television programming into their personal experience.

We learn and remember 40 per cent of what we discuss with others. Suppose you are listening to a lecture. You probably will remember 10 per cent of what you hear. Suppose you take notes during the lecture and see the points made in the lecture written on the chalkboard. This reinforces learning and remembering to 20 per cent. Now, suppose the lecture is over and you take part in a small group discussion on the topic of the lecture. This improves learning and remembering to 40 per cent if you seriously participate by listening to the other students, responding yourself, and concentrating on the teacher's remarks. In short, if you focus on the topic and integrate the ideas into your store of knowledge, you are more likely to learn and remember. A reasonable generalization could be: learning improves substantially when there is a discussion, particularly if the discussion focuses attention and calls for an exchange of ideas in which the learners participate. In other words, the more students contribute ideas, the more they get out of the discussion in the form of learn-

ing and remembering. Thus discussion, where the student is focused and participating, is appropriate at all stages of growth and development.

We learn and remember 80 per cent of what we experience directly or practise. Have you ever practised an experiment in science, gone on a field trip, practised giving a speech, participated in a role play, or participated in a demonstration? Did you ever practise a sport, or sing with a group? All of these activities could lead to 80 per cent learning and remembering, primarily because they all require your active, undivided attention. If you are really concentrating on playing a game, learning a song, demonstrating a lesson, giving a speech, or observing during a field trip, then your mind is focusing attention on the task at hand. The 80 per cent level of learning and remembering suggests that the activity you are involved with promotes or encourages a long attention span where your mind is focused on a specific task, and this direct experience helps you to learn and remember. Direct experience, of course, is the most appropriate way of learning for the first two stages of growth and development from birth through age seven (class one), and it is also the most effective when dealing with concrete and abstract learning. If students experience an event and integrate that experience into their own understanding of that event, then they are most likely to comprehend (understand) it and to be able to retain it longer.

We learn and remember 90 per cent of what we attempt to teach others. Even without research confirming it, common sense and perhaps your own experience informs you that if you teach something to someone else, you are organizing and reinforcing for yourself the content you are teaching; and this activity leads to the highest percentage of learning and remembering. In short, when you are asked to explain an idea to others, the act of explaining actually clarifies the meaning for yourself. This makes sense, simply because in order to teach, you have to focus your entire attention on the task, and further, sustain that attention for an extended period of time. Almost all teachers know that they really learned their subject after they had started teaching it in school. Furthermore, studies suggest that cooperative learning and peer teaching are powerful ways to focus and reinforce what has been learned. Some have suggested that turning students into teachers (tutors) of other students will produce the highest percentage of learning and remembering for those doing the "teaching". Attempting to teach others is particularly appropriate for the second, third, and fourth stages of growth and development. In short, Programme Hodja had it right: the most effective learning occurs when "those who know explain to those who don't".

In Summary

Do not forget, when citing the percentages on learning and remembering, that because of preferences for different learning styles and the different age levels of the four stages of growth and development, these percentages are approximations. The learning pattern for no one pupil would likely fit exactly the percentages of any of the categories. But given an entire class or number of classes, the percentages offer a useful way to view how the students might respond and learn. Lecturing is the least effective way to help students learn and remember. When lecturing to students, however, you could enhance the learning and remembering of your students to 20 per cent by providing experiences, including teaching aids, audio-visual materials, and instructional resources that illustrate what you are trying to say.

Further, learning and remembering are greatly enhanced to the 40 per cent level through class and small group discussion where most students participate, with an even higher level of remembering (at 80 per cent) occurring when students experience directly or practise the skills or behaviours they are expected to know and acquire. When students teach other students, as in peer teaching, the student doing the tutoring is most likely to learn and retain information and understanding at the highest 90 per cent level. Thus, while passive and unfocused teaching will yield the least learning and remembering, in contrast, active and focused teaching will facilitate greater learning and remembering. In other words, the greater the opportunity for the student to focus attention and experience quality time on a task, the higher the percentage level of learning and remembering that will be achieved.

Though we have some understanding of the four stages of growth and development from a previous chapter and of the percentages on learning and remembering under different conditions, this does not indicate how we could effectively use this information in the classroom. We have said that knowing the stages and percentages should guide how we work with children and youth. What follows are eleven effective teaching practices that illustrate how to use this knowledge in the classroom.

Eleven Effective Teaching Practices to Focus Attention

These eleven practices to focus attention and to promote learning and remembering are identified as follows:

1. Accommodating
2. Challenging
3. Providing feedback
4. Goal setting
5. Integrating
6. Modelling
7. Reinforcement
8. Rewarding
9. Encouraging self-direction
10. Building self-esteem
11. Self-fulfilling prophecy

How do you now apply what you know about the percentages of learning and remembering that take place and the four stages of growth and development to teaching in the classroom? Summaries of research on effective teaching practices have consistently identified these eleven strategies that seem to be the most promising. As suggested earlier, the *key to learning is focusing attention on the task at hand.* Just how does a teacher focus that attention? What is it that a teacher could do in the classroom to focus students' attention on a task? The following eleven effective teaching practices can be a guide to this.

Focus Attention by Accommodating

Practise accommodating: Effective teaching accommodates students' needs and learning styles. This is particularly important to remember when working with special students, those who are mentally or physically handicapped. It is obvious that all students do not come to the classroom at the same stage of maturity, the same level of intellectual achievement, or the same level of skill development. Accommodating is literally "providing for", which means adapting and adjusting to the different needs and learning styles of students. Learning styles refer to the students' tendency to learn better through seeing, hearing, or participating in the lesson, which in turn reflects their ability to understand both concrete and abstract experiences. Accommodating is finding alternative ways of appealing to different learning styles at all stages of growth and development. Some alternative techniques to accommodate different learning styles in teaching the same lesson might be lecturing, or class discussion, or a panel discussion, or peer teaching, or having a guest speaker. The use of two or three of these techniques might be appropriate ways to accommodate different learning styles and enhance the percentage of learning and remembering.

Focus Attention by Challenging

Practise challenging: Effective teaching involves providing a challenging experience which questions, disputes, raises doubts, or suggests a reasonable risk. A challenge requires the full use of a pupil's abilities and energies in order to perform a task. For example, some challenging situations might include oral reports, role play, or debating the best way to promote a healthy environment. The students might identify a community study, projects, speakers, all of which would challenge the class to define and to maintain a healthy environment. A challenge can be a field trip to meet new and different people. Of course, some familiar challenges from teachers to students are to perform well on tests, to work hard on completing projects, and to pay attention in class. In short, the challenge in the classroom is to focus the children's attention on completing a task that requires a risk or a performance on the part of the student. Challenging experiences will vary according to the different stages of growth and development, with concrete experiences being more effective in the early stages. Students, when actively challenged, will most likely learn and remember at a higher level of thinking.

Focus Attention by Providing Feedback

Practise providing feedback: Effective teaching provides an opportunity to offer feedback to both teacher and students. Traditional feedback has been in the form of grades on a test or evaluation of an assignment. The knowledge that a response is correct greatly increases the likelihood of that response being learned and remembered. Positive feedback can be a teacher saying to a student, "Yes, that's a good idea."

An example of feedback might also be saying, "I liked the way you handled that situation, you've done a good job today", or "I'm pleased with your improvement." When a student puts forth considerable effort, you want to acknowledge it; but the praise should also include emphasis on achievement, such as, "Bernard, you have worked hard on the project. Your attention to detail and the good organization of your ideas have been quite outstanding." Positive oral feedback is important in the early stages of growth and development before children learn to read and write well. Teachers should also look for ways to provide private feedback. Private conversations, written comments on papers, tests, and on other assignments give the teacher opportunity for praising accomplishment. Feedback is extremely important in the learning progress. Students want to know about their progress, and teachers want to know if their instruction is effective. At times, progress on a lesson cannot be continued until there is feedback; particularly in stage four of the child's growth and development.

Focus Attention by Goal Setting

Practise goal setting: Effective teaching results from a clear idea of the goal to be accomplished. The setting of goals is one of the reasons for identifying the objectives for a lesson. Setting goals is important to learning and remembering because it focuses attention on what is to be learned. Research shows that when students know the goal or reason for the lesson, they are more likely to successfully complete that lesson and really learn from it. What the goal does is to focus attention on the task at hand. Knowing what the task is, students can direct their attention to what is to be learned. For example, if the teacher announces a goal at the beginning of a class, students are more likely to understand what is required of them. It seems to be important to learning and remembering if students

know (1) where they are going, (2) how they are to get there, and (3) what the outcome ought to be. This is true for all stages of growth and development.

Focus Attention by Integrating

Practise integrating: When children enter school for the first time, they come to that experience with an integrated understanding of their world. Integrated means that the children make sense of their world by understanding how different things, objects, events, and people all fit together (see Figure 1.1). The school experience begins by breaking that integrated sense of the world into exact and separate words, facts, definitions, descriptions, concepts, and generalizations. The formal school experience continues, through primary and into higher education, to separate knowledge into fields or disciplines called history, math, science, art, or music. The trend in modern education is to fragment knowledge into ever smaller bites, and from bites into mini-bites.

The primary teacher, however, is encouraged to integrate the child's experiences in class. For example, when talking about family, the lesson should integrate geography (place or village where the child lives), history (family history), social relations, culture, and change. Also integrated with the topic "family" might be music, art, and language. The point is that children can more easily identify the relationships between the different subject areas that are studied in class if these areas are integrated according to the children's personal experiences.

Focus Attention by Modelling

Practise modelling: Effective teaching requires modelling the behaviour that the teacher wants the student to practise at their stages of growth and development. Modelling means serving as an example to be imitated. For example, if the teacher wants students to have self-respect and respect for other people, to exhibit tolerance, be open-minded, have a willingness to try, be cooperative, demonstrate readiness, and to show impartiality, then the teacher should model these same behaviours. Social studies teachers who use a problem-solving, critical-thinking approach should model open-minded attitudes, allow students freedom to investigate, or should practise the skills and attitudes they want their students to have, and should encourage that behaviour from students. In short, good modelling requires the teacher to "Do as I say *and* as I do."

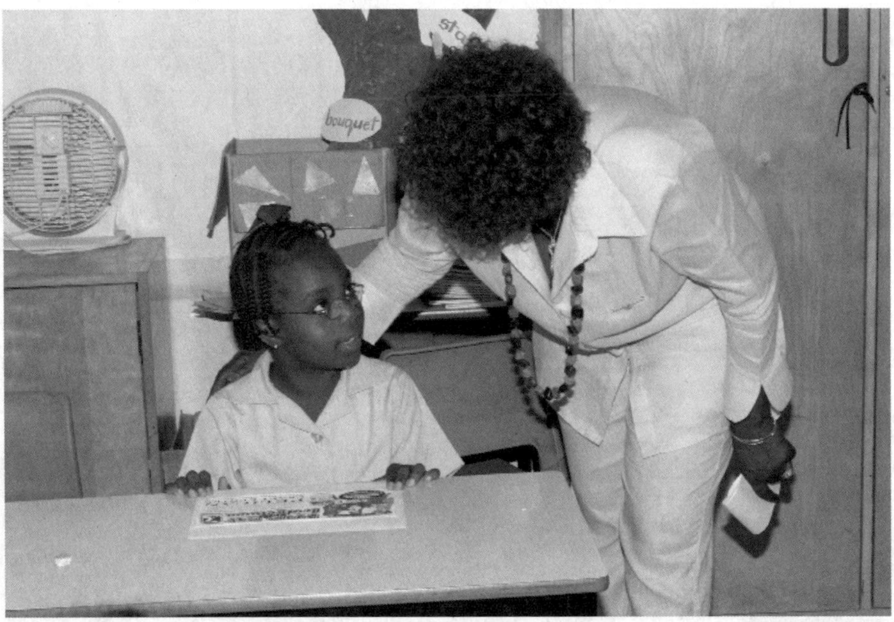

Focus Attention by Reinforcement

Practise reinforcement: Effective teaching should build in powerful reinforcement of ideas by repeating the same ideas in different forms of presentation. The more and varied the kinds of associations that are built around an idea or topic, the better is the learning and retention of the idea. "Hear it, say it, read it." For example, in a map location exercise, the social studies teacher might have a large map of the West Indies in the front of the room on which the teacher would point to Anguilla, Grenada, and St Kitts. A student or students would be called to the map to point out the same locations. Then students would have, at their desks, papers on which they would draw a map of the West Indies and mark the location of Anguilla, Grenada, and St Kitts. This exercise would have repeated the locations of these islands three times, but each time in a different form of presentation, thus also accommodating different styles of learning. Another example of reinforcement is giving a test and then using the test, after it has been evaluated, to reinforce through class discussion what should have been learned. Reinforcement could also involve having students *read* a passage or article, then students in small groups would *identify* the important points in the passage and *report* those points to the entire class. Reinforcement is effective at all stages of growth and development, and depending on the strategy of reinforcement used, it can lead to 80 per cent retention of learning and remembering.

Focus Attention by Rewarding

Practise rewarding: Effective teaching is rewarding for both teachers and students. The term "rewarding" implies a satisfying, mutual experience that is shared by both persons. For example, a teacher who wants to encourage and motivate performance, achievement, and participation will set incentives, such as field trips or free play time, as rewards for students to work towards. How does a teacher convey to individual students the positive rewards of success? We recommend public praise (reward) that is an acknowledgement to the students and the class that the student has accomplished a task well. However, the public praise (reward) should focus on the accomplishment rather than just the effort. While you want to acknowledge the effort, the praise should also include emphasis on achievement. As with feedback, the teacher should look for ways to provide private praise. Private conversations, written comments on papers, tests, and other assignments also give the teacher opportunity for praising accomplishment. Rewards are often a visible recognition of success. Types of rewards may vary in the four stages of growth and development, but it is an effective practice at all stages.

Focus Attention by Encouraging Self-Direction

Practise encouraging self-direction: Effective teaching encourages self-direction, which means self-management or supervision of one's own learning. One of the purposes of education is to encourage students to set their own goals and to learn how to work towards accomplishing those goals. Self-direction can be encouraged through students planning their own projects, engaging in small-group work, or in student-directed research. Some methods of teaching, such as problem solving, specifically promote the practice of self-direction where students identify and scientifically study several issues and problems. Self-direction becomes particularly important in the later stages of growth and development. For the Carib-bean Examinations Council examinations, for example, the school-based assessment (SBA) projects are largely self-directed research which students are required to undertake. *By practising self-direction from as early as primary school, students will be well equipped for these activities later.*

Focus Attention by Building Self-Esteem

Practise building self-esteem: Effective teaching sets a climate of warmth and trust and enhances the self-esteem of both teacher and students. In short, self-esteem is pride in oneself. Self-esteem is extremely important because it has to do with students' beliefs about their abilities and possibilities of achieving success in the classroom. Studies have shown that students who do not have a good self-image do not perform well in class. Building self-esteem, therefore, is important at all stages of growth and development. Teachers help students to build self-esteem by saying such things as, "You are a good student and I know you can do the work" or "This class has done excellent work and I know this quality of work will continue." Classrooms that emphasize a positive attitude, where social studies teachers believe students are capable, and where students know they can achieve some success, are likely to be effective places of learning.

Focus Attention by Self-Fulfilling Prophecy

Practise self-fulfilling prophecy: Effective teaching uses the principle of self-fulfilling prophecy. Prophecy is a prediction. The accomplishments or successes of students will depend on the teacher's treatment and expectations of them. If students are taught as though the teacher thinks they cannot learn, they probably will not learn. If, on the other hand, students are told that they are in an excellent class that can learn, they are more likely to learn. Students become what they think is expected of them. That is a self-fulfilling prophecy. What you think you can do, you probably can do and will do. When students know that teachers believe them to be capable, then it is easier for students to be challenged to new tasks. In short, believe you can, believe you cannot, either way you are right, and that is a self-fulfilling prophecy.

What We Have Discovered about How Children and Youth Learn Best

In summary, research on effective teaching, including percentages of learning and remembering and the four stages of growth and development, leads to the conclusion that students will remember information and develop skills and positive attitudes if they focus their attention and spend quality time on a task. If teachers are willing to "challenge" students with active learning by "modelling" learning behaviour, "rewarding" and "reinforcing" good performance, enhancing "self-esteem" by providing "feedback", "personalizing" instruction, permitting some "self-direction", while holding "positive expectations" for the class, and proposing clear "instructional goals", then they can expect to be effective teachers.

Looking Ahead

The application of effective teaching practices will be illustrated in the topics to follow, on methods, learning activities and strategies, and on the application of these. Many of the concerns of Caribbean teachers about student performance and learning could be successfully addressed if the effective teaching suggested here was actually practised in the classroom.

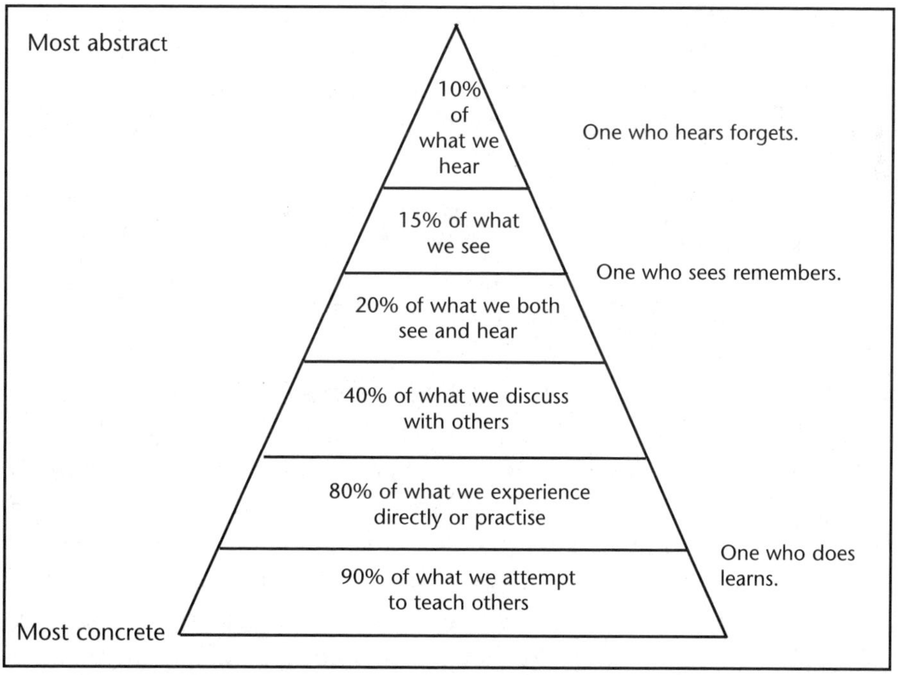

▶ **Figure 3.2:** Learning and Remembering

4

Methods, Learning Activities, and Strategies for Teaching Social Studies

Introduction

If you were to build a house, think of the building materials that would be necessary. You might consider the design of the house or think about what it should look like and how it should meet your needs. Planning to teach is much like building a house, the building materials are methods, techniques, and strategies, and the design is your unit and daily lesson plans. Your classroom will be your students' "house of learning".

The quality of your house of learning will depend on how imaginatively you organize the method, techniques and strategies, and this is why knowing about the many different building materials (techniques) and design (planning) is important.

Rationale for Learning about Methods

Telling is *not* primarily teaching. It is quite easy to think that teaching is telling. After all, teachers have been subjected to a great deal of telling in their education, and they tend to imitate that "model". In addition, there is a tendency to want to share one's vast store of knowledge by telling others what one knows. Another reason is that beginning teachers are usually afraid that their questions will provoke no response. Finally, it is much easier to tell than to make people think. But students are not

sponges, and ideas are not absorbed like water. No, telling is not primarily teaching.

There are times, of course, when a teacher ought to elaborate on a point or give students some background information that they do not yet have. But these times should be reduced to the minimum and teachers should not look upon their classes as captive audiences to which they should lecture at any school level. Teaching and learning takes place best when students are able to discover, to explore and to prove, under the guidance of a teacher who is understanding, yet challenging. The job of the teacher is to discover every possible means for arousing interest, encouraging critical thinking, stimulating questions and promoting deep thinking. The effective teacher examines ideas, issues, problems, countries, people, and institutions with students. Real teaching and, by extension, real learning, is the process of probing, discovering, analysing, and examining: in short, creating knowledge. The goal of all social studies teaching is the maturing of future participating citizens in a democratic society.

Trends and Directions of Teaching Citizenship Education

The following are contemporary twenty-first century trends (see Chart 4.1) that are found in social studies curriculum guides for the future. These trends are also based upon what is known about how students learn best. It is these changing ideas or trends that require a greater professional knowledge of methods, techniques, and strategies.

Trends Chart	
Change from past citizenship education	To future teaching of citizenship education
1. Aims	
Amassing information.	Changing behaviour; acquiring attitudes and understandings; developing skills; acquiring useful knowledge.
Stress on the past and transmitting the culture.	Stress on the present and future; past used to illuminate them. Transmitting culture and some attention to transforming it.
2. Course of Study	
Based solely or largely on society's needs – often from the past.	Determined by teachers with some help from parents and based on needs of boys and girls for living in society today and tomorrow.
3. Methods	
Teacher planning; use of single textbook for entire class.	Some teacher-student planning. Active learning includes improved use of textbook and/or use of several reading references plus a variety of experiences such as trips and audio-visual aids.
Lecture and recitation.	Variety of activities, including committees, panels, reports and projects.
Largely teacher dominated.	Group centred, with teacher as expert guide. Cooperative learning and learning centres.
Classroom as sole location for learning.	Classroom, school, community, nation, and the world as locations for learning.
History, geography, civics as separate and often very distinct subjects.	Social studies is the integrated concepts from history, geography, and civics along with other social sciences such as psychology, sociology, economics, anthropology and global studies.
4. Evaluation	
Objective tests giving little or no chance for the exercise of judgement or development of organizing ability.	A variety of types of evaluation, including observation of behaviour, tests of skills and attitudes. Many types of test questions representing both objective and subjective.

▶ **Chart 4.1:** Trends in Teaching Citizenship Education

Do the Trends and Research Suggest Methods for Effective Teaching?

The research on learning and remembering (see chapter 3) supports the future trends in the trends chart. Can you recall some of the significant points made about good teaching in the previous chapter? One such point is, "The key to learning and remembering is helping students to focus attention on a task." A second point you should remember is, students learn better - learn faster, remember more, and derive greater enjoyment - when they are actively involved in learning. It is for this reason that teacher-training courses should begin with the assumption that methods, techniques, and strategies should emphasize active learning. The aim of classroom instruction is to focus students and to help them retain attention through the planning of effective teaching practices. In support of this aim, we offer Chart 4.2 on active versus passive learning. The chart summarizes the research findings on how students learn best, and thus

Active vs Passive Learning Chart	
Students learn best:	Teaching practices/benefits to be derived:
A. When there is 1. clarity (which means students know what they are supposed to do) 2. enthusiasm 3. a positive attitude 4. A specified goal to be accomplished	These four goals are related to the effective teaching practices of **goal setting and building self-esteem.**
B. When they are 1. asked stimulating questions rather than being lectured to 2. asked questions at different levels	Students who ask stimulating questions focus attention and encourage the effective teaching practices of **providing feedback, challenging, modelling, rewarding, and integrating.**
C. When teachers respond to their actions in an encouraging manner, 1. with constructive positive feedback on their work 2. by teaching them as though they are expected to succeed	These points are related to the effective teaching practices of **providing feedback, accommodating, and self-fulfilling prophecy.**
D. When there is student-to-student interaction. This means there is a discussion in which they participate in an exchange of ideas.	This point is related to the effective teaching practices of **providing feedback, reinforcement, and encouraging self-direction.**

Chart 4.2: Active vs Passive Learning

should be the foundation used by modern teachers to build a philosophy and psychology of teaching.

You know from personal experiences that active involvement is likely to help focus attention and help you to remember. All students in a class are not usually actively involved with each activity. You may, for example, organize the class into small groups. Out of a class of forty, twenty may actively participate, while twenty may be passive and indifferent about grouping. As you already know from research on learning, at any given moment during a lecture, only 10 per cent of the class is actively, thoughtfully listening. Students are skilled at taking notes, staring at the teacher, appearing to be actively involved when, in fact, their minds are somewhere else. Students are mentally tuning in and out of a lecture from moment to moment, thus a teacher can never be quite sure which 10 per cent of the students actually heard and understood what was being said. The key to learning is active attention to the task at hand.

Any Strategy for Teaching Social Studies Should Include Several Techniques

The point is, teachers need to use a variety of techniques in the hope of focusing and retaining students' attention. During an average class period, at least two or three different techniques are needed to keep students' attention active, depending on the length of the class period. All students are not equally attracted to each technique. Some enjoy and

actively watch films, some sleep (are passive) through films. Five or six students might actively participate in class discussion, while thirty-five sit silent and passive. Lecturing is a favourite technique for a few students but ineffective for many. Teachers are, therefore, encouraged to use a variety of techniques. A variety will increase chances of reaching a greater number of students and improve their quality time on a task. It is for this reason that you should identify a *method* and variety of *techniques* which you plan as a *strategy* to actively involve all students, at least part of the time.

Before introducing the definition of methods, be aware that teacher educators may have different definitions of methods, techniques, and strategy. The fact that these definitions may differ because they reflect different fields of study should not cause you great concern. What you should focus on is the relationship between method (overall approach), techniques (activities performed in class), and strategies (the order in which the techniques are carried out in class). Why discuss methods, techniques, and strategies? Because they describe how a lesson is going to be taught, starting from the general method to the specific techniques as part of a strategy that is called planning. In short, methods, techniques, and strategies describe what the teacher will do and how it is going to be done.

Defining the Relationship between Method, Technique, and Strategy

In many countries, the word "method" is assumed to mean planning, evaluation, use of teaching aids, techniques, and strategies; in short, almost anything a teacher does in the classroom. In this chapter, a distinction is made between the three terms: method, technique, and strategy because each has a different role in planning to teach.

Methods, techniques, and strategies are just names for three different levels of planning that a teacher thinks about when preparing to teach. Admittedly, the three levels may sound confusing, but is there a real difference in meaning between the three? Method refers to a teacher's approach to instruction, whereas technique means the specific activities performed in class, that is lecture, grouping, or discussion. Strategy describes the sequencing of the techniques during a class period. For example, a teacher may say, "My method for today is a problem-solving approach. I am going to achieve problem solving by using the techniques of small group, panel discussion, and field trip. My strategy is to sequence those techniques in the following order: first a short field trip, followed by grouping of students by interest to discuss what they have observed on the field trip, and finally a panel discussion with one member of each group participating on the panel." Having identified a method, techniques, and a strategy, the teacher has automatically planned the lesson for the day; in other words, what the class will do and how it is going to be done.

What Is Meant by a Method of Teaching?

Keep in mind that a method is a teacher's overall pedagogical approach to a lesson. Some educational authorities believe there are actually only two general methods (approaches) to teaching. One method emphasizes *transmitting* (meaning to hand down, convey, or impart) subject matter. In brief, the teacher's approach is expository, where the teacher dominates the instructional process and tells the students what they need to know. That method is called *knowledge transmission.*

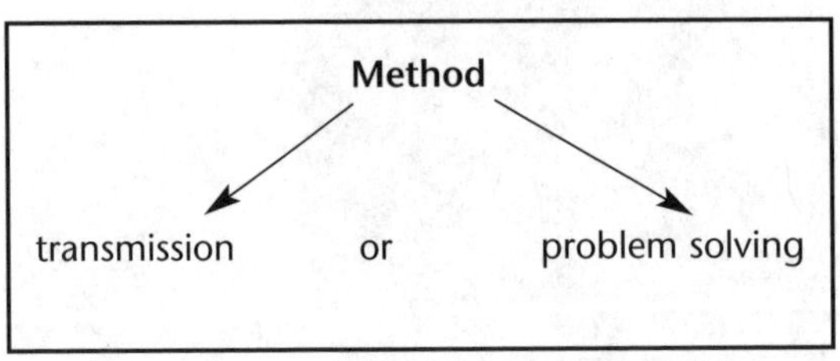

Figure 4.1: Methods of Teaching

The second method is *problem solving* (meaning to examine, investigate, and explore the subject matter). Problem solving includes the following categories of reflective thinking: discovery, critical thinking, decision making, enquiry, reflective thinking and reflective enquiry. Under this method, the students are challenged to do the examining, investigating, and exploring. In brief, the teacher's approach to the lesson is to organize a series of activities, such as field trip, small groups, and panel discussion, in which the students are working on a problem. Very simply, teachers tend to emphasize one or the other of these two methods - although, of course, teachers at times use a mixture of both. Generally speaking, teachers who lecture and have recitation and discussion almost all of the time, lean towards the transmission method. Those who emphasize discovery, investigation, and reflective enquiry can be said to favour a problem-solving method.

In summary, method is defined as the systematic way teachers generally approach their teaching. The method indicates how the teacher intends to proceed with the lesson. One teacher may intend to proceed by presenting the information, while another teaching the same lesson may intend to proceed by problem solving where the students are required to work on a problem. The transmission teacher might plan a lecture on the content of the text. The problem-solving teacher might plan projects in which the students are required to be self-directed problem solvers. If a method is how a teacher generally intends to systematically approach the lesson, what then is a technique?

What Is Meant by Technique?

Technique is simply what teachers ask the students to perform in the classroom, that is, listening to a lecture, writing out a work paper, or answering questions. In short, technique is an action performed to achieve the method. When approaching the teaching of a lesson, how do you know what techniques to use? The method suggests the appropriate techniques to be used (see Figure 4.2).

For example, if we assume the method is problem solving, then techniques to achieve that method might call for student participation in projects, grouping, role playing, or simulation. If the method is transmission, then the techniques might be lecturing and recitation, or workbook exercises. Another way of expressing the relationship between method and technique is to ask the questions, "What do you want to do? What is your intent?" If the answer is, "I want to cover the subject matter in the chapter," this suggests the transmission method. Or, "Specifically how are you going to teach the material in the chapter?" Answer, "By using the techniques of lecture and recitation." Now I know your method, which is transmission, and your techniques, which are lecture and recitation.

Method is the approach to instruction.	Technique is an action performed to achieve the method.
1. Transmission method *or* 2. Problem-solving method	• lecture • recitation • discussion • workbook exercise • teaching aids • grouping • debate • panel discussion • oral report

▶ **Figure 4.2:** Method versus Technique

What Is Meant by Teaching Strategy?

Strategy is simply the sequencing or the ordering of the techniques a teacher has selected to teach the lesson. In chapter 3, eleven different effective teaching practices were identified. For example, one of the eleven was *reinforcement,* in which the teacher planned a strategy sequence of three techniques or activities. First, the teacher pointed to the map to identify locations; second, a student was asked to come up to the map and also point out locations; and for the third activity, the students filled out the location on their own maps. In short, the teacher planned a strategy of reinforcement that included three techniques to teach map locations. All of the other ten strategies described in chapter 3, such as modelling, rewarding, self-direction, and so on, imply the same sense of sequencing of activities or techniques.

Increasingly, teachers talk about strategies, a term popularized by the military, which suggests the plan for winning a battle – in this case, in the classroom. How does strategy relate to method and technique? Very simply, strategy refers to sequencing (organizing) a given selection of techniques based on a particular approach.

For example, if one were to select such techniques as introductory lecture, grouping, and panel discussion, these techniques sequenced one after the other are called a strategy. This implies that there is an appropriate ordering of the techniques. Suppose the panel discussion depends upon a grouping of students and a lecture, then the proper sequencing of the techniques to achieve the transmission of content would be (1) lecture, (2) grouping, and (3) panel discussion (see Figure 4.3).

Technique is an action performed to achieve the method.	Strategy is the sequencing of techniques to achieve the method.	
• lecture • recitation • discussion • workbook exercise • teaching aids • grouping	Lecture, then discussion, then workbook exercise.	Sequenced to achieve the method of transmission.
	or	
• debate • panel discussion • oral report	Field experience, then projects, then written/oral reports.	Sequenced to achieve the method of problem-solving.

▶ **Figure 4.3:** Technique versus Strategy

Summary of Definition of Method, Technique, and Strategy

It is not the case that citizenship is inherently more passive than other subjects. Nevertheless, it is the case that many students complain about how uninteresting, dull, lifeless, and obscure citizenship education can be. If teachers use one or two techniques, they should be prepared to face students who are silent, passive, bored, and uncooperative. If, however, you wish to reach a greater number of students, be prepared to plan a strategy using two to three techniques per lesson, depending on the length of the social studies lesson. No one can really tell you what techniques you must use. But it is important that whatever techniques you do select should *emphasize active participation,* because this is what the research and the trends for teaching suggest. It is important to understand that any given technique may be either passive or active. For example, lecture, grouping, oral reports, field trips, debates, panel discussions, or simulations may be either active or passive, depending on whether students are focused and spend quality time on the lesson. The relationship between method, technique, and strategy is summarized in Figure 4.4.

Method is the approach to instruction.	Technique is an action performed to achieve the method.	Strategy is the sequencing of techniques to achieve the method.	
1. Transmission method *or*	• lecture • recitation • discussion • workbook exercise • teaching aids • grouping • debate	Lecture, then discussion, then workbook exercise.	Sequenced to achieve the method of transmission. *or*
2. Problem-solving method	• panel discussion • oral report	Field experience, then projects, then written/oral reports.	Sequenced to achieve the method of problem solving.

▶ **Figure 4.4:** Method, Technique, Strategy

Techniques: The Building Blocks of Effective Teaching

If techniques are truly the building blocks in your students' "house of learning", then there is good reason why you, as a teacher, ought to know and be proficient in many different techniques. Suppose at this moment you were asked to list ten different techniques you might use to teach a lesson. When you get beyond lecturing, discussion, and reading the textbook, what other techniques do you think about? Can you think of a reason for knowing not only three techniques, but one hundred different techniques. Have you said to yourself: some students learn well by reading, others need to hear, see, practise, talk, or touch objects? Some learn well by themselves, while others need group participation. In short, different students learn differently. Having a variety of techniques at your command opens your mind to many ways of meeting differences.

Start with 180 Techniques

The following 180 techniques, with more to be identified later, are organized according to the categories of learning and remembering in chapter 3. As you have already discovered, how a technique is to be applied depends on a teacher's general approach or method (transmission or problem solving). Thus, naming a technique does not suggest how it is to be applied. How techniques are planned into a teaching strategy is addressed in the next chapter. For the moment, be excited by the almost infinite number of techniques that you can use in the classroom.

180 Techniques Based upon Percentages of Learning and Remembering

Hearing Techniques

We learn and remember 10 per cent of what we hear.

1. Lecture by teacher
2. Recitation: oral question by teacher answered orally by students
3. Listening to a panel presentation by instructors or students
4. Listening to individual student oral reports
5. Listening to student-group reports by committees from classes
6. Teacher playing music to illustrate a culture
7. Listening to recordings: records, tapes, CDs
8. Listening to radio programmes
9. Verbal illustration: use of anecdotes and parables
10. Listening to story telling by students
11. Teacher relating a trip or experience
12. Listening to a resource person for whom students have prepared a series of questions

(Use your imagination, think of other techniques that require hearing. Be excited about the endless possibilities.)

Seeing Techniques

We learn and remember 15 per cent of what we see.

13. Reading textbook assignment
14. Reading assignment in journals, monographs, etc.
15. Reading assignment in supplementary books
16. Use of maps, globes, transparencies
17. Open textbook study
18. Use of chalkboard by teacher as an aid in teaching
19. Use of diagrams, tables, graphs, and charts by teacher
20. Use of exhibits and displays by teacher
21. Viewing reproductions of famous places, people, and events
22. Viewing motion pictures without sound
23. Teacher-made timelines

24. Teacher-made units of instruction organized by topics
25. Portraying abstract ideas using posters
26. Reading local history
27. Using free and low-cost materials such as local and national promotional materials, or tourist agency materials, as classroom resources
28. Collecting and using old magazines
29. Making and using coloured slides
30. Students following the activities of a world leader (in the newspaper)
31. Students read novels and poetry for different perspective
32. Pantomime (drama without a spoken word) on historic events
33. String a clothesline across classroom, and using clothespins to pin current event dates in sequence

(Be excited by the endless possibilities. Think of other techniques that require seeing.)

Both Seeing and Hearing Techniques

We learn and remember 20 per cent of what we both see and hear.

34. Lecture-demonstration by teacher
35. Lecture-demonstration by guest speaker
36. Using flannel board to help students tell a story
37. Use of slides with sound
38. Use of theatre motion pictures with sound
39. Use of television
40. Using word association (both say it and see it)
41. Students reading aloud
42. Inviting elder citizens to present local history to class, including displaying artefacts (clothing, tools, pictures, other objects)
43. Students watching a skit (planned dramatic play)

(Don't limit your imagination to this list. Be excited by the endless possibilities.)

Discussion Techniques

We learn and remember 40 per cent of what we discuss with others.

44. Class discussion
45. Discussion groups conducted by selected student chairperson
46. Presentation by student panels from class: class invited to participate

47. Debates (informal) on current issues by students from the class
48. Class discussions conducted by a student or student committee
49. Forums (open discussion)
50. Small group tutorial with teacher
51. Socratic small group with teacher as leader of small group
52. Discussion – task-oriented small group focused on specific project
53. Brainstorming in small groups, students identify a list of learning activities and strategies that best fit their class
54. Fortune-telling game: class predicts what will happen in the future because of some major news event

(Think of other ways [techniques] to use discussion. Your imagination is the only limit.)

Experiential or Participatory Techniques

We learn and remember 80 per cent of what we experience directly or participate in.

55. Students creating bulletin board
56. Participating in small group projects
57. Choral speaking (the class reads together)
58. Students collecting items: newspapers, magazines, pictures, bottle caps, and so on, for class use
59. Assignment to outline portions of the textbook
60. Assignment to outline certain supplementary readings
61. Students participating in formal debates
62. Working crossword puzzles
63. Cooking foods of places studied
64. Student construction of vocabulary lists
65. Vocabulary drills
66. Students keeping diaries
67. Performing dances of places or periods studied
68. Construction of summaries by students
69. Dressing dolls to illustrate different customs or people or periods of time
70. Students writing term papers
71. Students creating a class media centre
72. Students preparing and presenting biographical reports
73. Reports given by students on published research studies and experiments
74. Research on topics or problems
75. Written book reports by students

76. Making flags of selected countries
77. Jigsaw-puzzle maps made by students
78. Students setting up a "Hall of Fame" by topic or era (military or political leaders, heroes)
79. Simulations of local government (an imitation of event)
80. Student-made flash cards
81. Student-made flow charts
82. Student interviewing resource people
83. Creating mobiles on specific topics
84. Audio-tutorial lessons (individualized instruction)
85. Making models, collages
86. Taking field trips to view local landforms
87. Drama, formal and informal
88. Student-initiated committee projects
89. Keeping a journal, noting personal impressions and feelings
90. Students constructing murals
91. Class-selected school/community service projects
92. Individual projects selected according to students' interests
93. Quizdown gaming
94. Modelling with clay, papier-mâché, and other substances
95. Corresponding with pen pals from a different district, region, country
96. Students taking and showing photographs
97. Performing experiments on the environment (testing soil, water, air)
98. Use of dramatic plays – free association based on life experiences
99. Student construction of diagrams, charts, or graphs
100. Students making holiday posters
101. Students drawing pictures or cartoons
102. Compiling case studies of people, places, or things
103. Use of puppets
104. Construction of exhibits and displays by students
105. Role-playing to illustrate an important point, to stimulate imagination
106. Students using sand tables
107. Student planning and undertaking service projects for the community
108. Students preparing a list of community, local, regional, or district resources
109. Student survey of community needs and interests
110. Practising good oral reporting techniques
111. Student use of workbooks
112. Student making classroom teaching aids such as ink, paints, or dye from local materials

113. Student construction of scrapbooks
114. Student-made timelines
115. Practice of good study habits during class period
116. Oral history: collecting stories from elders in the community
117. Student use of computer-based instruction
118. Writing a caption for a chart, picture, or cartoon
119. Students holding a mock or real election for class monitor, prefect or other position using leaflets, slogans, and other electioneering paraphernalia
120. Preparing editorial for school paper or local newspaper
121. Attending local government meetings
122. Exchanging "things" (stamps, coins, crafts)
123. Preparing and making announcements of coming events
124. Taking part in community elections, census survey, community development project
125. Students playing music from other countries or times
126. Compiling a list of elder citizens as resource people
127. Inviting students from different schools
128. Students visiting an "ethnic" restaurant (traditional, Chinese, Italian, French, American)
129. Students doing specialized research on one country, district, or village
130. Starting a campaign ("Save the Environment", "Don't Litter", "Talk Reason, Don't Use Violence")
131. Students investigating a life: national personality, family tree
132. Assisting an immigrant as a "big brother" or "big sister"
133. Students preparing an exhibit
134. Collecting money for a reputable cause
135. Electing persons to a "Hall of Fame" for males: athletes, artists, teachers, musicians, statesmen, world figures
136. Electing persons to a "Hall of Fame" for females
137. Constructing a "salt" map (see chapter 6)
138. Writing and producing a drama
139. Preparing a presentation for elder citizen group
140. Preparing mock newspaper on specific topic or era
141. Students drawing a giant map on the floor or ceiling of classroom
142. Researching local historical (archaeological) site
143. Exchange programme with schools from different communities or countries
144. Weaving on a loom, or operating some other traditional machinery
145. Preparing mock clay tablets
146. Carving objects from soap

147. Carving potatoes for printing
148. Constructing toy carts as illustrations of present and past
149. Making marionettes and putting on show
150. Helping teacher make homemade compass
151. Visiting the museum to view exhibits of historic culture
152. Students detecting propaganda in advertising and editorials in newspapers and magazines
153. Using games and toys to study family, communities, and countries
154. Constructing balloon globes from papier-mâché for studying world current events
155. Identifying a systematic set of career exploration experiences
156. Students develop criteria to judge the relevance of their social studies textbooks
157. Working in cooperative learning groups
158. Use of manipulative learning aids such as board games and puzzles
159. Students setting up classroom learning centres
160. Teacher creates a classroom where children act upon, modify, or transform knowledge through the creation of collages and murals
161. Students prepare a class or school history album including photos, short biographies, or creative works

(This list is just a beginning. Imagine other techniques to help students experience or participate.)

Suppose the class were studying the environment.

162. Catalogue natural resources in the community or parish
163. Locate and map local natural features (rivers, lakes, hills)
164. Locate and map local man-made features (roads, bridges, railroads)
165. Students classify man-made features according to function (transportation, shelter, recreation)
166. Students locate sounds or odours in their community that are natural and man-made
167. Bring to class small animals to study (include insects, reptiles, birds – animals with which students share their environment)
168. Students collect plaster casts of footprints – human and other animals as signs of what has lived in the environment
169. List forms of life found in warm or wet seasons and compare with those found in the cool or dry season
170. Students examine microscopic specimens, through a microscope, of local rainwater, pond water, or school drinking water
171. Locate old and recent newspaper articles on community environmental issues to identify change

172. Students collect litter items from outside school and ask what story the individual items suggest about life in the community
173. Identify and name sources of energy that students use in daily life
174. Compare lifestyles of communities having different energy sources: wood, coal, gas, water, electric, nuclear

Attempt-to-Teach-Others Technique

We learn and remember 90 per cent of what we attempt to teach others.

175. Students making oral reports
176. Student groups making committee reports to class
177. Using students' collections of stamps, coins, crafts, and other hobbies in class as presented by the students
178. Tutorials: students assigned to other students for assistance, peer teaching
179. Producing a pageant to illustrate a series of events
180. Roundtable of students summarizing current events

The list should be endless. Your imagination is the only limit.

It may be true that some social studies teachers, because of the school curriculum, are primarily focused on one of the social sciences or history. Thus, some teachers would be interested in techniques particularly for the teaching of geography, history, government (civics), or perhaps even environmental studies. Besides the 180 social studies techniques listed above, under the categories of how a child learns best, we now add an additional sixty-seven techniques which are categorized by subject area.

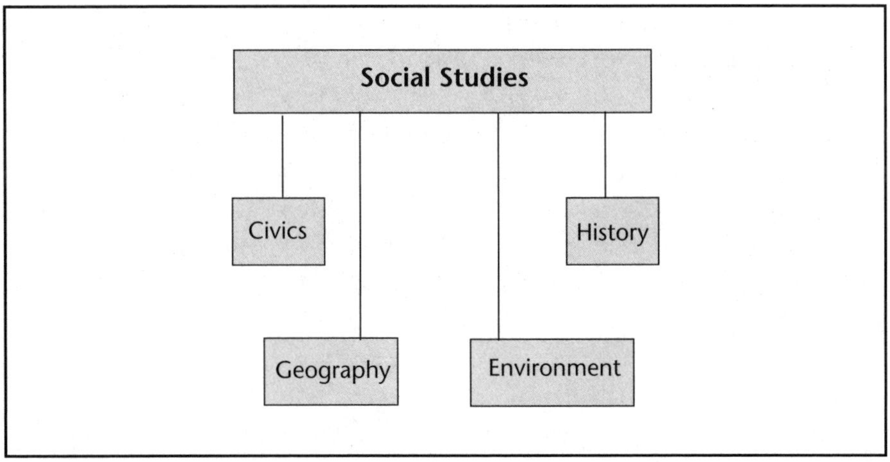

Figure 4.5: Subject-Specific Areas in the Social Studies

Techniques and Strategies for Subject-Specific Teaching

When one examines the content of many social studies or citizenship education programmes, one finds that the specific subjects most commonly drawn on are geography, history, civics, and environmental education. At times, the content of the subject areas are integrated (meaning parts are joined to make a new, meaningful, and reputable whole). Since the specific subject areas are so prominent in many citizenship programmes, they should be noted and especially treated in terms of the methods, techniques, and strategies discussed earlier. Though the list of 180 techniques is relevant to all social studies curricula, there are techniques and strategies that should be particularly helpful when one is thinking about effectively teaching subject-specific geography, history, and civics. With the 180 techniques already listed, we can now add an additional sixty, making for a total of 240 suggested techniques to stimulate your imagination and to be a continuous guide and reference for classroom instruction.

Why Teach Geography as Part of Social Studies or Citizenship Education?

Every day we make important decisions about our well-being, and every day we use geographic knowledge in our lives. We interpret complicated geographical factors to determine the places where we choose to live – physical characteristics such as climate, topography, and drainage influence where we can build safe, secure, and desirable housing. Cultural factors include quality housing and schools, convenient transportation routes to work and for leisure. All of these factors affect our quality of life.

A sound geographic education provides the background, information, concepts, and skills to understand ourselves, our relationship to the Earth, and our interdependence with other places and peoples of the world. Geography reinforces and extends the process of critical thinking and problem solving on decisions we make in our country. Thus, geography is often integrated into social studies lessons. In primary school social studies, geography provides an effective means for asking questions about places on Earth and their relationships to people. Geographic education focuses on five central themes (location, place, relationships within places, movement, and regions), and we examine below how these themes follow a scope and sequence throughout the social studies curriculum.

The primary role of geography is (1) to present information and facts about the world: to introduce and reinforce the concepts of location, place, relationships within places, movement between and among places, and the region; (2) to examine values and attitudes towards environments; and (3) to sharpen intellectual and practical skills. Students bring to the classroom a wide range of incidental and systematic information about geography, and, where possible, teachers should use students' prior learning. In their own fashion, these students have learned how to find their way from place to place, have observed how their surroundings have changed, and have experienced how these changes have affected sites, paths, boundaries, and culture. In the primary grades, geographic education offers children a unique opportunity to explore and understand their immediate life space, as well as other areas in their country and in the Caribbean. Children will acquire not only geographic knowledge but also will develop essential skills for gathering, interpreting, and portraying geographical information.

Suggested Techniques for Dealing with Geographical Issues

1. Make maps of different kinds, including salt maps, clay maps, moulded maps, papier-mâché globes. (See chapter 6 on "Audio-Visual Aids for Teaching Social Studies".)
2. Collect and mount pictures to be used for picture study in the class.
3. Build a collection of slides, through photography or making slides of your own. (See slide construction in chapter 6.)
4. Collect, mount, and use all kinds of travel posters.
5. Interview students from other parts of the country or persons who have travelled in other parts of the world.
6. Plan trips to some other Caribbean island – plan the transport, clothing, time.
7. Correspond with persons on another island or country. (Family members, friends of friends are sources of names and addresses.)
8. Read novels, poetry, biographies, and autobiographies set in or about people of various islands to deepen understanding of other people throughout the Caribbean.
9. Take trips in the community to see geographical features: the landforms that make the region unique, how and where people live, possible environmental problems.
10. Visit museums to learn about the Earth at different points in its history and to see exhibits on earlier peoples who lived in the West Indies and in your country.
11. Exchange materials made in your school with those in a school overseas. (Start by writing UNICEF asking for addresses.)
12. Compare and contrast accounts of geographical features, activity, or country in a variety of textbooks.

13. Take, draw, or collect pictures of the local community of other islands or in other countries, showing geographical features or people and their way of living, then prepare a bulletin board or display.
14. Participate in some aid programme for a group of people in another part of the world through CARE, UNICEF, UNESCO. Are there people in the world who could use your interest and help?
15. Become an expert on a particular part of your country. Display what you have gathered as an expert on a flannel board or other medium.
16. Read in the daily newspaper accounts that involve geography. Do news stories include geographic content: landforms, people, and environment? Collect clippings for a scrapbook.
17. View TV programmes or listen to radio programmes that tell about the Earth, space, or people of the world.
18. Arrange an exhibit for the school on some geographical topic such as resources, transportation, or the environment either in your community, island, or another Caribbean country.

In chapter 5, "Applying Methods, Techniques, and Strategies", there is a special section on teaching maps and globes. Consult that section to identify how maps and globes should be developmentally taught throughout the primary school. Also, see chapter 6, in which the construction of maps and globes is described.

Why Teach History as Part of Social Studies or Citizenship Education?

Like literature, philosophy, and the arts, history is a way of looking at human experience – at the lives of the individuals who are its "parts", and at the life of the society, which is the sum of its parts. What is history's importance to the Caribbean in the twenty-first century? What does it have to say that is of value? Why teach history?

First, history is a response to the eternal desire of man to know about himself and others. For this reason, it is fundamentally a humane study, emphasizing the importance of people, their individual choices, the values they hold, the way they see themselves and the world. One of history's most valuable contributions is that it puts the present in its proper place.

Second, history is concerned with societies as well as with individuals. Historians are interested in how, and hopefully why, people have acted together as social beings. History observes how men have developed their institutions, what they have used them for, and how they have ordered their lives. Today's society can distill something from the past that may be useful for its guidance, for history has a kind of built-in warning system for those who know how to listen to it.

Third, history emphasizes the uniqueness of human experience. However attractive the parallels between past and present may be, we learn that the past is not really repetitive, that history never does quite repeat itself. History, in fact, warns us that we cannot exactly repeat experiences, and thus we cannot say that what worked once, or failed once, will do so again. History serves as a corrective measure to remind us that we are very, very human.

The purpose of history, then, is not merely to locate and understand the facts of human experience, but to transcend experiences by giving them values that are stimulating, suggestive, and relevant to the students' life, to the problems the students understand, and to the citizenship decisions the students must make.

Suggested Techniques for Dealing with Historical Issues

1. Novels and biographies can often give a better "feel" for a person or period of history than any textbook can.
2. Plays and poetry can also help students to understand, emotionally, parts of their history.
3. Maps should be used extensively. A large map of the West Indies is an absolute necessity. Maps in textbooks should be studied rather than merely looked at. A variety of maps based on themes can be made and posted in the room for use by the class. (For help in how to construct maps and globes, see chapter 6 on audio-visual aids.)
4. Socratic small groups is a useful technique. For example, a class may be divided into the east, south, north, and west in order to understand how these different areas of the Caribbean reacted in general to such issues as the need for economic development, political independence, or national security.
5. Museums can be rich resources for class trips or trips by individuals or committees both during and outside of class time.
6. Pictures should be collected and used to help students to "see" events and persons in the past. Sometimes, they can be shown to advantage through the overhead projector. The students can make their own transparencies. (See chapter 6 on audio-visual aids.)
7. Radio and television programmes can often be used to enrich learning. In some cases, they can be given as homework assignments, keeping in mind that today's news is tomorrow's history.
8. Trips, if well planned, can enhance learning, especially if the community has many historic places. Every community has a history.

9. Simple research can be undertaken by students, especially those who are interested in history, but also to build interest.
10. Mount bulletin-board displays of community history, both past and present.
11. Current events should be used to help students to see that old problems are still with us, even if in different forms, or to show how the past helps to explain the present, and to help us make decisions today.
12. Timelines are most useful for helping to establish time concepts.

For other good suggestions on teaching historical issues, see the section "Suggested Techniques for Environmental Education" in this chapter.

Why Teach Civics as Part of Social Studies or Citizenship Education?

Primary school civics programmes attempt to achieve several goals. Among these are helping students to understand their social environment and develop sensitivity to political issues and problems. Teachers need to remember that the reason for including civics in the curriculum is to draw on civics perspectives to help students attempt to think about their problems and those of the community and the nation.

Current civics programmes include such concepts as power and authority in the family, the school, and the community. Attention is given in civics to (1) public employees; (2) public services such as education, protection, and recreation; (3) city planning and redevelopment; and (4) urban planning in order to solve transportation, traffic, and other community problems. Studies often include concepts such as authority, separation of powers, processes of government, and democracy; materials on law and powers, and processes of government; and materials on law and government.

The study of civics should be a lively confrontation and should provide realistic and predominantly first-hand experiences as much as possible. The test of the success of civics content should be the improvement of daily living in the home, school, and community, and the eventual participation by students in political life, in a democratic manner, whether by voting, canvassing for a candidate, or posing questions at public meetings.

Suggested Techniques for Dealing with Civics Issues

1. Make a collection of clippings on current problems, and mount them

for the class or school to see, taking care to have several viewpoints represented.

2. Make a similar collection of cartoons on an issue, again presenting two differing points of view.
3. Listen to a radio or television programme on an issue of current importance. Report the issue to the class as a cartoon or drawing, or by oral report.
4. Present a *panel* discussion before a class, school assembly, local club, or other organization in your community, after the panel members have become "experts" on the topic or issue.
5. Draw a world map showing the different types of government now existing.
6. Study the life of a Caribbean or world political leader, past or present.
7. Interview local officials on their duties and problems.
8. Interview an older citizen about the changes in government or politics during the citizen's lifetime.
9. If there is one, examine your student government, and try to suggest ways in which it might be improved. If there is not one, draw up a proposal for one.
10. Organize a class "resource squad", "acquiring audio-visual materials squad", or "homework squad" to encourage and assist other students with homework or some other classroom service activity. Let the students learn to participate.
11. Plan a survey of school traffic or traffic hazards near the school, or make some similar survey that will benefit your school or the community.
12. If school elections are a feature of your school, suggest improvements in the ways of holding them.
13. Make a list of services rendered by your local government, and check the ones that help you as an individual, directly or indirectly.
14. Take pictures of local government activities, and mount them in your classroom or school.
15. Arrange a debate on some current issue such as traffic problems, community health, community development, sports facilities.
16. Start a campaign to collect books and magazines as resources for your class or school.
17. Conduct a poll of citizens on a current issue, being sure to word your topics without bias and to protect the answers of the persons interviewed. Analyse and debate the results.
18. Encourage student participation in community activities as you attempt to build democratic attitudes.

Why Teach Environment Education as Integrated with Other Social Studies Courses?

Citizens in the Caribbean should be concerned about the development of their environment. They may see in the future a diminishing quality of their lives. What your students and their families may witness is deterioration in water quality, urban sprawl, decreasing open spaces, vanishing forests and vegetation cover, increasing noise pollution, landscapes scarred by highways, litter and blight, all of these threatening the future quality of their lives.

Action to conserve the remaining natural environment, and to maintain it, will require a sense of responsibility on the part of every citizen. Unthinking people pollute the environment. Thinking people can effect a new environmentalism dedicated to restoring as well as protecting, bringing beauty to cities as well as the countryside, minimizing the waste of technology as well as of natural resources.

This, then, is environmental education: a recognition by citizens of their interdependence with the environment and all of life, and their responsibility for developing a culture which maintains that relationship through policies and practices necessary to maintain a quality environment.

The inclusion of environmental education in the school programme is a response to a need – a need for citizens who are students in your class, who can identify and resolve problems affecting the quality of the environment. The objective of environmental education is the development of strong, rational attitudes that are essential to the resolving of environmental problems.

Suggested Techniques for Dealing with Environmental Issues for Five- to Eight-Year-Olds

1. Have students trace the foods used in a single school lunch to the communities where they were grown or produced.
2. Have students collect pictures of traced foodstuffs (activity 1) while they are growing or being processed. If the source or processing plant is close by, take students there on a field trip, and have them either take or make their own pictures. *Note:* A similar set of activities could be developed for the clothes the students are wearing, the houses they live in, the water they drink, or the products they use in any one day.
3. Have students interview people who produce or process the foods, and ask questions about the processes involved.
4. Have students imagine what their room would be like if all the prod-

ucts from a given resource were removed, that is, forests, water, iron ore, clay, cotton, and so on.

5. After taking a walking tour through the community, have students develop a map of their neighbourhood and locate predominant natural features on the map (rivers, lakes, hills, ponds, etc.). On the map, draw in the predominant features that are man-made (roads, bridges, railroads, houses, businesses, factories). On the map, have the students identify their own homes.
6. Have students classify man-made features on the basis of function, such as those used for transportation, shelter, food, distribution, utilities, or recreation. Have students imagine how their community may have looked before the man-made features appeared. Have them draw pictures of how the school or some other area may have looked at that time.
7. Have a long-time resident of the community visit the class and describe how the community looked when that person was a student. Students should be able to identify changes that developed during that individual's lifetime and be able to construct a timeline.
8. In addition to the visual changes identified in the above activities, students might close their eyes and identify sounds or odours that are man-made, and sounds or odours in their community that are natural.
9. After a rain shower, the students might take a walk in the community and look for animal tracks, tracing where the animal came from and where it went. They could also construct an inference of what type of animal it was and what it did. (The sets of tracks we would find in an urban area would not be the same as those we might find in a rural or suburban area.)

Suggested Techniques for Dealing with Environmental Issues for Eight- to Eleven-Year-Olds

1. Photograph or draw pictures of environmental problems or issues discovered during a field trip.
2. Write a story that describes how the life of a frog or a bird is affected by pollution.
3. Role-play a citizen living in this community in the year 2025.
What might the community's environment be like at that date?
4. Ask the students to prepare a panel debate, class play, mock television programme, or multi-media programme depicting how the destruction of a local water supply might affect the quality of life for them and their community.

5. Take a field trip to a chosen area, and observe it during different seasons:
   a. List forms of life found in wet, warm season as compared to forms other countries might observe in their winter.
   b. Have students make inferences about what happens to different life forms during the winter or dry season.
      i. Where have the birds gone?
      ii. What happens to frogs during the winter in cold climates or during the dry season.
6. Look outside during a downpour of rain, and have students take notes on observations made.
7. Trace the runoff from a service station, a farm, or factory during or after a heavy rainfall.
   a. What pollutants do you think were there before the rain?
   b. Where did they go?
   c. What effect do they have on the local water supply?
   d. What suggestions do you have to improve this environmental problem?
8. Photograph or collect pictures that demonstrate how water is used in your community.
   a. In what way is water being misused?
   b. What suggestions do you have for reducing water consumption or the wastage of water.
9. Survey the school to determine how wisely water is being used.
   a. Develop a water-use plan for the school.
   b. Develop a water-use plan for the student's home.
10. Let students collect live specimens of various insects and small animals. Locate a safe place for students to collect them. Look after them. Do research on their life cycles and activities.

A Final Thought: Techniques Require Skill Development

Many experienced teachers do not use a variety of teaching techniques and activities. What teachers discovered as they tried some of the 247 techniques listed above is that students may not have the skills to perform the techniques in class. Teachers often assume incorrectly that students have the skills to give an oral report, perform in a role-play, work effectively in small groups, research a project, debate an issue, take effective notes, perform as a member of a panel discussion, or conduct an interview. These techniques may not work if students do not have the proper skills. Thus, a special obligation rests upon the teacher to provide training and guidelines for the proper application of any activity.

Ordinarily, primary school teachers expect to develop the students' skills, but this does not necessarily apply to all teachers, some of whom are concerned only with course content. If your interest is rooted in covering content, with no time to develop the necessary skills of reading, comprehension, oral communication, writing, and researching, then you can hardly effectively use the problem-solving method and active techniques with your students. If, however, teachers develop a plan to improve students' oral, written, reading, and research skills, then their students will be prepared to participate in the problem-solving method and active learning techniques. It must be realized that the successful practise of these techniques requires a sufficient level of student skill development. If the technique does not work, it probably means that the students are not sufficiently skilled. Do not abandon the activity, but rather develop the students' skills to ensure that the method and techniques do work.

Active Learning in the Classroom Requires a Variety of Learning Techniques

Now that you have seen a listing of 247 techniques, it is perhaps important to again repeat a suggestion made at the beginning of this unit. Now that you can imagine 247 different techniques, it is realistic to understand why active learning in the classroom requires about two to three techniques during each lesson. It is perfectly well understood that a variety of techniques planned as a strategy will help students in the classroom to be effective learners. The key thought is holding students' attention to the task at hand. Holding that attention is best accomplished through the use of a variety of techniques.

Summary and Conclusion

This chapter has drawn a distinction between methods, techniques, and strategies; applied the research on how children learn best as to methods, techniques, and strategies; and finally, listed 247 techniques that were intended to stimulate interest and act as a reference. The point was made that there are only two general teaching methods, transmission and problem solving. However, there are an infinite number of techniques that could be used in the classroom. A strategy is merely the plan by which the activities are sequenced to accomplish the method. Teacher educators are unanimous in their recommendation that teachers use active learning techniques with the hope, of course, that by encouraging students to participate, they will be increasingly motivated to learn and remember. But active learning does not just happen by accident. Active learning must be planned. The rationale for study about methods, techniques, and strategies is that these are basic to planning lessons and to catering to individual differences among students.

Looking Ahead

The following chapter, "Applying Methods, Techniques, and Strategies", is a discussion on how you the teacher can apply the techniques in a strategy, how you prepare the students with the skills necessary to successfully use the techniques, and finally, how to evaluate the techniques when given a set of standards of performance.

5

Applying Methods, Techniques, and Strategies

Introduction

The 247 techniques listed in the previous chapter are important because they demonstrate the wide variety of different ways subject content can be presented in the classroom. However, merely listing techniques does not explain how they should be used; and it is the purpose of this chapter to select from the 247 techniques the most widely used ones in order to illustrate how they can be applied in the classroom. In addition to the four well-known techniques of (1) lecturing, (2) effective use of textbooks, (3) recitation, and (4) discussion, eight other basic techniques to be discussed in depth are (5) grouping or cooperative learning, (6) drama or role-playing, (7) oral report, (8) debate, (9) panel discussion, (10) games or simulation, (11) audio-visual aids, and (12) learning centres (multi-media programmes).

Skill Development

You are reminded of the admonition in chapter 3 that effective teaching practices, in the form of techniques, require the development of certain skills. In short, student research projects require research skills, reading requires reading skills, writing requires writing skills, and oral reports require speaking skills. If the students do not have the skills and the teacher is unwilling to develop these skills, then the techniques will not work. Skill development is required for all techniques. In this chapter, we will discuss how teachers can assist students to develop skills and evaluate progress when using a particular technique.

The Four Most Frequently Used Techniques

Without question, the four most popular and frequently used teaching techniques are (1) lecturing, (2) use of textbooks or workbooks, (3) recitation, and (4) discussion. They are the most popular with teachers and the easiest to use, but they are not the most effective techniques, although every student knows them well. The truth is, many teachers believe that lecturing, the use of textbooks, recitation and discussion are the most effective when working with a large class of students because these techniques help the teacher control their behaviour. Teachers also believe that these four techniques usually do not require as much skill development as do other techniques. In brief, lecturing, textbooks and workbooks, recitation and discussion are easier to plan and use in comparison to the eight other techniques illustrated in this chapter.

Techniques and Passive Learning

Though these four techniques are not naturally passive, they are so often remembered as standard classroom practice and used by teachers that, through repeated use, they become passive (the same thing every day) for students. But then, this is true for any technique if overused. There is therefore nothing basically wrong with these four most frequently used techniques, provided they are not, as with all other techniques, used in such a way as to lead to passive student learning.

Lecturing Techniques

You hardly need an introduction to lecturing, having experienced this technique most of your life. However, because you have experienced it often does not mean that either the lectures were well planned and skilfully presented or that you know how to deliver a good lecture. We are not saying that lecturing is not an important technique. It is obviously important, and actually you will use this technique often to introduce, summarize, explain, share and provide information. But we are talking about using successful effective lecturing that focuses students' attention and actively involves their minds, holds their attention and gives them reasons to think.

The problem with lecturing is holding the student's attention. Research on attention span at different age levels suggests that lecturing effectively for a full class period is difficult, some would say impossible. Why? Because students have a finite attention span, ten minutes for young children and fifteen to twenty, at most, for older students. And as the limits of that attention span are reached, they begin to "tune in and out". In short, their minds wander. You will recall from chapter 3 that we learn and remember only ten per cent of what we hear. However, we believe that a well-planned and skilfully presented lecture can be an exciting learning experience. Lecturing should fit effective teaching practices by focusing students' attention. The following are guidelines for the effective use of lecturing.

1. Use the lecture to focus students' attention; for example, to
   a. introduce a lesson,
   b. summarize a discussion or lesson, or
   c. explain an activity.

   When you plan a lecture, prepare an introduction that will grab students' attention. In other words, the introduction should create "high interest" and act much like a springboard – launching the class into the lesson. When ending a lecture, a brief summary will focus attention on the main points of the lesson. The teacher's responsibility is to clarify and summarize the points of the lecture so that students can identify patterns – in short, can learn and remember. Closure, or ending a lecture, is the point at which the class should start the next day. For example, a teacher might say: "Do you recall the ideas we talked about yesterday? Would you find in your notes the summary of those ideas (from the previous day's closure)? Do you remember we talked about the colonial period and that today we would discuss the European explorers who first laid claim to different parts of the Caribbean? Would you now turn to your atlas and find the map of the Caribbean?"
2. A lecture is an efficient way to give information, but not information that students can get from their textbook, reading materials, or student handouts. Use a lecture to impart new information. As already noted, chapter 3 indicates that students will learn and remember more of what they see than what they hear. Visual aids and discussion, together with questions, will measurably improve students' retention of points made in the lecture.
3. Keep lecturing to a minimum, and combine it with other active teaching and learning activities in a single class period. Two or three different techniques in a class period will prolong students' attention and increase students' quality time on task. Several short lectures, combined with other techniques, represent an effective use of the lecture.
4. Based on the average attention span of students, lecture sessions should last no more than ten minutes for primary students, and no more than fifteen minutes for junior secondary forms (ages twelve

and thirteen). The longer you talk, the less students will focus attention on the lesson.

5. Lecture from notes. Do not read a prepared script. An outline of the main points of your lecture should be written on the board, an overhead projector, or in a handout. The outline will help students focus as you lecture and help them find "where you are" if their minds wander. A lecture, interspersed with higher-level, thought-provoking questions, will also encourage students to focus attention and increase their learning and remembering. (See chapter 8, for some tips on the skill of asking different levels of questions.)

The Effective Use of the Textbook through Reading Comprehension and Study Habits

Teaching from the textbook, which is a transmission technique and probably the most common today, is also known as the "assign-study-recite-test" strategy. It is a strategy because the teacher sequences four techniques from assignment through testing in order to transmit the subject content. Textbooks usually feature a series of materials graded for use at different levels. They also present a framework, which provides the teacher with direction. The textbook is particularly useful for inexperienced teachers who may benefit from such systematic guidance. However, the strategy by which the textbook is used is not effective for many school-age students. The major criticisms of the assign-study-recite-test strategy include the following:

1. Some teachers consider the textbook as the only material to which the child should be exposed, which means the textbook becomes the only curriculum material for the entire course.
2. Some teachers expect all children, at a certain age level, to be able to effectively read a textbook's content, which means that the textbook is considered appropriate for all reading at a given grade level. But of course, this is almost never true, given the individual differences between students.
3. Some teachers expect to cover the entire textbook content during the school year. Teachers should realize that the textbook was not meant to be covered page-for-page and cover-to-cover throughout the school year.
4. The textbook strategy stifles teacher creativity by causing dependency on the text as the only source of teaching, which means the teacher is not encouraged to seek additional source materials or teaching and learning aids.

The following is a list of other reading resources, apart from the textbook, that can be used:

- newspapers
- magazines
- encyclopaedias and almanacs
- dictionaries
- phone directories
- pamphlets
- travel guides and timetables
- atlases
- government publications

Although the social studies curriculum is often based on the textbook strategy of "assign-study-recite-text", we know that many students are not, for a variety of reasons, successful in learning and remembering from the textbook and workbooks. The typical social studies programme is a series of age-level textbooks, essentially a "reading" course, and many students find the subject of citizenship education, in the form of social studies and social science, to be uninteresting and unmotivating.

Given the general and persistent use of this textbook strategy, the problem for the teacher is how to be more effective with the strategy. The answer lies in skill development. The skills of reading and studying require discipline. What the teacher must improve is students' reading comprehension through a disciplined approach to reading and through students' study habits.

What we want to discuss in this chapter is how to effect this improvement. Teaching citizenship education is predicated on the assumption that students have the skills to read and study. So let us be clear on what you, the teacher, are being asked to do. In theory, students have practised reading skills at least since age five. What you are asked to do is work specifically on reading comprehension, which is simply helping students to effectively use study habits to gain the information from the social studies textbook. As reading is not equal, learning to comprehend textbook content requires a special skill. How do you teach this skill? We recommend the following strategy, which will increase reading comprehension when using the textbook.

A Reading Comprehension Improvement Strategy

The strategy is called SQ3R, which states that the best way to comprehend what has been read is to quickly survey (S) or glance over the assessment, then turn each heading into a question (Q), then read (R) to answer the question, recite (R) a response in your own words, and finally review (R) your questions and answers. Thus SQ3R means *survey, question, read, recite, review.* At first, this may seem rather tedious and difficult, and requiring a great deal more time than just skimming through the assignment. But once the strategy disciplines the reading behaviour, the students' reading comprehension skills will dramatically increase, and the strategy will require little extra time. The following is an explanation of the SQ3R reading strategy for the effective comprehension of a textbook lesson.

SQ3R: Survey, Question, Read, Recite, Review

Survey

Have students glance over the headings and the illustrations (maps, pictures, charts) in the textbook chapter in order to identify the main points. Also, read the final paragraph (which is usually a summary), if the chapter has one. This survey should not take more than a few minutes and will identify the core ideas around which the chapter is organized. This survey will help students organize the ideas as they read them later.

Question

Now have students begin to read. Many students ignore headings when, in fact, the heading is the clue to the meaning of the paragraph. Have them turn the first heading into a question or a series of questions. For example, a heading on Population of the Bahamas may be "Early Inhabitants". The heading can be turned into: Who were the early inhabitants of the Bahamas? Where did they come from? What did they do here? How did they live? Why did they leave? This will arouse their curiosity and so increase comprehension. It will bring to mind information already known, thus helping students to understand the section more quickly. Turning a heading into a question can be done instantly upon reading the heading, but it demands a conscious effort on the part of the reader to make this a question for which an answer must be found.

Read

Have students read purposefully to answer their questions based on the heading. This is not a passive plodding along each line, but rather an active search for the answer to the questions asked.

Recite

Having read, have students look away from the book and try briefly to recite the answer to their question. They should use their own words and try to include an example. If they can do this, they are more likely to learn and remember. If they cannot, have them glance over the section again. An excellent way for students to do this reciting from memory is to jot down cue phrases in outline form on a sheet of paper. Make these notes brief.

Now have students repeat Question, Read, Recite on each subsequent headed section in the textbook chapter. That is, have them turn the next heading into a question, read to answer that question and recite the answer by jotting down cue phrases in outline form. Have students read in this way until the entire lesson is completed.

Review

When the lesson has been completely read, have students look over their notes to get a bird's-eye view of the main points and check their memory of the content by reciting the major sub-points under each heading. This checking of memory can be done by covering up the notes and trying to recall the main points. Then expose each major point and try to recall the sub-points listed under it.

A final reminder: Keep in mind that we are not talking about leisure reading. We are talking about reading to identify ideas and to remember those ideas. Reading comprehension, an effective use of the textbook for instruction, requires reading that identifies ideas and the remembering of those ideas.

Using Study Habits Effectively

Improving a student's reading comprehension is only a part of the discipline necessary for effective use of the textbook. The other part is improving their study habits.

Knowing how to learn is an important part of citizenship and lifelong education. Create the proper learning habits with students at an early age, and they will have a better chance to achieve. Good study habits include the following practices. Students should do the following:

1. Make and keep a study schedule. Keep the same schedule from day to day.
2. Study in a suitable place, the same place each day. Proper surroundings will help in concentrating. The amount of time is not what counts; it is focused attention and quality time on task that counts.
3. Collect all the materials needed before beginning. In the study area, all materials should be at hand so that study can be accomplished without distraction or interruption.
4. Do not wait for inspiration. We can learn a lesson about studying from observing athletes. They train strenuously every day whether they think they want to or not. Like the athlete, students get into training by disciplining themselves to comprehend the lesson.
5. Have a well-kept notebook; this can help students achieve. Teachers know that there is a definite relationship between the orderliness of students' notebooks and their achievement.

6. Make a careful record of assignments. Knowing just what is expected, and when it is expected to be done, is the first step towards completing important assignments successfully.
7. Keep good notes, for without good notes rereading the whole assignment may be needed before a test. Following a simple SQ3R will help with good notes.
8. Aim to "over learn". This is the secret of remembering and learning for the future. Over learning is continuing to study the material beyond what is just enough to barely recall it. One- fourth of the original study time should be spent on over learning the materials. Students who over learn the materials tend to remember the materials four times as well after a month as those did who did not over learn.
9. Undertake frequent reviews, since this will pay off well in achievement. Without review, the average student can forget 90 per cent of what they have read in just two weeks. The first review should come shortly after studying the materials for the first time. This early review acts as a check against forgetting and helps remembering far longer, and this is the reason for using SQ3R, which requires a review.

As a final consideration in using a textbook, examine the following standards. We include these standards so that a teacher might check reading effectiveness against a standard of excellence. These standards should act as a guide to the actions taken in the classroom in order to improve students' comprehension and study habits.

Standards of Excellence for the Use of the Textbook

Check yourself to make sure that you are following some or all of the standards when using a textbook.

1. *Study techniques:* Are efficient study techniques (SQ3R and study habits) presented and discussed with the class, then gone over and rehearsed from time to time so that students will automatically use them?
2. *Vocabulary building:* Are new terms or definitions related to the content explained to students, and are their understandings of terms periodically checked?
3. *Supplementary materials:* Are materials with different points of view presented so that students can learn to distinguish fact from fiction, recognize biased statements, and evaluate what they read?
4. *School resources:* Do you make use of special personnel or services when necessary, for example, library audio-visual aids, resource people, community resources?

5. *Individualized instruction:* Do you plan for, or take into account, students who have special needs?
6. *Explicit instructions and assignments:* Are instructions and assignments worded so there is no doubt as to what is expected of students (complete performance objectives)?
7. *Related events:* Do you suggest outside activities related to class work, such as holidays, commemorations, and community events that are related to the development of citizenship?

Recitation Technique

Recitation and the following activity, discussion, both engage the class but for different purposes. How would you distinguish recitation from a class discussion? Recitation is the student's oral delivery of memorized materials normally addressed to the teacher, a cognitive-memory or convergent-level response. For example, a recitation is when the teacher asks the class, "State the three major reasons found in the textbook for the independence movement in Barbados?" The only way to answer that question is to have read the text and memorized the three reasons. Reciting the reasons is called recitation. Discussion however is a purposeful consideration of a topic by class members addressed to other class members and the teacher, and is usually at a convergent, divergent, or evaluative level. For example, "What are your views on garbage pollution in Belize City?" Now you can identify the difference between recitation and discussion.

Discussion Technique

Try to understand the difference between the preceding recitation that calls for three reasons from the textbook and the following lesson taught by discussion techniques drawn from the students' experience.

The teacher in her age six to seven social studies class in St Vincent says, "I would like to discuss with the class the topic 'What We Learn from Our Community'."

The Lesson: "Proverbs and Wisdom"

Teacher Lesson Plan

Purpose: Practise recalling customs of the community.

Objective: Processing information (established meaning).

Method: Problem solving or discovery.

Strategy sequence: Introductory lecture, discussion.

Effective teaching practices: Building self-esteem, integrating, accommodating. Recalling and reciting proverbs encourages up to 40 per cent learning and remembering.

Duration: One class period.

Audio-visual aids: Chalkboard.

The lesson: Teacher explains that this is a lesson on proverbs and social customs. The teacher might continue by saying, "There is much wisdom in the community and that wisdom is often found in the form of proverbs you students have heard and memorized. For example, in some neighbourhoods it is often said, 'When the community is in sight, you don't need a guide.' " As the students recite proverbs, the teacher writes them on the chalkboard for the purpose of discussion in which the students attempt to identify the meaning of the proverb and determine whether the proverb is an expression of wisdom.

The following are examples of proverbs:

- Night does run till day catch it.
- Cockroach has no place at fowl-cock fight.
- The higher the monkey climb, the more he show his tail.
- What goes around, comes around.
- There is more in the mortar than the pestle.
- If you behave like grass, the cow will eat you.

Is it clear why the lesson "Proverbs and Wisdom" was a discussion and not a recitation? Classroom discussion that calls for a purposeful consideration of a topic might commence with a question such as, "How do you account for the fact that the liberation movement from colonial rule took the form it did?" This question calls for knowledge about the liberation movement, but also calls for speculation or personal opinion on why that movement was successful. In chapter 3, it was stated that we learn and remember 40 per cent of what we discuss with others. Of course, that is 40 per cent if the members of the class participate. If only two students are actively discussing with the teacher, and the other members of the class are passive and indifferent, then only two students may be getting the full benefit from the discussion. Participation by all students is important because active interest encourages learning and remembering.

The following are guidelines for the teacher for developing effective discussion learning activities:

1. Clearly identify the purposes or objectives for the discussion. In short, be sure there is a point to the discussion and that the students know what the teacher wants. For example, "The lesson we are going to discuss is on the environment."
2. Suggest and guide the development of the topic to be discussed. For example, "First, identify the conditions that led to the environmental problems we face as a country here in Jamaica."
3. Assist students in maximum participation in the discussion. Be sure

to include all students in the class by skilful use of different levels of questions. (See chapter 8, for practising the skill of asking different levels of questions.)

4. Accept student contributions as worthwhile no matter how limited the value may be. In fact, encourage students' questions; this is one of the best techniques to encourage focused, prolonged attention. Students asking good questions is the sign of a successful discussion.
5. Suggest appropriate time schedules for how long the discussion will continue. For example, "We will discuss the conditions leading to the environmental problems in our country for five more minutes."
6. Either the teacher or a student should provide the summary remarks or conclusions based on what students have discussed. If the teacher wishes to check the class understanding of the topic, it is often a practice to ask students to summarize.
7. Evaluate the discussion activity – what went well and what needs to be improved. For example, how many students participated? Do you believe you are getting the 40 per cent learning and remembering that discussion is intended to achieve, or does the participation suggest more like 10 per cent? Do your discussions often become lectures? Was it actually your intention to lecture rather than have a discussion?

Teaching Current Events through Discussion Techniques

Why should the teacher have current events as part of a social studies programme? Because current events do two things. First, the foundation for developing an informed citizen should be provided in the primary school. Informed citizens are a requirement for an effective democratic society. Second, current events provide immediate relevancy from the abstract textbook content – whether historical, geographical, or civics – to the concrete personal experience, showing how what is being studied has currency in real life today. Students must become informed about issues and must acquire the skills necessary for being informed. Since a current-events activity is the one means of providing a contact for students with topical problems and issues, a current-events activity is a must.

Five- to six-year-olds have entered a period of readiness training, which means students are introduced to the relationship between the content in the social studies programme and the lives they lead. From the next age level on, current events should be an integral part of the social studies school programme from age six through to high school.

Integrating Current Events into Class Lessons

One suggestion on how to integrate current events into textbook content is to follow the "extended current events" idea. This is simply to encourage or require students to find in the newspapers, radio, television, magazines, any other media, or personal experience, examples of how what they are studying reflects on a current problem or issue that potentially affects the students' lives. Encourage collections of current events articles or items so they may be put on the bulletin board for regularly scheduled class discussion. See the following example of an extended current events discussion technique.

Topic: "There's No Place like Home, But . . ."

Teacher Lesson Plan

Purpose: Practising map skills, decision making, and current events.

Objective: Examining values and beliefs. Example of "extended current events".

Method: Problem solving.

Strategy sequence: Audio-visual aids, discussion.

Effective teaching practices: Accommodating, challenge. Discussion encourages approximately 40 per cent learning and remembering.

Duration: One class period.

Audio-visual aids: Large map of West Indies divided into four regions: north, south, east, and west.

The lesson: Each class member must pick a region, and in that region, a city or town where he or she would like to live. The following must be taken into consideration: climate, location's opportunities or attractions, city or town size (some atlases give population next to a city's name in the index). See if students can find some current news event from newspapers, radio, television, or magazine about the area they have chosen. Have students indicate their choices on the map by pinning their names to the locations. Hold a discussion on how students made their decision, and what were their reasons.

- How many chose where they currently live?
- What was the farthest location chosen?
- What was most important in making the choice: climate, attractions, or size?
- What attractions or opportunities featured most?

Grouping Activity and Cooperative Learning

Grouping students for the purpose of instruction has become popular with many teachers. Officially, grouping is defined as assembling students in groups for the purpose of instruction. Grouping has become popular because this technique emphasizes active student participation. Participation in small group discussion may help students learn and remember up to 40 per cent of what they are exposed to, according to the research. Keep in mind that the 40 per cent of learning and remembering may occur if students are actively participating in the small-group discussions. However, if in groups of five students, only two students do the task assigned to the group, and three remain passive, then those three are not spending quality time on the task. Thus, the learning activity is not working for those three students.

It is difficult for a teacher with a large class to provide an opportunity for every student to participate during each class period. Grouping offers one learning activity by which students in groups participate among themselves and in so doing become actively involved in class work. Students who are reluctant to participate in class recitation or discussion can be encouraged to be involved in small group discussions. Some teachers dislike grouping because they feel that many students are willing to waste time by not focusing attention on the assigned group task. It is true that grouping will not work well unless the task assigned is understood and unless the students are cooperative and actively participating. Also, it is understood that large classes and inflexible classrooms make this activity difficult to practise. But grouping can be effective. Consider the six types of grouping below and how you might use each of these to effectively teach your class.

Six Types of Grouping Strategies

The most recent development in grouping has been the identification of at least six different types of grouping for instructional purposes. The six types are as follows:

1. *Task-oriented small group* for the purpose of focusing on a specific project or proposal.
2. *Brainstorming small group* for the purpose of discussing, freely and uninhibitedly, a topic which is problem centred or solution centred.
3. *Tutorial small group* for the purpose of emphasizing individual instruction, usually of a remedial nature, or to evaluate an independent study project.
4. *Discussion small group* for the purpose of encouraging free and uninhibited discussion of a topic which has some previous structure and relevance to the material under consideration.
5. *Socratic small group* for the purpose of bringing students and teacher(s) together to discuss a problem posed by the teacher for which an answer can best be determined through the open and honest exchange of informed opinion.
6. *Cooperative learning,* a popular recent strategy that combines task-oriented and tutorial grouping with other teaching techniques.

Successful Grouping

Grouping often fails when students do not have clear instructions about what to do in their groups, which means the group is not focusing on the task at hand. How should teachers focus the students' attention to achieve a good purpose? The following are keys to successful grouping.

1. *Assign students to groups.* There are four suggestions:
   a. arbitrarily assign them
   b. do it by interest groups or topic
   c. when students enter class, hand each student a piece of coloured paper, and determine groups by the colour of the paper
   d. have students count off by number of groups desired
2. *Assign a leader for the group.* Either appoint a leader or have the group select a leader if needed.

3. *Make provision for notes or report.* Who will give a report? Do notes need to be taken? Who will take notes? Either the teacher or the group will make these decisions.
4. *Set a time limit if that is appropriate.* The teacher or the class should determine how long it will take to accomplish the purpose of the grouping. Groups will fill whatever time you give them. Suppose the task could be done in ten minutes. If you give them no limit, they might take the whole class period and still not be finished. The class that takes an hour to do what could be done in ten minutes is not practising quality time on task, and this could lead to discipline problems.
5. *Evaluation.* A common complaint in a group is that a few students do most of the work, while the other group members are passive and unfocused. Also, not all students work well in or enjoy grouping. There is a need for evaluating what is happening in the group and what students think about grouping. Be sure the class knows that you will be asking for an evaluation that identifies those who did not contribute and for students' attitudes about grouping. Be sure to see the instrument for "Evaluation of Self and Group" at the end of this section.

Strategies That Illustrate Grouping Techniques and Evaluation

Merely to know the names of the six different types of small-group organization and the keys to successful grouping is not necessarily to know how to use these small groups in classroom activities. The following lesson illustrates a task-oriented small group attempting to develop the processing skill of classifying and categorizing.

The Lesson: What We Need in Order to Live

Teacher Lesson Plan

Purpose: Practise the skill of classifying and categorizing.

Objective: Using and refining information.

Method: Problem solving.

Strategy sequence: Task-oriented grouping, teaching and learning aids, discussion.

Effective teaching practices: Accommodating, self-direction, integrating. Discussion encourages approximately 40 per cent learning and remembering.

Duration: Three class periods.

Audio-visual aids: Magazines, newspapers, brochures, whatever the teacher and students can collect as resource materials.

The lesson: During the first class period, divide the class into task-oriented small groups of four or five students each. Have each group cut out pictures of things students think are necessary in order to live. Groups should place similar things in paper folders, for example, a folder for clothing, one for shelter, one for heat, one for health, one for food, and so on.

For the second class period

- Have one folder labelled "Group Problems" for pictures that do not easily fit into a category such as clothing, shelter, heat, health, or food.
- Have a class discussion.
- Have each group show its folders to the entire class.
- Do other groups have folders of similar categories?
- Put similar pictures from all the groups together and label each category, for example, clothing, food, tools, and so on. Then have each group look at its problem pictures, such as television set, car, electrical appliances.

In the third class period, groups should discuss each problem picture to see if it fits a category, needs a new category, or if the item is not necessary. Teacher should help groups as they work.

Cooperative Learning

Cooperative learning, a strategy to promote peer teaching, is the sixth type of grouping. This type of grouping is distinctly different from the other five, but is related to task-oriented and tutorial small groups. The emphasis in cooperative learning is on working *as* a small group, as opposed to working *in* a small group. *Cooperative learning means that each student must work as a contributing member to the group's objective.* Working in groups means all individuals contributing to their own goals, which does not necessarily require teamwork such as in brainstorming, tutorial, discussion, or Socratic groups. Team work, not the competition in a traditional classroom, is the key to cooperative learning. In other words, each student in the group is responsible for the academic success of the other members of the group. Group success can be accomplished only by the individual achievement of each group member. You might recall that peer teaching results in 90 per cent learning and remembering and is thus the most powerful way for students to learn and remember. Cooperative learning is based on peer teaching, that is, the group members become each other's tutors on a given subject or project.

Primary school teachers expect their students to learn to interact with their classmates, to get along with others, and to take responsibility for themselves. If students are expected to do this beyond the classroom, teachers then have an obligation to make sure that students learn how to interact, to be responsible in the classroom, and to practise the attitudes of tolerance and cooperation. All these skills and attitudes are found in cooperative learning. A benefit of cooperative learning is that it supports the development of democratic citizenship, that is, learning how to cooperate in small groups to accomplish democratic goals. In short, cooperative learning is consistent with the real-life situation of citizens who, throughout their lives, must learn to work with others, to tolerate differences, and to contribute to the goals of a democracy.

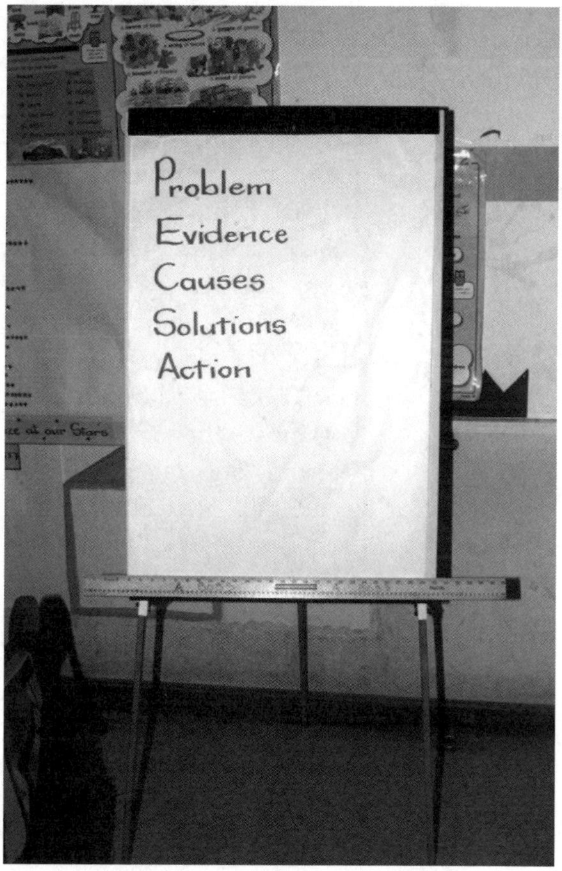

However, cooperative learning strategies conflict with the traditional values of a schooling system that favours the competitive academic curriculum. When teachers reward and encourage students for being "first" or "best", or when they stress individual achievement to the exclusion of group achievement, and when schools organize their programmes to create the impression of superior student achievement, then cooperative learning strategies do not work well in that traditional school environment.

How Does Cooperative Learning Work?

Cooperative learning groups are given a task that should include the efforts of all the students in the group. Students need to directly interact with each other. They do not just sit silently next to each other working on their own assignment. In addition, cooperative learning includes the element of individual accountability. Each student is held accountable for learning the subject matter or contributing to the task. Accountability is often accomplished through tests, or through teacher and student evaluation of group work and presentations. To encourage group effort, in some classes, there is a group grade on a test, as well as on a presentation, so that the more able members of the group take some responsibility for teaching (tutoring) the materials or skills to all members of the group. In short, *group pressure* from one's own group to conform by cooperating and performing is enforced by the school and the classroom teacher.

There are a number of different ways to organize cooperative learning. The following is an illustration of one of those ways. In cooperative learning, the teacher organizes students into groups whose members reflect a variety of interests and abilities. After the groups are formed, the teacher gives each an assignment that needs the attention and involvement of each group member. It is best when group members have many talents and enthusiasms to share in each group. This allows individual students to deal with parts of the overall project that match their own interests. The completion of the assignment usually results in a "product": a play, oral report, research report, panel discussion, debate, or some learning aid such as a model. Group members are graded on this project.

Activities performed by group members can be quite different. In the production of a play, for example, different students could act the part of head writer, general editor, set designer, and so on. Students in a group receive the same grade, and this acts as a group pressure for them to join their talents so all benefit in a good final evaluation. While the groups are working on their assignments, the teacher observes each group carefully. Problems and misunderstandings may need to be cleared up, and the groups encouraged to complete the work to produce the final cooperative product.

Summary of Planning a Cooperative Learning Strategy

1. Design a lesson with a clear objective for the task. For example, designing a play, a poster, a model, a panel discussion. See chapter 4 for the list of 247 different activities that students can try.
2. Select the group size and composition. Early primary students may work best in groups of two; more mature students in groups of three to five.
3. Define roles, identify materials, and consider room arrangements.
4. Students select a role such as editor, writer, set designer for a play; or research coordinator for a panel; or designer of a model.
5. Each student is involved in preparing their part in the overall project.
6. Students pool their talents, such as in presenting a play, a panel discussion, an exhibit.

7. Assessment of learning content and of attitudes.
8. Judging how well groups did. (See "Evaluation of Self and Group" below.)

Below is an "Evaluation of Self and Group" form. Students can evaluate their own participation within the group and the group's participation as a whole. If the learning activity of grouping is used often in class, then a form such as this should be periodically administered.

Evaluation of Self and Group

Instructions: Select the response that best fits your feeling about yourself and the group you have been working with.

Date: ________________

Name: ________________

Circle the letter.

A most of the time **B** frequently **C** average **D** not often **E** did not do

Self

1. I participated by making suggestions, arguing, and discussing.	A	B	C	D	E
2. I cooperated by listening to others and tried to work out difficulties (compromised).	A	B	C	D	E
3. I am satisfied that I did my best to accomplish the group task.	A	B	C	D	E

Group

4. The group made a real effort to accomplish the group task.	A	B	C	D	E
5. The group worked well together by cooperating with each other.	A	B	C	D	E
6. The group shared the responsibilities; no one was left out.	A	B	C	D	E

▶ **Figure 5.1:** Self-Evaluation

Drama or Role-Playing Technique

The technique of drama involves the students in a dramatization of some event or feeling. This technique encourages students to learn through dramatization, by expressing in their own words the drama of the event. Some authorities classify drama under the heading of role-playing and, of course, most of what happens in drama is role-playing.

In drama, students experience something directly or practise it, which encourages 80 per cent learning and remembering. Many teachers have begun to take role-playing seriously because this technique does force students to be actively involved in historical, political, or social events. The dramatization provides an active situation in which the student not only participates but must interpret, thus developing feelings and attitudes, and reinforcing knowledge. This is an exceptionally good technique for focusing quality time on task. Normally, drama is used in one of two ways in the classroom: extemporaneous (impromptu) drama or formal (skits, scripted) drama.

Many teachers use an extemporaneous form of drama. Extemporaneous, meaning without preparation, emphasizes the student's response to a situation or a set of feelings without prior practice. Teachers also use a formal, written drama, or scripted plays, to emphasize certain historical or contemporary events. The teacher might ask students to dramatize a historical situation: for example, role-playing the first meeting of native islanders and the Europeans or recreating a historical event particular to a Caribbean country. The plays and skits are often written by students or by the teacher and are acted before the class.

The following illustrates a drama technique where students learn to identify differences between fact and opinion by role-playing stereotypes. (A stereotype is a commonly held opinion or mental picture that we have about something or some people that may or may not be true.)

The Lesson: I Am Role-Playing a . . . Stereotype

Teacher Lesson Plan

Purpose: Identifying differences between fact and opinion.

Objective: Using and refining information.

Method: Problem solving.

Strategy sequence: Teaching and learning aids, role-playing, discussion.

Effective teaching practices: Reinforcement, challenge, feedback. Discussion encourages approximately 40 per cent learning and remembering.

Duration: One class period.

Audio-visual aids: Small cards with the name of an occupation or person that is often stereotyped: for example, doctor, community official, teacher, grandmother, store keeper, farmer, bus driver, police officer.

The lesson: Have each student draw a card with the name of occupation or person, and role-play that occupation or person. Can the class guess who or what occupation is being role-played? Discuss characteristics commonly used to stereotype each specific occupation or person.

For example:

- Are the characteristics true to life?
- What are other characteristics common to this occupation or person?
- Suppose you worked at this occupation, would you try to practise a different set of characteristics?
- Are stereotypes of occupations or persons helpful or harmful when trying to understand the world of work?

Oral Report Technique

One of the favourite techniques among experienced teachers is the oral report. Normally, this technique requires a student to report to the class on a particular topic. Teachers have traditionally favoured this technique because it has placed emphasis upon research and oral presentation, both of which are thought to be important citizenship skills. Oral reports can be informal, such as when the students are asked to report on some personal incident of which they have knowledge, or they can be formal, as when the student is required to research a topic and give a report.

The fact that oral reporting is a favourite technique also suggests that, as a learning activity, it is often abused. The obvious intention of the teacher is to encourage the student to have something to say (through research, personal experience, or reporting results) and thus to practise the skill of communicating this to the class. The oral report tends to be inappropriate when there are no criteria set out for a good presentation. The practice has been for teachers to concentrate on research activities and other means of gathering information, but teachers have not offered equal standards for making oral presentations. Keep in mind that oral reporting as a technique can be effective if there are criteria (standards) by which the student and the teacher can judge the quality of the presentation.

Students cannot improve their oral presentations if teachers cannot identify the difference between a good and bad oral report. As a minimum,

- set limits such as time limits: for example, two minutes or five minutes;
- encourage preparation; and
- develop criteria by which the reports will be evaluated.

The following is an oral report checklist which students may use as a guide to prepare oral reports, and which teachers may use to evaluate the presentations. The checklist does offer the criteria by which students and teachers can judge the quality of the presentation.

Oral Report Checklist

____

Student's Name

Instructions: Evaluate the student's performance by checking the appropriate box.

	Well done	Satisfactory	Needs attention
1. Approved outline			
2. Writes subject on chalkboard			
3. Faces class, speaks slowly			
4. Identifies sources			
5. States time and place of subject			
6. Relates subject to what class is studying			
7. Gives report from notes (no reading)			
8. Writes difficult names and words on chalkboard			
9. Summarizes			
10. Is ready for class questions			

Comments:

Figure 5.2: Oral Report Checklist

Using the oral report checklist, have students prepare oral reports, such as in the following activity.

The Lesson: Oral Report

Teacher Lesson Plan

Purpose: Identify historically important persons, places, or events.

Objective: Gaining knowledge.

Method: Transmission.

Strategy sequence: Research, oral reports, teaching and learning aids.

Effective teaching practices: Challenge, self-esteem, reinforcement. Making an oral report to the class encourages approximately 80 per cent learning and remembering, and listening to and watching the reports encourages 20 per cent.

Duration: Presentation of reports as appropriate to the development of the lesson.

Audio-visual aids: List of historical persons, places, or events for students to report on.

The lesson:

1. Assign, or let students select, a topic to report on from teacher-prepared list. Allow adequate time for students to research topics.

2. Have students find or draw a picture or prepare a poster about the event, person, or place they have researched.
3. Have students dress up as the person they researched, if they wish to.
4. Have students locate on a map where the person they researched lived or where the event they researched took place. A little flag with the event or person's name might be pinned to a map where the event took place.
5. Pupils should report orally to the class, displaying their pictures and explaining who or what their person, event, or place is and why it is important.

Debate Technique

Debate encourages deliberation, argument, and discussion of opposing points of view. This technique *allows students to actually apply the knowledge they have acquired.* It is also used to help students develop the skill of preparing arguments for one or another side of an issue. Debate is used in either a formal or informal way. Some teachers like to require their students to learn formal rules of debate. The intent is to teach students the procedures for developing formal argumentation. Most teachers, however, use debates in an informal way, that is, with modified rules of debate that are appropriate to the class. The informal learning activity is intended to prepare students to defend a particular point of view, argument, stand, or position. Informal debates permit the teacher and student to develop their own set of rules. It is intended that the students be *actively involved in preparing and defending an argument.* Teachers often use this technique to illustrate that there are many different points of view that can be debated. In short, the debate focuses attention and can generate quality time on task for the purpose of examining problems and issues.

The following illustrates one use of the debate as a learning activity.

The Lesson: Do We Need Rules?

Teacher Lesson Plan

Purpose: To examine problems and issues.

Objective: Using and refining knowledge.

Method: Problem solving.

Strategy sequence: Discussion, grouping, debate, discussion voting.

Effective teaching practices: Challenge, reinforcement, rewarding. Participating in debate encourages approximately 80 per cent learning and remembering.

Duration: As needed to complete activity.

Audio-visual aids: List of rules suggested by class, debate, and task-oriented small groups.

The lesson: Have students think of rules that control their lives. For example, the family has rules, school has rules, community has rules, country has rules, sports and games have rules. List on the chalkboard the rules students suggest control their lives. Divide the class into small debate teams of four or five members. Assign one team to defend several of the rules, and assign another team to argue that those same rules are unnecessary. Continue assigning selected rules to teams to defend or challenge until all teams have a position to defend. Give teams time to prepare.

Have one set of teams (one team defending and one team challenging a specific set of rules) debate their set of rules in front of the whole class. For example, each team has five minutes to argue for or against a rule. Continue allowing sets of teams to debate until all teams have had a turn. As a conclusion to the activity, ask the class to express their opinion by voting for or against each rule listed on the board.

Panel Discussion Technique

Teachers use panel discussions to present information to the class. The panel often consists of a number of students who are assigned to act as a team to research and present a particular topic. Normally, the panel orally reports their findings on the topic to the class. Some teachers also require that the report be written as well as orally reported. The panel differs from debate in that it is not intended as a means of stimulating debate among the panel members but rather as a systematic way for a team of students to present together their report on a topic. The following is an activity using the panel discussion technique.

The Lesson: Researching the Latin American Region

Teacher Lesson Plan

Purpose: Investigate several selected countries in different parts of Latin America.

Objective: Gaining knowledge.

Method: Problem solving.

Strategy sequence: Grouping, research, panel.

Effective teaching practices: Self-directing, integrating, goal, self-esteem, challenge. Participating in a panel discussion encourages approximately 80 per cent learning and remembering.

Duration: Two weeks.

Audio-visual aids: Resource materials, list of Latin American countries, small group, research, panel.

The lesson:

1. Divide class into task-oriented small groups (each group will act as a panel). Either assign or ask each group to select countries from the list of Latin American countries provided by the teacher.
2. Each group will research its set of countries using the following questions:
   a. Where on the map is the country found? (Cognitive-memory type question)
   b. Why is the country important to study? (Convergent type question)
   c. Suppose you could visit that country, what would you want to see, do, and find out? (Divergent type question)
   d. How would you feel about living in that country? (Evaluative type question)
3. Each group may be requested to turn in a written report on its findings.
4. Each group will act as a panel to report to the class in an oral presentation. Each panel member will deliver some part of the panel report so that all panel members have a chance to participate.

Game or Simulation Technique

You know what a game is, essentially a competition with a set of rules where people play to win in a contest. But what is a simulation? A simulation is a pretending, an imitation. Simulation is also a game, but there are not necessarily winners or losers, depending on the purpose of the simulation. Role-playing is often a part of simulation. For example, students in a simulation would role-play the process by which laws are made in a country, whereas a game in class could be students teamed for a competition such as spelling or locating countries on a map. The team that spells the most country names correctly wins the game. The difference between gaming and simulation is that in gaming there is usually a winner, but in some simulations there may not necessarily be winners or losers. Illustrations of gaming and simulation will help to demonstrate the similarities and differences.

Benefits of Gaming and Simulation

Gaming and simulation are included as techniques because they can be of value by enriching the effectiveness of a teacher's instruction. Simulation also fulfils most of the practices suggested to achieve effective teaching, such as self-directing, accommodating, integrating, challenging, providing feedback, and rewarding, as suggested in chapter 3. In short, a simulation, when properly presented, is the most powerful technique for generating creative thinking and effective learning. Gaming and simulation are motivational techniques because students enjoy games, meaning that they generally have a positive attitude towards participating. Some of the advantages of using games and simulations are to

- review content as in a quizdown;
- encourage critical and creative thinking;
- offer an opportunity to teach role-playing;
- teach content as well as process; and
- add variety and a change of pace to your teaching.

Illustration of a Game Activity

The Lesson: Quizdown Name Game

Teacher Lesson Plan

Purpose: Practise map skills, locating, naming, and spelling the names of different countries.

Objectives: Gaining knowledge.

Method: Transmission.

Strategy sequence: Audio-visual aids, quizdown game.

Effective teaching practices: Reinforcement, challenge, rewarding. Participating in a game encourages approximately 80 per cent learning and remembering.

Duration: One class period per game.

Audio-visual aids: Maps or globes.

The lesson: Using maps or globes for reference, the first student names a continent such as Asia or Africa. In this case, the continent's name ends with the letter "A". The second student must name a country or city in Asia or Africa that also ends with the letter A. A third student then names a country or city that also ends with the letter A. Students continue naming countries until no more countries or cities ending with A can be found. The last student to name a country or city with the letter A wins the game. That student then selects the name of a different continent, and the game continues. Students must also be able to locate on a map or globe the country or city they named. The game could also be played by teams.

A variation of this name game is "Twenty Questions". Have one student leave the room. The class then picks the name of a country, city, or landform, and so on, in a continent or country. The student returns and tries to guess the place by asking twenty questions that can only be answered by Yes or No. For example, Is it small? Is it a body of water? If not successful in guessing, the game starts over with another student. This could also be played by teams. Below is an illustration of a simulation technique. You should clearly identify that all the games above had winners. When a student won the game, the game would then begin again. Simulation techniques will emphasize problem solving, where students are not necessarily competing but rather trying to think about how best to make choices.

The Lesson: Who Gets to Go?

Teacher Lesson Plan

Purpose: Practise rule making and decision making.

Objective: Examining values and beliefs.

Method: Problem solving.

Strategy sequence: Task-oriented grouping, simulation, discussion.

Effective teaching practices: Challenge, self-direction. Participating in a simulation encourages approximately 80 per cent learning and remembering.

Duration: One period.

Audio-visual aids: List of individuals requesting to go to domed city on the moon.

The lesson: This activity is a contemporary problem in selection for colonization. This activity involves selecting appropriate people for a colony and anticipating problems that might arise in the new colony.

A domed city with controlled climate and life systems has been built on the moon to house a colony of seven settlers. A national selection committee has been established to determine which persons should be transported to the domed city.

1. Divide the class into groups of four to six students per group.
2. Each group should imagine or pretend that it represents the national committee with the responsibility of choosing seven people from the list to go to the domed city.
3. The list of seven that the group chooses must be approved by a majority of the members of the group.
4. After the small groups have completed their lists, the entire class should compare and discuss the different groups' lists. Allow each group, as a panel, to defend their choices. Then encourage the class to arrive at a *consensus* of who should go to the moon. Keep in mind that the very life (survival) of the new colony may well rest on the right choice of people. There is no "correct" list of the seven people who can go.

(The following list is just an illustration. Teachers should make up their own lists according to students' age level.) Individuals requesting to go to domed city:

1. Thirty-five-year-old carpenter who is going blind.
2. Thirty-year-old Syrian who is a computer expert.
3. Sixty-eight-year-old retiring Iranian army officer.
4. Thirty-three-year-old doctor suspected of selling illegal drugs.
5. Twenty-five-year-old female electrician with a history of emotional problems.
6. Thirty-seven-year-old primary teacher with a retarded son, who will go only if her son can accompany her.
7. Forty-eight-year-old farmer and his wife, who is a special education teacher. They will go only if they can go together.

8. Forty-year-old musician who is going deaf.
9. Thirty-five-year-old politician.
10. Twenty-three-year-old art teacher.

Using Audio-Visual Aids

We have said up to this point that, as alternatives to lecturing, when using textbooks, recitation, and discussion techniques, teachers ought to think of: grouping, drama or role-playing, oral report, debate, panel discussion, game or simulation. These techniques, if properly applied, should focus attention and help to motivate learners by encouraging student participation. According to research, active learning through participation should help students learn and remember well. One additional way to be effective is through the use of teaching and learning aids. The activities that illustrate the various techniques of teaching in this unit also show that audio-visual aids are an important part of the strategy.

The use of audio-visual aids is particularly important because much of the content in social studies and social science are abstract concepts such as democracy, freedom, change, social control, scarcity, and interdependence. It is important to illustrate past history, it is important to visually demonstrate concepts, and it is important to provide models for students to touch. We need not belabour this argument, for few teachers would argue that illustration is not a significant part of teaching, and those illustrations which most reliably transmit a clear picture are the best audio-visual aids.

The following is an illustration of the use of audio-visual aids.

The Lesson: Investigating a Society

Teacher Lesson Plans

Purpose: Identify the effects of environment on societies and cultures.

Objective: Gaining knowledge.

Method: Transmission

Strategy sequence: Grouping, research, audio-visual aids.

Effective teaching practices: Goal, self-direction, accommodating. Creating a visual presentation encourages approximately 80 per cent learning and remembering.

Duration: Two weeks.

Audio-visual aids: Materials as needed.

The lesson: Divide the class into task-oriented groups. Each group must choose a society or culture to study. Students research to learn about the land, people, customs, government, food, housing, religion, arts, and so on. Each group must decide how to present its information in the form of a visual aid to the rest of the class. For example, they might choose one of the following:

1. *Mobile:* Each item hanging from mobile must represent something in the society being reported on. Each member of the group will have several things hanging on the mobile to explain and perhaps elaborate on to the class.
2. *Diorama:* Group will need to construct a diorama to represent the society being reported on. Different parts of the diorama can be constructed by individual members of the group, making sure, however, that the diorama is a complete visual aid when finished.
3. *Drama:* Group prepares role-play or drama that includes costumes, scenery, props, singing, dancing, food, and so on. That is representative of the culture or society being studied.

Importance of Audio-Visual Aids

Because of the importance of audio-visual aids, an entire chapter has been devoted to identifying different aids, how to construct them, and how to use them in the classroom (see chapter 6). Turn now to a discussion of visual aids, maps, and globes. The use of audio-visual aids is complex because, as teachers, we need to know that aids are appropriate at a specific age level. The following is an illustration of the use of maps and globes at primary school level.

Learning to Interpret Maps and Globes

You have learned in chapter 2 that there is a sequential development of learning how to interpret maps and globes. The following are suggestions on how to teach maps and globes in the primary grades according to the growth and development of children.

Kindergarten or Reception: Age Six

For kindergarten and the first grade, the scope of map and globe study includes the use of relative terms for size, such as nearer, farther, larger, smaller; the directions north, south, east, and west; recognizing that familiar places can be represented in map form; and relating the student and his community to the country and the world. Suggested techniques and strategies include the following:

1. Development in students' ability to explain relative terms such as "larger" and "nearer" as places are mentioned in stories.
2. Make a floor plan of the classroom on the chalkboard or flannel board, using symbols suggested by the class to represent various features of the room.
3. Lead the class on a tour of the school building, then make a floor plan of the building based on students' observations.
4. On a large map of your island, locate for the students places where they or their relatives have travelled.
5. Make a simple map of the neighbourhood. Have students locate the position of their homes on the map.

Ages Six to Seven

Skills for this age group include using directions on a street map of the community; using north, south, east, west directions on a map; recognizing your island on a map; locating students' own area on a map; using a world map to locate countries related to experiences and stories; and distinguishing between land and water areas on a map.

Suggested activities and strategies include the following:

1. Have student point out, on a neighbourhood map, the route they use in coming to school.
2. Use a compass to determine the directions that the classroom walls face. Then place N for north, S for south, E for east, and W for west on the correct wall.
3. Help the class to make a mural or a pictorial map of the school neighbourhood.

Ages Seven to Eight

In this age group, the study skills would include determining compass directions on a globe; using pictorial symbols on a map; using grid lines to locate places on a map; locating the equator and the poles; recognizing different climates; learning and locating the oceans, continents, and boundaries between countries; learning to differentiate between islands and countries and cities and towns; and recognizing lakes on a map or globe.

Some suggested techniques and strategies include the following:

1. Discussing the meaning of symbols used on a pictorial map.

2. Have students label the continents and oceans on an outline map.
3. Have the class draw up lists of warmer countries and colder countries using climate maps.
4. On an outline map of your island or country, have students locate areas they have studied.
5. Locate places of interest on a large map of your town or village such as students' homes, schools, parks, playing fields, beaches, lakes or ponds, rivers, historical sites, or churches.

Ages Eight to Nine

Skills suggested for this age group include locating the tropics, locating and identifying the hemispheres; understanding warm, cold, and temperate climates; locating and identifying important countries, rivers, islands, and mountain ranges; using a simple scale of kilometres (miles); using special purpose maps that depict rainfall or population; using geographical terms; and introducing the terms longitude, latitude, parallel, and meridian.

Some suggested activities and strategies include the following:

1. Present a list of names of countries and have students use maps to decide on which continent and in which hemisphere each country is located.
2. Have students write descriptions of life in the various climatic regions.
3. With a picture collection, show comparisons in housing, clothing, and products raised or used in various climatic regions.
4. Present a list of pairs of cities such as Nassau–Bridgetown or Basseterre–Port of Spain, and have students use scale of kilometres (miles) on a map to give the approximate distance between each pair of cities named. The activity may be made more interesting if students in groups are asked to pair off the cities beginning with the same letter (for example, Belize–Basseterre or Castries–Charlestown).

Ages Nine to Ten

Skills for this age group include: using latitude and longitude; using abstract symbols and legends on maps; using a scale of kilometres (miles) to find distances; interpreting altitude using the map legend; tracing the course of a river from its source to its mouth; interpreting information on distribution maps; and freehand drawing of simple maps.

Some suggested techniques and strategies include the following:

1. Have students locate cities using latitude and longitude.

2. Have students make representation, with salt map mixture or papier-mâché, of the common land and water formations.
3. Provide a sample legend for a map, and have the class give written explanations of each symbol.
4. Name a certain latitude and ask students to list the countries through which this latitude passes, beginning at the prime meridian.

Ages Ten to Eleven

By age ten, students should be fairly competent at gaining various types of information from maps and globes, but these skills need reinforcement. The activities at this age level place special emphasis on various types of map projections, on how they are made, and on advantages and disadvantages of each kind. Some suggested activities and strategies include the following:

1. Have students explain the reasons for distortions that appear on various map projections.
2. Have students decide which map projections are most accurate and helpful in studying various regions of the Earth.
3. Give students practice in determining dates on either side of the International Date Line and computing time in various parts of the world.
4. Have students gather census figures for population densities, which should guide them in making their own population maps of their island or country.

For additional suggestions on the use of maps and globes, see "Learning Outcomes" in chapter 2. We turn now to the final topic that illustrates the application of techniques and strategies.

Learning Centres (Multi-Media Programmes)

The concept of a learning centre is not new, it is simply a new restructuring of a strategy that orders activities in a particular way. A learning centre is a designated area (usually in the corners of the room) containing a specific number of learning stations where resources and teaching aids, selected by the teacher and contributed to by students, are provided to guide individuals and groups of students in specific learning activities.

One of the reasons for considering learning centres as a strategy is that they relate to the effective teaching strategies of accommodating, challenging, feedback, reinforcement, and self-direction, as described in chapter 3. That chapter also indicates that, according to research, students will learn and remember 80 per cent of what they experience directly or practise. Learning centre activities offer students that direct experience and practice.

Many teachers believe that students should take responsibility for their own self-direction, one of the eleven effective teaching strategies mentioned in chapter 3. Student participation in learning centres should not be restricted to special times or to enrichment for the more able learners. When learning centres are provided, students plan some of their activities, interact with each other, confer with the teacher, move freely from activity to activity, evaluating their progress, projecting and exploring their interests, working individually, in pairs, or in small groups, testing their ideas, using multilevel texts and materials, enquiring, and experimenting.

The teacher's goal, school curriculum, and student growth and development all help to determine the themes and topics for learning centres. The centres may be designed

- for the students to acquire information through problem solving;
- to provide practice in the use of skills and opportunities for concrete manipulative experiences;
- to reinforce material previously learned;
- to stimulate creativity; and
- to build habits of cooperation.

The pattern of students' involvement in learning centres and the length of time necessary for study of the organized themes and topics will vary. Not all students need to complete the activities in any one centre, nor do the activities have to be performed in the same order by each student. Thus, learning centres promote individualism. One of their great strengths is that they require continual "doing" of citizenship education, and communicating the findings of investigations in various ways. Each station can be a study in itself, but together the stations become a powerful source of individualized instruction.

The keys to developing successful learning centres include the following:

1. Select a problem, idea, theme, or topic worthy of sustained examination by students.
2. Set up an attractive display. Students will respond positively to a colourful display with easy-to-read descriptions of how to perform the centre's activities.
3. Provide clear instructions. This means easily read directions, using familiar vocabulary, listing directions in appropriate sequence, providing examples or illustrations where necessary, explaining how work is to be evaluated, and what is to be done with the work when it is completed.
4. Include a variety of activities in each centre. Because students differ in needs, interests, learning styles, and levels of achievement, the teacher needs a variety of activities to accommodate all the students.

An example of a learning centre for early primary students might focus on the theme, "Who am I: The Child Is the Curriculum". Such a centre would have several stations with appropriate activities at each station. One set of stations might be labelled "Exploring My Outside". Another might be labelled "Exploring My Inside" and, under that label, one of the individual stations might deal with the topic "Friends". At this station, activities would attempt to help students distinguish between different kinds or types of friendships and how to identify the characteristics of each. Students could classify friendships as friend, not a friend, best friend, and could identify what behaviour leads to each classification. For example, when is someone a best friend? The station could contain pictures of students in various situations and groupings.

Another type of centre might deal with attitudes, and be designed to make the students more aware of their own individuality and more sensitive to their feelings and the feelings of others. One activity in the centre might be to make a "Mood Book". The materials needed in the centre would be magazines, paper, glue, writing implements, and scissors. The student would take given pieces of paper and, at the top of each page, write one word describing a mood: happy, sad, angry, silly, and afraid. Students would look through the magazines and cut out one picture that illustrates each of the moods. They would paste the picture on the page with the appropriate mood word, and under the picture, they would write why they think the people in the picture feel the way they do. They might complete the "Mood Book" by making a cover for it from coloured construction paper.

Looking Ahead

As you will have noted, many of the teacher's lesson plans in this chapter called for audio-visual aids, as illustrated by the "Mood Book" activity above. The use of audio-visual aids is such an important topic that it deserves special treatment as part of the application of techniques and strategies. Though audio-visual aids have been introduced as one of the basic techniques of teaching, their use in teaching strategies will be explored more fully in the following chapter.

6

Audio-Visual Aids for Teaching Social Studies

Introduction

Do you question the use of audio-visual aids for your social studies classroom? Many teachers do. Data obtained for a study on the use of instructional materials and equipment in selected countries revealed that of all subjects surveyed, social studies was the lowest in the use of audio-visual aids. Thus, we are led to conclude that even though the class size in primary school is often quite large, the teachers do not use *many, or any* instructional materials to teach social studies: no maps and globes, bulletin boards, posters, murals, slides, television, radio, or filmstrips – virtually nothing other than the text. You should be asking some questions. Here are a few:

1. What can audio-visual aids do for the learning of my students, and is there any evidence that students learn more if they have concrete experiences through the use of audio-visual aids?
2. What audio-visual aids can I think of using to teach my class?
3. Suppose my school has few, perhaps no, audio-visual aids, can my students and I be creative and self-sufficient, through the use of local resources, to create necessary audio-visual materials?

Question 1

What can audio-visual aids do for the learning of my students, and is there any evidence that students learn more if they have concrete experiences through the use of audio-visual aids?

What does the research in chapter 3 say about audio-visual aids? Clearly, students learn better, meaning they remember and are ready to apply the information, if the teacher uses audio-visual aids. Research on learning and remembering suggests that seeing an illustration, map, movie, filmstrip, pictures, or reading an assignment encourages the learning and remembering of approximately 15 per cent of what is seen or read. But if students were to both see and hear a lecture using a map or globe, then the use of both the audio and visual aids encourages 20 per cent learning and remembering. However, 80 per cent learning and remembering can be encouraged if students themselves make and demonstrate audio-visual aids such as maps, globes, charts, pictures, posters, graphs, models, dioramas, and mobiles. *In short, the more students are involved in the concrete illustration of the abstract idea they are discussing in class, the more likely they are to learn and remember.* In other words, audio-visual materials focus students' attention on a task, and hence learning and remembering are strengthened by the use of these.

Concrete and Abstract as Related to Learning and Remembering

Note how learning and remembering is related to the *concrete* and the *abstract.* Concrete is when you directly experience an event, something actually seen or done. For example, some activities you actually participate in, such as going to school or eating a meal, are concrete experiences. The opposite of concrete is abstract, meaning to create a mental image of abstract concepts such as freedom, joy, hope, peace, and faith. Examine the following cone of experience (page 137) as it relates to learning and remembering.

An Important Question: Does Effective Teaching Require Audio-Visual Aids?

You will note that the most abstract experience occurs at the top of the cone where lecturing results in approximately 10 per cent learning and remembering. Whereas at the base of the cone, 80 per cent learning and remembering results from a concrete experience such as a field trip, the creation of an object, or the practice of a skill. Is there evidence that audio-visual aids would help teachers to be more effective? The evidence is clear: the more concrete the experience, the more likely students are to integrate new ideas into their present store of knowledge, thus understanding and retaining new ideas.

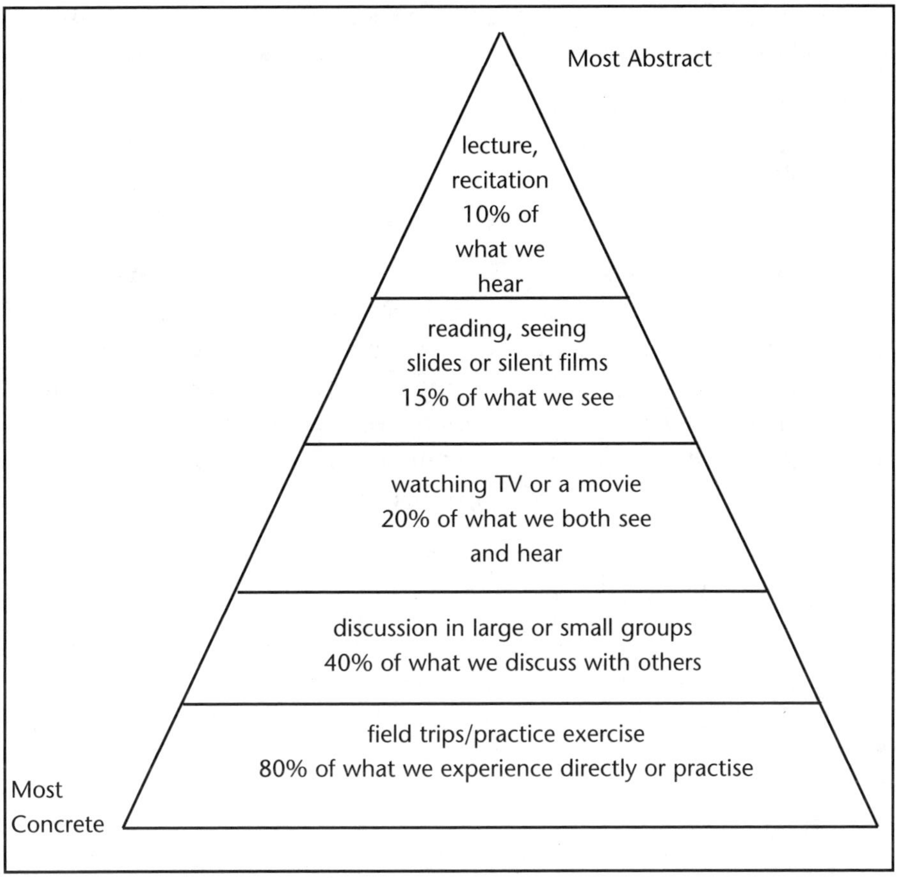

Figure 6.1: Cone of Experience as It Correlates with Learning and Remembering

You can, therefore, conclude that most of the research evidence on learning and remembering suggests that effective teaching, in fact, requires the use of audio-visual aids. In particular, social studies and the social sciences, because of their inherent abstract content (for example, concepts such as democracy, development, self-reliance, freedom, and social harmony) need concrete illustrations, which audio and visual materials can provide.

Question 2

What audio-visual aids can I think of using to teach my class?

Before the question of what audio and visual aids to use, you must first be able to think about the alternative types of teaching aids that are available. Then you can plan how to select and use the audio-visual aids most appropriate to your class.

One way of classifying audio-visual aids is by separating them into four basic categories:

1. Display boards
2. Three-dimensional materials
3. Graphic materials
4. Electronic aids

Each of these audio-visual aids will be discussed in terms of its advantages and disadvantages. As you read the description of each, think of how you might use this aid to teach social studies. If you or your students need to create these aids, see the section in this chapter titled "Construction of Audio-Visual Aids by Teacher and Students". As you already know, if students make the audio-visual aids, this substantially strengthens their learning and remembering.

Category 1: Display Boards

The following types of display boards may be used:

- chalkboard
- flannel board
- bulletin board
- poster
- collage
- mural

Chalkboard: The chalkboard is perhaps the most widely used visual aid in the world. No special talent, other than writing, is required to use a chalkboard. It fits the pace of instruction, and mistakes can be easily erased. The chalkboard also offers opportunity for student participation. Chalkboards can even be made portable to move from class to class. However, work done on the chalkboard is not permanent and may be lost.

Flannel board: The flannel board has a rough background cloth that is usually placed on a board or hard surface. The materials that are to be displayed on the board, pictures, drawings, symbols, and so on, are backed with a rough surface and will stay in place on the flannel board when pressed lightly. The flannel board is easy to construct and easy to use. Children respond well to this visual aid, and an advantage is that the display pieces can be moved around and then stored for use over and over again.

Bulletin board: Bulletin boards, also referred to as news boards or display boards, make excellent decorative, motivational, and instructional display areas. Boards can vary in size and shape, but they are usually made of a material into which pins and thumbtacks can be stuck without damage to the board. Bulletin board displays can easily be changed. They are a good place to display students' work, and children can be assigned to plan and prepare bulletin board displays as projects. See how to construct bulletin boards in the section titled, "Construction of Audio-Visual Aids by Teacher and Students".

Poster: The purpose of a poster is to attract attention and deliver a message quickly. Effective posters stimulate student learning and remembering, and their construction is an excellent learning experience for students.

Collage: The collage is a form of poster, using layers of specifically chosen materials. The texture and layers of materials form a symbolic picture and deliver a message.

Mural: A mural is art work that usually covers a wall or section of a wall depicting a single topic or theme. It often depicts, in visual form, a topic being studied in class. Students can work on a mural individually or in groups. Some topics for murals are "Everyday Life from Early Age to Modern Times", "Growth in Cities and Towns", "Road to Independence", "Industry in the West Indies", "Varied Landscapes in the West Indies", "Farming Activities and Rural Life", or "City Activities and City Life".

See how to construct the above displays in the section titled "Construction of Audio-Visual Aids by Teacher and Students".

Category 2: Three-Dimensional Materials

The following three-dimensional materials may be used:

- model
- mobile
- diorama
- sand table
- salt map

Model: A model is a representation of a real thing and can be either larger or smaller than the original that it represents. A model may be complete in detail or simplified for instructional purposes. When possible, students should be encouraged to handle and examine a model. Model construction allows students to turn abstract ideas into a concrete three-dimensional form.

Mobile: A mobile is a moving sculpture, usually hanging from an overhead source, and in most cases is simply a three-dimensional poster which moves, thus providing changing visual effects. A mobile usually centres on a single topic. As with many visual teaching aids, its construction is a valuable learning experience for students. (See the section titled "Construction of Audio-Visual Aids by Teacher and Students".)

Diorama: A diorama is a three-dimensional depiction of some scene or event. This visual aid is usually made from a box with one side or parts of sides cut off, and with the remaining part of the box used as background. Objects to complete the scene can be constructed of paper, cardboard, or modelling clay, appropriately painted and positioned in the box. Diorama construction teaches students about reproducing objects to scale and using perspective to more accurately depict a scene or event.

Sand table: The sand table is exactly what the name implies: a table or section of the classroom floor with built up sides and filled with sand. The sand can be moulded to portray a map or the background for scenes, events, or to picture landforms. It can then be smoothed and used over and over again. For schools with limited resources in the form of pictures and paper on which to draw, the sand table can be an inexpensive and effective teaching aid.

Salt map: A salt map is related to the sand table but is more permanent. One cup flour, one cup salt, and one-half cup of water, well mixed, provides a substance that can be moulded into contours. When the mixture dries, it hardens and can be painted or coloured. A salt map is an effective visual aid for illustrating landforms, and students enjoy making the maps. Salt maps can be hung on the wall to become permanent audio-visual teaching aids.

Contour maps can also be moulded from a mixture of one-half cup liquid starch and one cup powdered detergent, whipped with an egg beater until thick enough to mould. This can be painted when dry. If starch is not available, powdered detergent and a small amount of water can be beaten by an egg beater until thick enough to mould. This can also be painted when dry.

Other three-dimensional aids that teachers often find useful and easy to make are small weaving looms, clay tablets, compasses, miniature carts, soap carvings, and puppets.

Category 3: Graphic Materials

The following graphic materials may be used:

- maps and globes
- diagrams
- charts
- graphs

Maps and globes: Maps and globes are almost indispensable aids in teaching the social studies curriculum, and they may be the only instructional aids available. Maps and globes can help students read symbols and see relationships such as landforms, water forms, distances, climate, and location. They show the position and size of countries and their relationship to the rest of the world. Maps and globes should be used and referred to frequently. However, if they are not available, the teacher and students can make their own. (See section titled "Construction of Audio-Visual Aids by Teacher and Students".)

Diagrams, charts, and graphs provide visual representations of abstract ideas.

Diagrams: These are most frequently used to illustrate a structure or explain a series of steps that would be hard to visualize from just the spoken word. The diagrams we are most familiar with are those that explain how to assemble some object or piece of equipment.

Charts: These are most commonly used to show relationships. For example, a timeline can visually illustrate a series of events and their chronological relationship. An easy timeline to make is a rope or wire strung across the classroom and divided into centuries. Students can attach important dates and events to the appropriate place on the timeline with plastic clothespins.

Graphs: These are visual representations of statistical or numerical information. Bar, line, or circle (pie) graphs provide a visual image of percentages, quantities, growth, and change, and so on.

Category 4: Electronic Aids

The following electronic aids may be used:

- radio
- television
- tape recorder
- overhead projector
- slide projector
- film-strip projector
- movie or film projector
- computer

Radio: This audio teaching aid is a basic, easy-to-operate instrument for listening to the news and obtaining up-to-the-minute information. It forces one to visualize a picture from the spoken words or sounds from the radio. In many countries, radio transmission is used to provide long-distance supplemental instruction.

Television and video-tape recorder: This teaching aid provides both visual and audio information, as well as news. With the recorder, programmes can be recorded and replayed at an appropriate time in the lesson. However, television and television recorders are sometimes complicated and may take more than one person to operate. A television or video camera is an additional aid that can be effectively used to tape student activities and social activities and events, and these can be replayed later for evaluation or reference. This teaching aid requires careful maintenance and storage.

Tape recorder/player: This is an easy-to-operate teaching aid that plays pre-recorded tapes. In addition to pre-recorded programmes, a teacher can record student presentations for evaluation. Tapes can easily be erased and reused, but they do require careful storage.

Overhead projector: This is a popular teaching aid that projects materials prepared on transparencies. Transparencies can be prepared ahead of time and stored; or the teacher can write directly on the transparency, which can be wiped clean and reused. A strong advantage of this aid is that the teacher can face the class while using it. A room need not be completely dark to see the projection. Colours can also be effectively used on the transparencies.

Slide projector: Slides are attention-capturing illustrations. One can regulate the pace of showing the slides to coincide with instruction, and slides can be easily rearranged or re-shown. However, slides, if not properly cared for, can be lost or get out of sequence, or fade over time. Slides can be produced by the teacher without a camera. This will be explained later in the section titled "Construction of Audio-Visual Aids by Teacher and Students".

Filmstrip projector: This aid uses easy-to-store short films. The illustrations on the film always remain in sequence, and thus can never be rearranged. As with slides, filmstrip projection can be matched to the pace of instruction.

Movie or film projector: Films easily capture student attention. They provide scenes or events that students might never get to see in person. Films can speed up or slow down action so that a process can be clearly observed. Since films are shown uninterrupted, students must be prepared for what they are to see, and they should be provided with a related follow-up activity.

Computer: This aid provides active, individual instruction at the student's pace. It gives instant feedback. The drawback is that normally only one student, or perhaps two, can use a computer at any given time, but it is an effective teaching aid and will continue to gain importance in the future. It is becoming common practice for students at all grade levels, to be using a textbook, writing materials, and a laptop computer in this twenty-first century. The question is, What will the role of computers be in the classroom? Given the demands of a highly technological society, the first application will be computer literacy, which simply means learning how to use the computer, perhaps programming the computer in one of the computer languages. The second application would be learning to use the computer as a database, which simply means gaining data information, and then processing that information on the computer. The third application would be learning to use the computer for computer-assisted instruction, which allows the student to work at his or her own pace. A fourth application involves students in surfing the Internet to access information from a variety of sources, as well as to establish contacts with students and schools in other parts of the world. Teachers can also use the computer to create visuals, and power-point presentations.

Question 3

Suppose my school has few, perhaps no, audio-visual aids. Can my students and I be creative and self-sufficient, through the use of local resources, to create necessary audio-visual materials?

Many teachers face being assigned to a school where the audio-visual aids are limited, if not non-existent. So an important question to ask is, What can I do if no aids are available? Unavailable aids might include glue, colours, ink, and other supplies which are necessary to make even the simplest teaching aid. If you face this situation, do not give up hope, but rather be creative and learn how to make audio-visual aids from the indigenous materials around the school. Not only can you make ink, but you can make colours, transparencies, slides, and other supplies, all from mostly indigenous materials. Perhaps the most important point is that you also can teach your students to become creative in making these aids, which means that your students never need to be without essential school supplies because these can usually be made from materials that surround the school, village, or town.

Construction of Audio-Visual Aids by Teacher and Students: Being Creative Using Community Resources and Local Materials

The following audio-visual aids can be constructed using community resources and local materials:

- flannel board
- bulletin board
- poster
- collage
- mural
- mobile
- slides
- slide projector
- transparencies
- globes and maps

Flannel Board

Materials:

- 50 × 75 centimetres (20 × 30 inches) of plywood or heavy cardboard
- 74 × 100 centimetres (30 × 40 inches) of flannel or rough cloth

Process:

1. Use as large a piece of wood or heavy cardboard as possible. Students will have difficulty seeing a small display from a distance.
2. Cover entire board with flannel, blanket, or other rough cloth. Fasten cloth to cardboard or wood with tape, staples, tacks, or glue.
3. If possible, use black, green, or grey coloured cloth because they are appropriate background colours.
4. The rougher the cloth used, the better the board will work.
5. If a board is not available, the cloth may be clipped to or draped over a portable chalkboard or placed on a simple tripod.

Flannel board display materials: Cut out whatever materials you want to display, for example, map pieces, graphs, or words. Cutouts should be large so students can easily see them. If the cutouts are on thin paper, they should be glued to cardboard so they will lie flat on the flannel board. Glue rough cloth or sandpaper to back of cutouts, so they will stay in place when pressed against the flannel board. (Sandpaper can be made by coating a sheet of paper with thin glue and sprinkling sand over it. Allow the sheet to dry and shake off excess sand.)

Bulletin Board

Bulletin boards can be made from the sides of large wooden or cardboard cartons, heavy cloth, or heavy wrapping paper. A reed mat also makes an excellent bulletin board. Two or more sides cut from a cardboard carton or wooden box, fastened together at the edges, can make a good bulletin board.

Poster

Good posters need to be carefully planned. They rely on a symbol that expresses a particular set of ideas. The size of the poster, lettering, and colouring, all depend on where the poster is to be displayed. A good poster should be simple; have a single theme or topic; have a concise slogan (should contain brief message); have bold lettering (so it can be read from every part of the classroom); and have accentuating colour (colours to help catch student's eye).

Collage

1. Select a topic or subject to depict.
2. Collect materials, for example, pictures, pieces of cloth, material, string, small objects, that have some relationship to chosen topic.
3. Choose a background for the display, for example, paper, cardboard, or wood.
4. Arrange the materials on the background, allowing them to overlap in layers. When an attractive display of the materials is achieved, paste or glue in place.

Mural

1. Select a topic, taking into consideration suggestions of topics from students.
2. Select a surface for the mural: a wall covered with paper or perhaps a long strip of plain coloured cloth.
3. Decide if this is to be individual or group work. If individual work, each student may be asked to draw a picture to show one section of the mural. If group work, each group could be given one section of the mural to complete.
4. At this point, some planning is required so that the pictures in the mural flow evenly from beginning to end.
5. Have students sketch in lightly with pencil the part of the mural they are responsible for.

6. Collect appropriate art supplies: crayons, charcoal, chalk, coloured paper to cut into shapes, paint, or whatever is available.
7. Carry out the art work.

Mobile

1. Pick the topic or subject to be presented, for example, maps, charts, pictures, names.
2. Select or construct materials that will fit the topic.
3. Construct a support from which to hang the separate parts of the mobile. This can be a wire coat hanger, a rod, a box, anything large enough to allow objects to twist and turn easily when hanging from it.
4. Prepare each display piece so it can be viewed from each side. Attach a string (yarn, thread, strip of material, sisal string, and the like) to the top of each display piece and fasten to support.
5. Displays hanging from support must be arranged to balance the support so it remains level and in the position required.
6. Attach string to top of support and thumbtack it to the ceiling or away from a wall where the slightest air movement will twist and turn the display. The mobile, in reality a moving poster, should turn to show its many sides upon which are placed the pictures of maps or names you wish the students to remember.

Slides

Materials:

- clear adhesive paper or tape (if using tape, the wider the strip, the better – two-inch-wide or even one-inch-wide tape will work better than quarter-inch)
- flat stick (like a doctor's tongue depressor)
- stiff acrylic or thin glass squares two inches by two inches
- scissors
- bowl of water
- printed matter or pictures from slick (clay-coated) paper such as magazines, catalogues, any shiny coated paper

You are going to transfer printing or a picture from paper to a slide.

Process:

1. Decide on printed matter or picture you wish to transfer. Remember the slide will be only two inches square.

2. Cover the printed matter with adhesive paper a little larger than two inches square. If you are using narrow tape, overlap each strip as you put it down.
3. Place a piece of paper over the tape (to protect it from scratches), and rub with the flat stick, pressing fairly hard to rub out all the little air bubbles under the tape. This seals the tape or adhesive paper to the picture.
4. Cut the picture covered with tape into a two-inch square (the size of a slide).
5. Lay the adhesive coated picture in a container of water and allow to soak for at least one or two minutes until you can begin to rub off the back of the picture on the tape.
6. Gently rub the back off the tape. The magazine residue will rub off leaving the transferred printed matter or picture on the sticky tape.
7. When all residue is removed, place the adhesive tape with the image (sticky side down) on the two-inch by two-inch acrylic or thin glass square.
8. Blot away excess water. Place a clean piece of paper over your "slide", and rub again with the flat stick (this seals the image to the slide).

Your slide is now ready to be shown in a slide projector or overhead projector.

Slide Projector

A simple slide projector can be constructed using a hand lens, tape, lamp and cord, lamp guard, small box such as a candy box, and a cardboard carton.

Cut round holes in the cardboard carton and the candy box a little smaller than the lens. Fasten the candy box and the lens to the carton with wire. Make a small hole in the carton and put the lamp cord through it. Cut off the cover of the carton and tape it together as shown in the diagram. Plug in the lamp and darken the room. Hold a slide in the back of the box. Move the slide back and forth until it shows on the screen or a blank wall. The projector should be quite close to the screen or wall and the lid of the box closed as much as possible.

Transparencies

Transparencies can be made in the same manner as the slides by overlapping tape on a magazine page. (Some schools have large, clear, adhesive sheets that are used to cover textbooks to protect them. These sheets make excellent transparencies.) After soaking off the back of the transparency, as described in slide construction, lay it on a thin acrylic sheet or a piece of clear plastic grocery bag. The transparency is then ready to be shown using an overhead projector. Transparencies can also be pressed against glass school windows. The sun shining through the transparency provides a good visual image and brightens the classroom.

Transparencies can also be made by coating the face of the picture with a coat of thinned rubber cement glue, using a brush and fast even strokes. Lay the picture aside to dry for seven to fifteen minutes. Take a sheet of clear acetate slightly larger than the picture. Sand or steel wool one surface in order to frost it. Wipe the surface clean of the dust and coat with rubber cement as done with the picture. Allow to dry. Carefully place the two rubber cemented sides of the picture and the acetate sheet together. Smooth out any air bubbles or wrinkles. As with a slide, place a piece of paper on the back and rub with a stick. Soak the picture in water, and peel the paper from the sheet of acetate. Allow it to dry. Another sheet of acetate laid on top of the transparency and sealed at the edges with tape will protect the picture.

Maps and Globes

Flat maps can be drawn on almost any surface, including the sand table mentioned above. Salt maps and other types of contour maps were described earlier. Globes have the advantage of showing the world from any position. Globes can be produced by soaking strips of newspaper in a thin glue solution and then layering the paper over two bowls of the same size. When the paper has dried and is lifted off of the bowls, the two pieces can be attached to make a ball, and continents and bodies of water can be outlined on the ball and appropriately coloured. A round gourd can also be turned into a globe. Globes can be made by covering an inflated balloon with papier-mâché and letting it harden. A globe can be made from a large ball of clay. Sometimes when students are trying to learn geographic terms, models made from moulding mixture help them visualize the terms. Models could be made for such features as canals, reservoirs, soil erosion, islands, plateaus, river sources, river mouths, deltas, harbours, bays, canyons, valleys, capes, or peninsulas.

Some Common School Supplies

Some common school supplies that can be creatively made by teachers and students from low-cost or free, indigenous materials include the following:

- charcoal sticks
- ink
- dyes and paint
- paste and glue
- finger paint
- illustrative models
- easels

Charcoal Sticks (for Drawing)

1. Cut wood into pencil-shaped sticks.
2. Put them into a can with a tight-fitting lid, filling about half the can. Punch a small hole (about the size of pencil lead in the centre of the lid).
3. Place the can on a low or medium heat. Heat the can slowly and watch carefully. White smoke (mixture of steam and gas) will begin to pour from the hole. Put a lighted match to the smoke to see if it will catch fire. Heat the can until the smoke will no longer catch fire.
4. Cool can before opening it.

Ink

- 22 cubic centimetres (¾ ounce) alcohol (or methylated spirits)
- 14 cubic centimetres (½ ounce) water
- 2 grammes ($^1/_{16}$ ounce) dry or powdered dye of a certain colour
- Mix ingredients and stir well.

One quick way to show children how ink is made is to hold a plate over a candle flame until black soot forms on the bottom. This is lampblack. Moisten a brush with oil or water, dip into the lampblack and draw or paint with it.

Dyes and Paints

A wide variety of roots, barks, seeds, and leaves can be used to obtain dye. Dye mixed with a little sugar or thin glue solution makes a good paint. The glue can be made from the residue of boiled bones or from the bark of certain trees. Some plants need to be boiled, and some need only to be crushed to obtain dye. For example, tomato plant leaves pounded and crushed with a little water in a mortar make an excellent green dye. Local craft artists who use dye for carpets, baskets and mats will be able to tell you what local plants make the best dye. The following have been found useful:

- dyers woad: blue (light or dark tones are produced by the length of time the plant is boiled)
- madder red: red (colour comes from the roots of the plant)
- walnut tree: brown (the thick, green rind of the fruit and the leaves make a green or blackish-brown dye)
- pomegranate tree: yellow to brownish yellow and brown to black (the fresh or dried skin of the fruit is used for dyeing)
- ox-eye camomile: bright yellow (dye comes from the fresh or dried flowers)
- buckthorn: deep yellow (unripe fruit, fresh or dried, makes the dye)
- spurge: yellow (all parts of the plant except the roots make the dye)
- bast hemp: brilliant yellow (not often used; often mistaken for a chemical dye)
- wild camomile: yellow (fresh blossoms in early spring produce the dye)
- three-leaved sage: yellow (leaves and stems, either fresh or dried, are suitable for dyeing)

Most of the above colour dyes must be boiled to extract the dye. However, there are some plants from which a quick dye can be extracted by crushing. Among these are the following:

- bougainvillea flowers: red and purple (extract the juice)
- geranium flowers: red or pink (squeeze the juice from the flowers)
- mulberry fruit: purple (crush the fruit)

Note: Because countries will have different indigenous plants, please consult local craft artists for appropriate plant colours.

Paste and Glue

To make flour paste from commercial wheat flour and water:

1. Remove all lumps from the flour by sifting through wire sieve.
2. Add water as needed to the flour to form a smooth paste.
3. Insecticides may be added in areas where insects are a problem. If insecticide is used, store paste out of reach of children, who sometimes eat paste.

To make rice paste, use a handful of rice and water:

1. Cook rice in water as usual until rice is moist and sticky. Do not allow rice to become dry before it is well cooked.
2. Allow to dry, drain off any excess water.
3. Press out lumps with finger when applying paste.

To make rubber glue:

- 5 grammes (¼ ounce) raw rubber
- Translucent, light-brown sheet (crepe soles from shoes, or some baby-bottle nipples may be used)
- 250 cubic centimetres (8 ounces) clear or uncoloured petrol

1. Put rubber and petrol in a jar with a screw top.
2. Let stand about three days until rubber has dissolved.
3. If any lumps of rubber remain, stir until dissolved. Rubber glue should be smooth and milk-coloured in appearance.

To make uncoloured petrol:

1. Take a clean tin can and puncture a hole in the bottom. Place a small piece of cloth in the bottom to keep particles of charcoal out of filtered petrol.
2. Fill the rest of the can with small particles of charcoal.
3. Hold the can over a bowl, pail, or other container, and pour the petrol over the charcoal.
4. Repeat step three as many times as necessary to remove all colour from petrol. You may have to change the charcoal after three or four pourings.

Warning: Petrol is highly flammable and must be handled with extreme care. Always work in open area so that petrol fumes cannot collect.

Finger Paint

- 250 grammes (8 ounces) starch
- 1.2 litres (40 ounces) water
- 125 to 250 grammes (4 to 8 ounces) soap flakes (optional)
- colour from dye

1. Stir a little hot water into starch to remove lumps.
2. Add water to the smooth starch mixture, and heat until clear and thick. Add soap flakes if desired and stir.
3. Stir in colour. If more than one colour is desired, separate mixture into several jars, and add a different colour to each jar.

Illustrative Models

Illustrative models are figures and maps that show contours (mountains, valleys, rivers, or communities). The objects modelled can also be globes. Many of the modelled objects when hardened can be displayed on the wall of the classroom.

Substances for Modelling Objects

- 250 grammes (8 ounces) flour
- 250 grammes (8 ounces) salt
- 125 millilitres (4 ounces) water

1. Mix until of modelling consistency. (This is the salt map mixture mentioned earlier.)
2. Shred newspapers or paper towels. Mix with starch and paste, and knead thoroughly.
3. Mix paste and sawdust. Add a little water if too dry.
4. Dissolve 250 millilitres (8 ounces) of starch paste in water to thin slightly. Add 375 millilitres (12 ounces) of plaster to 500 grammes (16 ounces) of sawdust. Knead to consistency of tough dough.
5. Soak small pieces of newspaper in bucket of water overnight. Remove from water, and rub wet paper between palms of hands until it is ground to a pulp. Mix 1 millilitre ($^1/_{32}$ ounce) of glue in 2.5 litres (80 ounces) of water; add 500 millilitres (16 ounces) of paste and 1 litre (32 ounces) of wet paper pulp. Knead to a doughy consistency.
6. Mix 250 millilitres (8 ounces) of dry clay powder sifted through a screen with 5 millilitres (¼ ounce) of glue in 250 millilitres (8 ounces) of water: add wet paper pulp, and knead to doughy consistency, adding more water as necessary.

Check to see if clay is available in your locality, you may need to dig only a bit.

Papier-mâché

Papier-mâché is a lightweight mixture that can be moulded to hold a shape. Tear paper into tiny pieces, and soak in a glue mixture. Mix to a consistency that can be moulded. If using papier-mâché to cover a balloon to make a globe, tear the paper into thin strips, dip them in a thin glue mixture, and then layer the paper strips onto the balloon. Continue adding strips until there is a thick, even crust built up before allowing it to dry.

Improvised Easels

Improvised easels can be used to support flannel boards, posters, collages, or to display the modelled objects suggested above. Students can also use easels to support paper when drawing maps and pictures. These may be two pieces of lightweight wood joined at the top or a piece of wood, such as wallboard, propped against the legs of an inverted school desk or chair, or stood in the chalk tray at the chalkboard.

Three-Dimensional Audio-Visual Teaching Aids

The following three-dimensional audio-visual teaching aids can be made using simple school supplies or low-cost items:

- weaving loom
- clay tablets
- compass
- two-wheel cart
- soap carving
- potato printing
- puppets
- marionettes
- longitude and latitude game

Weaving Loom

For students not familiar with the weaving process, a simple loom can be made from a heavy piece of cardboard. Notch the narrow ends of the cardboard and wrap the warp threads on tightly. Use a pin to weave the woof threads over and under the warp threads. Keep the weaving tight. The loom may be cut at the notched ends to remove the cloth. After some practice, students may want to use different coloured threads to produce patterns.

Clay Tablets

Cut heavy, preferably corrugated, cardboard into rectangular pieces about as big as a child's hand. Cover with some form of modelling clay. With a sharp pencil, students can write or draw on the soft tablet. Mistakes are easy to smooth out as long as the clay is soft. Allow tablets to dry before displaying them.

Compass

When students begin to learn directions – north, south, east, and west – a simple compass will interest them. Take a large needle, and very quickly pull it across one end of a magnet. Do this again and again, always pulling in the same direction. Stick the magnetized needle all the way through a cork, and place in a container of water so it floats. The magnetized end of the needle will point north.

Two-Wheeled Carts

To make a miniature cart, carve two wheels from wood. Cut a hole in the centre of each wheel, and put a stick through the holes, leaving a space between the wheels. Put a pin or small nail through the stick on the outside of each wheel so the wheel cannot slide off. Between the wheels, tie a layer of sticks with string. A string attached to the end of the sticks will allow the cart to be pulled.

Soap Carving

Older students can carve from bars of soft soap many of the items they have studied: Greek and Roman monuments, houses, buildings, statues, and so on.

Potato Printing

Cut a potato in half. Plan a design, picture, or letter, and cut it into the flat side of the cut potato. *Keep in mind that the design will print in reverse.* Press the cut side of the potato in lamp black or other thin layer of dye or paint and then on a piece of paper. The potato will make a print of only the parts that have *not* been cut away. Suggested prints might be family or village scenes, pictures of social gatherings, pictures of self, decorations for maps, or historic scenes.

Puppets

Puppets depict role-playing, historic scenes, national heroes and what they did. Puppets assist in story telling.

Paper-bag puppet: Small paper bags can be stuffed three-quarters full with wadded newspaper and tied closed. This is the puppet head, and features can be drawn on it or cut from coloured paper and pasted on. Cut thin strips of heavy paper, and fold them in accordion pleats for arms and legs, and attach to the head and lower part of the bag in appropriate places. Pieces of cloth may be tied to the place where the bag is tied closed to form a skirt or pants.

Paper-towel-tube puppet: Make a head of clay and attach to the top of an empty toilet tissue or paper towel tube. When head is dry, face features may be painted on and the body of the puppet (the tube) dressed with paper cloth.

Jointed spool dolls: Materials needed are several sizes of spools, heavy cardboard cylinder, wire or old clothes hangers, wood handles, and paint. Design dolls of people and animals by attaching various sizes of spools together with wire. The dolls can be made to stand, sit, or assume different positions by bending the wire. Paint, dress or otherwise decorate to suit the mood of the animal or figure.

Marionette

Make head out of clay. Insert paperclips in sides and neck of head while clay is still wet. Use stick for shoulders. Fasten head to shoulder with string or wire. Hang cardboard feet from shoulder stick. Make dress of cloth or paper. Hang dress onto shoulder stick. Tie control strings to sides of head.

Longitude and Latitude Game

Draw a long horizontal line on the chalkboard, and mark it *equator*. Draw a vertical line through the middle of the first line, and label it *meridian*. Draw a series of lines down and across on each side of the equator and meridian and mark with degrees. Divide the class into two teams. Make a small cross on the board where two lines meet, and ask one team to name the location (for example, 30 degrees north latitude and 15 degrees east longitude). The team with the most correct answers wins.

Another version of this is to make a series of small cards of the longitude and latitude chart, placing a cross on different locations on each card. A student draws a card and gives the location. If the response is correct, the student keeps the card. If not, the student replaces the card. The team that collects the most cards wins.

The Process of Choosing the Right Audio-Visual Aid

Now that you have reviewed the four categories of audio-visual aids, and how to create some of those aids, how do you choose what is appropriate? The effective use of teaching aids calls for systematic planning. When thinking about what is appropriate for your class, it would be well to consider the following:

1. Number of students in your class: Are you working with twenty students or fifty?
2. Students' age: Six or sixteen years old?
3. How abstract is the content to be learned (family as a concrete idea versus continent as an imagined idea)?

4. How complex is it to create or use the teaching aid (bulletin board or mobile versus a filmstrip)?
5. What teaching aids are available in home, school, or community?

Now be creative!

How Do I Plan to Use Audio-Visual Aids?

Imagine you are teaching a social studies topic. Identify aids from the given list of all aids previously discussed and describe how you might use those audio-visual aids to

1. Initiate the lesson
2. Develop the lesson
3. Summarize the lesson

- chalkboard
- overhead projector
- flannelboard
- slide projector
- bulletin board
- filmstrip projector
- poster
- movie projector
- collage
- computer
- mural
- model
- weaving loom

- mobile
- clay tablet
- diorama
- compass
- sand table
- two-wheel cart
- salt map
- soap carving
- maps and globes
- potato printing
- diagram
- puppets

- charts
- marionettes
- graphs
- radio
- television
- tape recorder

What Will Audio-Visual Aids Do for My Students?

Suppose you were lecturing to your students but wished to increase their learning and remembering. Select an aid from the given list of audio-visual aids above, and describe how you might use that aid to increase learning and remembering.

Looking Ahead

Can educators describe children's potential development at each grade level in such a way that you, the teacher, can imagine what developmental instruction involves? Yes, and that developmental description is called a taxonomy, the subject of the next chapter.

7

The Three Taxonomies

Cognitive, Affective, and Psychomotor

In a previous chapter, the suggestion was made that thinking, skills, and attitudes can be sequenced according to the *intellectual* (thinking), *emotional* (attitudes), and *physical* (skills) development of children. At each year level, there are appropriate knowledge, skills, and attitudes.

The question is, How, as teachers, do we recognize the appropriate teaching and learning levels and apply them in the right grade level? A following question might be: How do we know that a child is at the appropriate age and grade or class level of skill, attitude, and physical development? Are there any answers to these questions? Yes, there are answers.

There must be some way to determine children's intellectual advancement from lower-level to higher-level responses, from lower-level skills to higher-level skill development, and from lower-level to higher-level emotional development. What a teacher attempts to do throughout the year at each grade or class level, is to bring the child *from* lower-level accomplishments, at the beginning of the school year, *to* higher-level accomplishments by the end of the year. But what is meant by accomplishment? At all grade or class levels, this means accomplishment in gaining knowledge, in maturing, and in skill development. In short, do teachers have a guide by which to evaluate students' *gain in knowledge,* their *maturity in attitudes,* and their *development in skills?* There is a guide, referred to as a taxonomy.

Taxonomy: A Guide to Teaching

This guide consists of three taxonomy domains. The taxonomies were developed by educational psychologists to help teachers decide how they were going to sequence and develop their lessons through a school year, so that teachers would know that children were moving *from* lower-level behaviour *to* higher-level behaviour. For example, the taxonomies are useful when writing objectives so that when teachers plan lessons throughout a year, they will have a guide to follow in moving from concrete behaviour to more abstract. Also taxonomies provide a guide to asking questions from simple recall questions (lower-level thinking), to questions that call for evaluation (higher-level thinking). Finally, the taxonomies provide a guide to the evaluation of children's progress so that evaluation materials cover the different levels of thinking, attitudes, and skills.

Three Taxonomies

A taxonomy is a method of classifying action, or behaviour, in an ascending order from simplest to most complex. And this, of course, is how teaching should proceed in the primary grades: from the concrete, or simplest, to more complex and abstract. There are three different categories of taxonomies. The first is called the *cognitive domain.* Cognitive means thinking or intellectual, and domain refers to a specific area or field of activity. The second taxonomy is the *affective domain,* which deals with emotional behaviour, a child's interest, attitudes, feelings, and values. The third taxonomy is in the *psychomotor domain* (Bloom et al. 1965; Krathwohl et al. 1964; State of California 1975). "Psycho" means mental or of the mind, and "motor" refers to muscular movement. Thus, psychomotor means the coordination between mental and physical ability, or simply muscular movement (eye, hand, body movement) as coordinated mentally.

Taxonomies (A System of Classification)		
Cognitive (Thinking)	**Affective** (Attitude)	**Psychomotor** (Physical)
1. Knowledge	1. Receiving	1. Perception
2. Comprehension	2. Responding	2. Preparation
3. Application	3. Valuing	3. Orientation
4. Analysis	4. Organization	4. Pattern
5. Synthesis	5. Characterization	5. Performance
6. Evaluation		

▶ **Table 7.1:** Taxonomies of Growth and Development

Taxonomy: A Guide to the Meaning of Progress

We all know that children are expected to make progress from the beginning to the end of the school year. Are we all clear on what is meant by making progress? Another way to ask the question is, Why should teachers, throughout a child's education, be interested in taxonomic classification systems that define progress when teaching social studies or any other subject? Is there a reason for this focus on developing higher-level cognitive thinking, a higher level of maturity, and a higher level of physical and mental coordination so that children improve their writing, reading, communicating, and other skills that require physical practice? If children are to be prepared to solve problems, to be decision makers, to think for themselves, to speak for themselves, then it is the responsibility of the teacher to help them practise thinking and acting as mature, responsible citizens. In brief, the taxonomies help guide the teacher in preparing children to become effective citizens. The following are short explanations of each of the three taxonomies, with the action words that direct the children as to how they are to act or what they are to do. These action words will be important when reading the chapters on asking questions, on writing objectives, and on the evaluation of teaching.

The Cognitive Domain

The taxonomy of cognitive educational objectives, known as Bloom's taxonomy, includes behaviour that emphasizes the intellectual, thinking level of a child. The six levels of this domain start with the lowest levels of thought, then proceed to the highest:

1. *Knowledge:* lowest level, action words – cite, label, recite
2. *Comprehension:* explain, report, reword
3. *Application:* use, show, practise
4. *Analysis:* examine, question, experiment
5. *Synthesis:* build, design, predict
6. *Evaluation:* highest level – assess, rate, support

Bloom's taxonomy implies, though it is not necessarily true, that it is difficult to perform at the comprehension level unless facts are known at the knowledge level. Also, higher-level synthesis is not usually effective unless the levels of knowing, comprehending, applying, and analysis are within the intellectual capacity of the children. The following action words demonstrate how logical intellectual activities could be performed. Although the words are presented in separate classification lists, remember that thinking is a process where children may start at different levels.

However, children should be encouraged to use all six levels, although those levels may not always be sequenced logically from lower to higher. In short, thinking is not always logically organized from one level to the next. Nevertheless, the six taxonomy levels do offer a means of evaluating students' progress in thinking from lower level 1 (knowledge), 2 (comprehension), 3 (application) to the higher level, 4 (analysis), 5 (synthesis), and 6 (evaluation).

1. Knowledge

Ability to know facts. Specific information remembered by students exactly as they learned it.

The following are action words that ask students to repeat information:

arrange	pick
check	point to
cite	quote
define	recall
find	recite
group	record
label	repeat
list	reproduce
locate	say
match	spell
memorize	tell
offer	touch
omit	underline
write	

For example:

Students will
- label the map with the major cities in the Caribbean.
- locate Barbados.
- spell the word taxonomy.
- define the word domain.
- memorize the three domains.

The story begins at the knowledge level:
The teacher gives an assignment to read the chapter on the European explorers' discovery of the West Indies, and to memorize the names of the explorers and their accomplishments as noted in the book for the next day's class.

2. Comprehension

Ability of students to interpret information learned which they can then explain in their own words.

The following are action words that ask students to explain this information:

account for	recognize
alter	report
change	restate
describe	retell
discuss	review
explain	reword
generalize	summarize
group	submit
identify	vary

convert – change, transform
moderate – make less severe
paraphrase – restate
transform – change form
expand – explain
interpret – clarify meaning

For example:

Students will
- summarize the accomplishments of the European explorers.
- submit a proposal for a project.
- describe how the national legislature works.

The story continues at the comprehension level:
The next class meeting, the teacher, in a recitation activity, asks a student to retell in the student's own words accomplishments of three explorers and in turn all the other students are asked to do the same.

▶ **Table 7.2:** Taxonomy of Cognitive Growth

3. Application

Information learned by students and put to a new use.

The following are action words that ask students to use the information:

apply	practise
adopt	profit by
collect	put into action
construct	put to use
consume	relate
demonstrate	schedule
dramatize	show
employ	sketch
give example	solve
handle	state as a rule
illustrate	transfer
make use of	try
operate	use
organize	utilize

exploit – utilize
mobilize – assemble, prepare
devote – apply full attention to
manipulate – influence
survey – examine closely

For example:

Students will
- apply rules of order to a class meeting.
- construct a model village.
- organize a new fire escape route.
- collect artefacts from old historical sites.
- make use of information from an older generation.
- schedule a time for an oral report.
- demonstrate a teaching aid.
- organize a class play.

The story continues at the application level:
The third day the teacher asks students, during a discussion, to dramatize at least one accomplishment of an explorer.

4. Analysis

Information learned by students who then break it apart to examine.

The following are action words that ask students to examine the information:

break down	inventory
calculate	investigate
categorize	outline
check	question
classify	screen
compare	search
contrast	separate
deduce	shift
diagnose	simplify
diagram	sort
divide	specify
dissect	subdivide
examine	survey
experiment	take apart
test for	uncover

analyse – separate into parts to examine
audit – examine records, verify
canvass – conduct, survey or poll
factor – determine, decide
differentiate – show difference between
scrutinize – examine carefully
section – separate into parts
study – examine closely

For example:

Students will
- compare and contrast rural and city life.
- survey voters for an election.
- inspect the city's water supply.
- categorize the different historical periods in the history of the Caribbean.

The story continues at the analysis level:
The fourth day the teacher asks students to compare and contrast life in the Caribbean at the time of the European explorers, with the student's present life in the Caribbean.

▶ **Table 7.2:** Taxonomy of Cognitive Growth *(cont'd)*

5. Synthesis

Information learned by students which they formulate in a new way.

The following are action words that ask students to formulate or hypothesize information:

assemble	hypothesize
blend	imagine
breed	invent
build	make up
cause	modify
change	originate
combine	plan
compile	predict
compose	produce
construct	propose
create	rearrange
design	reconstruct
develop	reorder
discover	reorganize
evolve	revise
formulate	suggest
generate	suppose
find a way	usual

conceive – form, imagine
effect – cause, bring about, construct
structure – construct, arrange
visualize – imagine

For example:

Students will
- formulate a new national constitution.
- compose a historical skit.
- originate a children's human rights declaration.
- imagine the future development of the Caribbean.

The story continues at the synthesis level:
The teacher on the fifth day asks the class to hypothesize about the future of the Caribbean in the twenty-first century, given its past history.

6. Evaluation

Information learned by students that will allow them to form their own opinions or judgements.

The following are action words that ask students to express their own opinions:

accept	rate
award	recommend
choose	referee
criticize	reject
debate	rule on
decide	select
defend	settle
estimate	support
evaluate	umpire
grade	rank
judge	value

adjudge – determine, decide
appraise – evaluate, estimate
assess – evaluate, estimate
arbitrate – judge, decide
critique – critically review
decree – order, decide
editorialize – express an opinion
justify – demonstrate, prove
prioritize – establish right to importance
weigh – measure, think about
censure – criticize severely

For example:

Students will
- choose the best person for the job.
- justify a position taken.
- support a proposed recommendation.
- criticize the new school dress code.
- rank the economic problems of the Caribbean.

The story ends at the evaluation level:
On the sixth day the teacher asks the class to write an in-class essay evaluating their future opportunities in the Caribbean if their hypothesis about the future were to come true.

Table 7.2: Taxonomy of Cognitive Growth *(cont'd)*

Summary of Cognitive Domain

Can you imagine how the cognitive domain taxonomy could act as a teacher's guide on the question: What is meant by making progress on thinking? Do you recall the story of the teacher and his six days of class? Throughout the week, the teacher used each level of thought during each class session. This teacher also practised working on different levels of thinking throughout the week. The objective was for the class to practise thinking at each of the six levels using action words such as list, describe, apply, classify, create, or rate. So each class period had an objective that matched the level of thinking the teacher wanted the children to practise. Some children could think at each of the six levels, but some could not and would need further practice. Thus the taxonomy was used to diagnose children's ability to think at lower and higher levels.

Suppose the teacher had wished to evaluate the children on a test at each level. Given the action words listed at each level, test construction of either objective or subjective questions would have been easy. For example, the teacher might have as an objective, "The children will apply the three reasons cited in the text to their personal experience." The objective would be evaluated by having the children write a paragraph in which the children *apply* (meaning they will think at the cognitive application level) the three reasons. In summary, the taxonomy helps to diagnose problems in thinking, and is useful in writing objectives and in constructing evaluation instruments.

The Affective Domain

The affective domain, known as Krathwohl's taxonomy, deals with the progress or development towards mature emotional behaviour. That behaviour includes interests, attitudes, feelings, and values. A value is a principle or a standard. Values determine whether objects are considered good or bad, right or wrong, desirable or worthless, important or insignificant. Children are evolving their values throughout primary school, and for this reason the teacher plays an important role in determining what is good or bad, right or wrong. Krathwohl's affective domain taxonomy deals with emotional behaviour and values development at five different levels:

1. *Receiving:* lowest-level, action words – listens, accepts
2. *Responding:* answers, volunteers
3. *Valuing:* supports, rejects
4. *Organization:* compares, challenges
5. *Characterization:* highest level – consistent behaviour, philosophy of life

Each level of the taxonomy is dependent on the levels below it. For example, it is not possible to *respond* (level 2) to a value problem without having *received* (level 1) information on the value problem. In brief, if you do not know there is a problem, you cannot thoughtfully respond.

What does this mean to you as a teacher? It means that children who enter the class with poor behaviour in "receiving", as well as the other four levels, are immature, and will need instruction, throughout the school year, that develops sequentially from "receiving" through to "characterization". This is the sequence that leads to progress towards developing mature behaviour.

Summary of Affective Domain

Can you imagine how the affective domain taxonomy acts as a teachers' guide to progress? Throughout the week, the teacher's objective in the story was to have children learn to appreciate the use of maps by willingly wanting to use them in a social studies class. The teacher started the week's social studies lesson on the first level by getting the class's attention (receiving). Once the class's attention was achieved, the teacher started the second level (responding), children opening the social studies book to find the map. At the third level (valuing), children learned to set a value on using maps with their social studies lessons. The fourth level (organization) followed with comparisons and discussions on various types of maps, and the class came to appreciate (value) how helpful different types of maps could be. Finally, at the fifth level (characterization), by the end of the school week, children were using maps because they had learned to value the helpful information that could be gotten from different types of maps. The students had reached the objective of *appreciation and willingly wanting* to use maps as part of their value system.

Affective (Attitude)	
Systematic progression from lower level 1, receiving, to higher level 5, characterization:	1. Receiving 2. Responding 3. Valuing 4. Organization 5. Characterization

▶ **Table 7.3:** Taxonomy of Affective Growth

1. Receiving (meaning "to get") This involves students' – awareness: listening to directions; – willingness to accept: quietly waiting for the teacher to begin reading a story; and – controlling or selecting information: listening for certain sounds. Action words: The student accepts endures is aware of listens notices submits to waits for The story begins at the receiving level: The teacher says, "Please quiet down and open your social studies book to the map of Jamaica." If the students hear (receive) the request and are ready to act, they are at the receiving level. If the students continue to talk and do not look for their books, they show a clear lack of awareness of the receiving behaviour. The class will definitely need to work on practising their affective behaviour level of receiving.	**2. Responding** (meaning "to react") This involves students – complying by following directions: opening textbook at teacher's request; – showing willingness to comply by volunteering: raising a hand to answer question; and – finding satisfaction in complying: feeling happy over teacher's positive response. Action words: The student adapts allows answers asks refrains from doing replies selects follows directions likes to participate reads when asked recognizes questions chooses when asked consults teacher volunteers to welcomes The story continues at the responding level: Having learned to receive a request to open the text to the map, the students follow directions by opening the book to the map of Jamaica.

▶ **Table 7.3:** Taxonomy of Affective Growth *(cont'd)*

3. Valuing

This involves students

- expressing acceptance of a task;
- defending viewpoints: defending concept of democracy; and
- revealing commitment: campaigning for a person or cause they agree with.

Action words:

The student

accepts	rates
adopts	rejects
appraises	sets a value on
criticizes	shows appreciation by
joins groups	specifies
persists	supports a viewpoint

The story continues at the valuing level:

Having opened the book and found the map, the students could show appreciation for the map by saying, "This is a good map because I can find where I live. Yet the map is old because it does not label the modern name for our town." The students critically accept the map.

4. Organization

This involves students

- committing to a set of values;
- comparing, discussing standards; and
- defining or formulating a system of values.

(Some things are more valuable than others.)

Action words:

The student
challenges others' values
compares standards
organizes (values or rules)
persists in
refrains from doing
shapes

The story continues at the organization level:

At the organization level, students compare the book map with other maps in an atlas and conclude that maps are helpful (a value statement) in finding where we live on the Earth, but they also discover that there are different types of maps, and that some maps are personally more valuable than others.

Table 7.3: Taxonomy of Affective Growth *(cont'd)*

5. Characterization
(meaning a distinctive quality)

This involves students
- behaving consistently with internalized value system;
- resolving conflicts in consistency; and
- acting in accordance with a philosophy of life.

Action words:

The student

can be counted on to ________
reveals outstanding qualities in ________
shows a distinctive value system in ________
shows habitual conduct ________

The story ends with the characterization level:

At the characterization level, students, when studying about communities in Jamaica, voluntarily (meaning without the request of the teacher) open their books and atlases, and turn to a map of Jamaica because they see value in using maps and have a personal internalized value to use maps as a consistent behaviour.

▶ **Table 7.3:** Taxonomy of Affective Growth *(cont'd)*

The teacher reached the objective of "appreciation" and the fifth level of "characterization" with most of the class. One child never got past "receiving", which means that he never paid attention. Three other children were at the "responding" level where they opened the book, but never went on to value maps. Do you comprehend how a teacher might use the taxonomy to diagnose and help these four children who did not achieve the highest level of affective behaviour (characterization)? Do you comprehend how the teacher might have written objectives based on the five levels and how the class could be evaluated on their performance at each level? Could you now, using the action words from each of the five affective levels (that is, receiving, responding, valuing, organization, and characterization), develop a teaching unit to include all five levels of affective behaviour, and also construct a test to measure your students' affective progress?

The Psychomotor Domain

"Pick up your pen, place it properly in your fingers and write the letter 'A'. Continue practising writing 'A' between the lines in your copy book." Do you remember a similar experience when you started school? The teacher was asking you to perform a psychomotor skill - correctly and comfortably holding a pen, and with the right mental coordination, drawing the letter repeatedly between the lines.

The psychomotor domain emphasizes motor behaviours involving mental or muscular coordination. This domain is particularly important for teachers who are working with an age group who must develop coordination of eye/hand/body/

mind in order to build dexterity for running, playing, and competing with others. The levels of progress for this taxonomy start with the lowest level (1) *perception,* which is a simple cue or a signal of awareness, and moves on to (2) *preparation,* (3) *orientation,* (4) *pattern,* and to (5) *performance,* the highest level. The levels of this taxonomy are not necessarily sequential, as they might be in the cognitive and affective domains. A child's response will start with perception or recall of an experience, but how the child will progress through the other four levels will depend upon the growth and skill development of that child while performing the action.

Children, of course, differ greatly in their coordination, and this is an important point to keep in mind when observing where a child fits best at a particular level in the psychomotor domain. The psychomotor progress level at which the child is performing most of the time will be observed by the teacher. From that observation, the teacher should be able to place the child in one of the five categories. The following action words will demonstrate how to recognize and organize different levels of psychomotor skill development.

Summary and Conclusion

The psychomotor development of children, like their intellectual and their emotional development, seems to follow a progressive, systematic pattern. As you have noted throughout this chapter, these systematic patterns are called levels of behavioural development and, in some general way, they are known and can be followed. These levels provide an opportunity for diagnosing the strengths and weaknesses of children's intellectual, emotional, and physical progress. The levels offer some of the action words for writing objectives, and finally the levels provide a guide for

	Psychomotor/ (Physical)
Systematic progression from lower level 1, perception, to higher level 5, performance:	1. Perception 2. Preparation 3. Orientation 4. Pattern 5. Performance

▶ **Table 7.4:** Taxonomy of Psychomotor Development

1. Perception	2. Preparation
Sensitivity to stimulus normally leading to action. Action words: cue (a signal) look hear sense listen watch Students would be – sensitive to a situation; – cueing, triggering an act, waiting for; – sensing timing; and – aware of differences in the classroom. The story begins at the perception level: The teacher's objective this school term was to practise eye, hand and feet coordination, knowing that the development of higher physical skills is important both mentally and physically to the overall progress of each child. The inability to run, jump, hold a pen, tie shoes, follow directions, all of which call for coordination, can seriously prevent a student from succeeding in school. "Class," the teacher says, "we are going to work on a social studies project." The teacher has just given the class a signal, a cue. Some children, having experienced projects, are excited, others pay no attention because they do not know what the teacher means. This is the level of perception.	Involves readiness to perform (possesses knowledge and mind set) Action words: hold wait prepare stand Students would – be ready to perform in class; – have knowledge of skill set necessary to act (how to hold pencil to write); – be physically, mentally, or emotionally ready (inward knowledge that one can succeed); – have mind/body arrangement for action; and – have favourable attitude, willingness to respond (desire to participate, work in group, draw, speak, listen). The story continues at the preparation level: "Please get out your historical atlas which has maps showing the Bahamas, during four historical periods." The teacher continues, "We are going to have projects over the four different periods represented by the four maps in the atlas that cover the historical periods. The class will be divided into four project groups, one group for each period." All of these instructions (getting out the atlas, the project, and grouping) are at the level of preparation.

▶ **Table 7.4:** Taxonomy of Psychomotor Development *(cont'd)*

3. **Orientation**	4. **Pattern**
Knowing and/or deciding on an appropriate response to be made. Action words: copies corrects imitates Students would be – applying preparation for past action to new or different action; – imitating, in class, a demonstration of a skill that needs to be learned; and – using trial and error selection (trying several actions to see what works best). The story continues at the orientation level: The class is divided into four groups, and each group is selecting which audio-visual teaching aids would be best to demonstrate their historical period. Through brainstorming, the group selects which aids to construct: diorama, mobile, poster. These aids will be used to illustrate the group's oral presentation, their historical period. The group's preparation represents the orientation level.	A learned response that is habitual, smooth, and confident (a skill pattern or low error response). Action words: drills learns practises Students would – display a learned response that is habitual; – have confidence in their own ability; – respond by applying an element of preparation; – exhibit a skill pattern; and – execute a relatively low error incident. The story continues at the pattern level: Over the next several weeks each of the four groups' projects are being prepared for presentation. The groups learn to cooperate in creating each of the teaching aids. They are developing confidence in their ability to accurately present their historical period. As the weeks pass, the groups display an increasing pattern of skill development, with each member knowing how to contribute to the success of the total project. The students are practising at the pattern level where their responses in the group show they have learned to be confident, to be skilled in their ability to work together towards a common good.

Table 7.4: Taxonomy of Psychomotor Development *(cont'd)*

5. Performance

Response that is a complex motor action involving a high degree of skill (polished behaviour, complicated responses, made with ease and control).

Action words:

competes
does skilfully
excels
plays

Students would

- perform complex motor action with a high degree of skill;
- respond to cues with a polished performance;
- spend minimum time and energy on skilled performance;
- produce complicated response without hesitation;
- make complex movement pattern with ease and control; and
- demonstrate proficiency in classroom activity.

The story ends at the performance level:

By the end of the marking period, the teacher has assigned the class to another project.
The students' final projects showed how skilfully most of the class members had become in working cooperatively and productively with the other members of the class. The projects at the end of the semester demonstrated the class's proficiency in producing teaching and learning aids, and showed a polished performance in reporting to the class. Thus by the end of the semester, the class was generally responding at the performance level because they could produce polished, complicated responses which they could not have done at the beginning of the marking period.

▶ **Table 7.4:** Taxonomy of Psychomotor Development *(cont'd)*

evaluating the child's progress, during a marking period, from lower-level to higher-level behaviour. Because the levels are known and can be followed, curriculum materials can be sequenced and developed to respond to those different levels. For example, a primary social studies programme based on growth and development of children, would be a demonstration of how knowledge, emotional development, and skills, together with concepts, topics, maps, globes, and other learning aids, can be planned in a scope and sequence throughout a school programme.

Looking Ahead

The three taxonomies justify, and specifically explain, the meaning of growth and development. Thus, it is your responsibility, as a teacher, to use these levels as a guide to develop your skill of questioning, your teaching unit plans, and, finally, your evaluation of your children's progress, as discussed and illustrated in the following chapters.

8

Practising the Skill of Asking Questions

Introduction

Questioning is the first among teaching skills. Why should this be true? Studies on what teachers actually do in class show that approximately 30 per cent of their class time is spent in verbally asking questions. Another quarter of the time is devoted to reviewing, giving, and grading test questions. In short, on the average, about half of the class time is devoted to asking questions of some sort.

You know from chapter 3 that students learn better when they are asked stimulating questions rather than being lectured to. This means that students learn best when they are asked different levels of questions and also, by inference, that students who ask stimulating questions focus their attention and encourage feedback.

If you, as a teacher, are likely to spend up to half of your class time asking questions, then does it not make sense that you learn about, and practise, the skill of questioning? Of course, your immediate reaction might be that having spent most of your life asking and answering questions, don't you already have the skill? *No, you don't necessarily have it.* If you have no training in asking questions, the research suggests that 90 per cent of the time, you will, like most teachers, *ask only low-level questions.* Why should we care about different levels of questioning when teaching citizenship courses? The goal of social studies in primary school is effective citizenship. Effective citizenship, in a democracy, requires citizens who are able to ask all levels of questions because they are intended to be problem solvers and decision makers. It would therefore be difficult for citizens to make effective decisions if they cannot think as problem solvers.

You will recall from chapter 7 how the taxonomies can help teachers. The taxonomy levels provide an opportunity for diagnosing the strengths and weaknesses of students' thinking, acting, and emotional behaviour. They offer some of the key words for writing objectives, and the levels provide a guide for evaluating a student's progress. In particular, the cognitive domain taxonomy identified six levels of thinking from knowledge to evaluation. It was suggested, in that chapter, that a teacher's major skill objective during the school year was to practise the six levels of thinking with the hope, of course, of preparing students to become problem solvers and decision makers. That preparation comes in the form of learning the skill of asking the lower and higher levels of questions. Both you, the teacher, and your students need to learn the skill, since effective questioning is basic to good teaching, and is also a basic skill to be practised in a democratic society.

Lower- and Higher-Level Questions

In this chapter, you will learn how to distinguish between the four levels of questions. These levels can be divided into lower-level and higher-level questions. Lower-level questions generally focus on the cognitive domain levels of knowledge, comprehension, and application, while higher-level questions focus on the analysis, synthesis, and evaluation levels of thinking. To simplify the skill of asking different levels of questions, the authors have identified four levels: (1) *cognitive-memory* questions, which deal with the knowledge taxonomy level; (2) *convergent* questions, which include the comprehension, application, and analysis taxonomy level; (3) *divergent* questions, which relate to the synthesis taxonomy level; and (4) *evaluative* questions, which include the evaluation taxonomy level.

Practising the Skill of Thinking at Four Levels

The remainder of this chapter is intended to give you practice in thinking and working at the four different levels of asking questions. Though the idea of different levels of questions may be rather easy to understand, it is also recognized that using the four levels of questions in order to teach is difficult because we may not have been required, in our own education, to practise thinking at the different levels. In short, the idea of developing a skill in asking different levels of questions may be a new thought for some teachers.

Cognitive-Memory Questions

Cognitive means knowledge, so cognitive memory refers to memorized knowledge (*list, label, recite*).

Cognitive-memory (CM) questions tend to be restricted to the lowest levels of thinking. Questions of this type seek *one right answer,* which usually requires students to respond with factual information or definitions that rely on recall or recognition. Answers to these questions tend to be short phrases or merely a single word. Students respond to cognitive-memory questions by recalling a fact, defining a term, noting something they observed, or simply giving an answer based on rote memory. The following questions are typical of the level of thinking elicited by cognitive-memory questions:

1. In the Federation, which is the largest in square miles, Nevis or St Kitts? (Clearly there is one right answer: St Kitts.)
2. What country in the Eastern Caribbean has the largest population? (Clearly the one right answer is Barbados)
3. Name the bodies of water that encircle the Caribbean islands.
4. Chance's Peak is located in which British Crown Colony?
5. Is Hackleton's Cliff located in Barbados?

To help identify cognitive-memory questions, the following introductory phrases are to be completed in the form of cognitive-memory questions.

Instructions: Complete each sentence.

1. *Recall* the name of _________.
2. *Identify* the reasons for _________.
3. *Are the* Falls of Baleine in _________?
4. *Define* exactly the meaning of _________.
5. *List* the most important _________.
6. *Designate* the right name for _________.

To further help you identify cognitive-memory (CM) questions, read each of the questions below. In the blank space provided, write CM if you think the question is cognitive-memory. If you decide that question is not cognitive-memory, then label it (N) for no. After labelling each question either CM or N, read the paragraph that follows to check your answers.

Identification Practice: label *CM* (for cognitive-memory) or *N* (for no) in the space provided.

A. Name the two-mile strait that divides Nevis from St Kitts. _________

B. Tell me why you think Anguilla is important. ________
C. Explain why development might create a pollution problem? _______
D. Recall the capital of Montserrat. ________
E. Identify the city with the largest population in the Eastern Caribbean. ________
F. Did Dominica gain independence in 1978? ________

If you marked questions A, D, E, and F as cognitive-memory questions, then you are on the right track. These four questions ask students merely to reproduce short, factual information such as names or dates. Although clear distinctions are sometimes difficult to make, questions B and C probably are intended to have the student develop a definition or engage in speculation, which is really higher-level questioning.

Key words when writing cognitive-memory questions are as follows:

Recall	Define
Identify	Name
Yes and No	Designate

Other key words are as follows:

Label	Recite
List	Spell
Locate	State
Match	Tell
Memorize	Write
Quote	Find

(For additional key words see the "Knowledge" level list in the Cognitive Domain Taxonomy for chapter 7.)

Writing Practice

Now it is time for you to try your hand at writing this level of question. On the lines provided below, demonstrate your ability to write three cognitive-memory questions. Choose any topic you wish. Use the key words above as a reference to write the questions.

1. ______________________________
2. ______________________________
3. ______________________________

Convergent Questions

Convergent means coming together as in converging one's thoughts (summarize, apply, organize).

Convergent (C) questions require students to establish a relationship between facts or ideas in order to construct an answer. Convergent questions are aimed at eliciting "right" or "best" answers. Generally, the information necessary for answering such questions is assumed to be known by both teacher and the students, such as when the teacher asks students to explain in their words, from the homework assignment, some event or idea. The question requires recalling certain facts, or ideas, organizing or associating them in some manner, and formulating an explanation in the students' own words. To cope with this level of question, the students are required to perform thinking operations that are more complex than those needed to answer cognitive-memory questions.

In short, there is one *best answer* or answers, which are often stated in the students' own words. Explaining, comparing, reviewing, and summarizing are words often associated with the specific level of thinking behaviour connected with convergent questions. Some examples follow.

Do you see a problem? Why?

Why is Grenada called the "Isle of Spice?" (If you had read the textbook assignment on this, you would probably be able to give a textbook answer in your own words. There is a correct answer according to the text.)

How are the cities of Port of Spain in Trinidad and Kingston in Jamaica alike?

Explain how Belize and Guyana are related.

Compare and contrast the Leeward and the Windward Islands.

State *in what ways* the Bahamas are unique as a "Caribbean" country.

To help you identify convergent questions, the following introductory phrases are to be completed in the form of convergent questions.

1. *Explain* the relationship between Antigua and ________________.
2. *Why* did Dominica ________________?
3. *Compare and contrast* cultural festivals in St Lucia with those in ________________.
4. *How similar* are St George's and ________________?
5. *Describe* the difference between the form of government in Anguilla and that in ________________.

In the set of questions below, use the letters CM, C, or N to indicate whether the question is cognitive-memory (CM), or convergent (C) or neither (N). The correct answers are in the paragraph below the questions.

Identification Practice: Label *CM, C,* or *N* in the space provided.

A. Explain the reason for the rise of tourism in St Kitts. ________
B. What is the name of the "Most magnificent pair of mountains" in the Caribbean? ________
C. Should the government put a priority on eliminating poverty?______
D. Name the famous English captain of the British fleet whose headquarters were at English Harbour in Antigua? ________________
E. Tell why the present economic conditions of citizens of the Eastern Caribbean are different from those of their ancestors? ________
F. What is the political relationship between Antigua and Barbuda? ________________
G. How are Trinidad and Jamaica alike? ________

Your task of identifying the different levels of questions in this set was more difficult than in the previous identification practice. If you labelled questions A, E, F, and G as convergent, you are progressing nicely. The use of key words "how", "why", and "explain" should have alerted you on three of these questions. Questions B and D are representative of the cognitive-memory level, while question C should have been marked N for neither. If you identified these questions correctly, move on to the next section. If you missed one or two, take a minute to review this section on convergent questions again. Key words when writing convergent questions are as follows:

Explain	Contrast
Describe	Why
Compare	How

Other key words are as follows:

Change	Summarize
Reword	Calculate
Interpret	Account for
Review	Paraphrase
Offer	

(For additional key words, see the "Comprehension and Application" level lists in the cognitive domain taxonomy from chapter 7.)

Writing Practice

On the lines provided below, demonstrate your ability to write convergent-level questions. The key words above for convergent questions would be helpful.

1. ____________________
2. ____________________
3. ____________________

Where have we been?

Cognitive memory: Recall, Identify, Yes, No, Define, Name, Designate.

Convergent: Explain, Describe, Compare, Contrast, Why, How.

Commentary on the Use of CM and C Questions

From the examples above, it is obvious that "how" and "why", "compare and contrast", and "explain" tend to act as key words for identifying convergent-level questions. Research studies, however, have found that student thinking can be restricted if cognitive-memory and convergent questions are utilized constantly because students will not think beyond the "right" answer. Students assume that the purpose of education and instruction is strictly one of finding the right answers, and they may become very defensive when asked to think beyond a simple response, and at a higher level.

Divergent Questions

Divergent means to hypothesize or inquire, to encourage a variety of answers, all of which are possible, yet can be supported by evidence (*change, combine, predict*).

Divergent (D) questions provide the student with much more freedom and independence in giving answers. Divergent questions allow for a variety of answers that can be supported by objective evidence. It is, however, more difficult to predict the actual answer a student might give. This level of question is often considered to be one that is thought-provoking. Teachers who ask divergent questions of their students are *seeking original or creative answers.* Divergent questions often confront students with problem situations, which force them to combine facts, concepts, and generalizations in new ways in order to create and develop plausible answers. Designing, evolving, predicting, modifying, reconstructing, hypothesizing, and inferring are the thinking operations typical of this level of question. Below are some examples of divergent questions.

How might life be changed in the Caribbean region if life expectancy were to increase by fifty years?

(There is no clear answer to this question, but the answer would need to include supporting evidence from the past fifty years suggesting changes that have happened because of rising life expectancy.)

Suggest a number of ways in which the standard of living could be raised.

Imagine what economic development will do to Grenada over the next twenty years.

Predict what would happen to our lives if motorized vehicles were eliminated from the Caribbean islands.

Reconstruct events as they might have happened during the early history of man.

Hypothesize about the effect on the Eastern Caribbean of a possible ten-year cycle of violent hurricanes.

To help identify divergent questions, the following introductory phrases are to be completed as divergent questions.

1. *Create* a lesson plan for ______________________________.
2. *Hypothesize* about the possibility of ______________________.
3. *Predict* the outcome of ______________________________.
4. *What would happen* if ______________________________?
5. *Originate* a theory for ______________________________.
6. *Plan* a programme for ______________________________.

It is obvious that more imagination and insight is needed to answer a divergent question than is needed to answer cognitive-memory or convergent questions. The divergent level of questions tend to stimulate and motivate the interests of students. Questions at this divergent level encourage students to speculate and to explore topics in more depth, the result being focused attention and a more favourable attitude towards the subject matter. Too often, teachers become so concerned with covering content by using cognitive-memory and convergent questions in recitations, that they neglect the divergent questions altogether. Consequently, they miss a valuable opportunity to help students develop higher-level thinking by asking them to extend their creative abilities.

By adding another level of questions to the set below, the task of correctly labelling each question becomes more difficult. Read each question carefully, and fill in the blanks in the space provided with either CM for cognitive-memory, C for convergent, D for divergent, or N for none. After labelling each question, read the paragraph that follows to check your answer.

Identification Practice: Label *CM, C, D,* or *N* in the space provided.

A. What do you hypothesize about the economic growth of Belize and Guyana in this new century? ________
B. Was Barbados the first Eastern Caribbean island to gain independence? ________
C. Formulate a plan to combat pollution in the major river in your country. ________
D. Summarize the major food crops produced and exported by the British Virgin Islands. ________
E. What would you predict would happen if the Caribbean established trade barriers against the European Community? ________
F. Construct a plan to deal with inflation. ________
G. Compare the effect of the French and English influences in St Lucia. ________

If you selected questions A, C, E, and F, as being divergent, you are correct. These questions would engage the student in hypothesizing and predicting. Question B, however, only requires recall and a yes or no answer as a cognitive-memory question. If you labelled D and G as being convergent you are doing well.

Key words when writing divergent questions are as follows:

Predict	Create
Hypothesize	Formulate
Originate	

Other key words are as follows:

Combine	Invent
Develop	Revise
Suggest	Modify

Construct Suppose
Discover

(For additional key words, see the "Synthesis" level list in the cognitive domain taxonomy in chapter 7.)

Writing Practice

On the lines provided below, demonstrate your ability to write three divergent questions. Use key words to write your divergent questions.

1. ______________________________
2. ______________________________
3. ______________________________

Where have we been?

Cognitive Memory: Recall, Identify, Yes, No, Define, Name, Designate.

Convergent: Explain, Describe, Compare, Contrast, Why, How.

Divergent: Predict, Hypothesize, Originate, Create, Formulate.

Evaluative Questions

Evaluative means to judge, justify or grade; to decide, to offer a personal opinion (*choose, judge, defend*).

Evaluative (E) questions deal with that area of thinking related to judgement, values, and choices. Evaluative questions tend to force students to organize their thoughts and knowledge in order to reach their own personal opinion. The students' judgement must be based upon some evidence and standards which the students or some other person or group establishes, but that evidence need not be objective or reliable. The following questions provide examples.

Do you think Grenada is making progress in diversifying the economy? (The question calls for personal opinion, but that personal opinion, in contrast to a divergent question, does not require support from objective evidence. Therefore, the personal opinion does not necessarily need to be rational or logical.)

What is your opinion about the restriction of fishing rights?

What do you believe should be done about the educational system?

Defend your position on environmental protection.

Justify your choice for a democratic way of life.

Recommend the best way to conserve our water supply.

Criticize the plans for economic development in St Kitts.

What is your ranking of the five top nations in the world?

To help identify evaluative questions, the following introductory phrases are to be completed in the form of evaluative questions.

1. *What do you think* about ____________________?
2. *In your opinion,* ____________________?
3. *Do you believe* ____________________?
4. *Defend* your choice ____________________.
5. *Which* is best ____________________?
6. *Recommend* ____________________.
7. *Judge* which of the following ____________________.

You have five different ways of labelling the following questions. In the practice below, use *CM* for cognitive-memory, *C* for convergent, *D* for divergent, *E* for evaluative, or *N* for none, to label each question. Read the paragraph that follows to check your answers.

Identification Practice: Label *CM, C, D, E,* or *N* in the space provided.

A. If Germany had defeated the Allies in World War II, how might that have affected Caribbean Colonial territories? ________
B. In your opinion, what is the best means for enforcing anti-pollution laws? ________
C. Justify your reaction to water rationing during the dry season. ______
D. Name the famous pair of mountains in St Lucia. ________
E. How do democratic governments compare with other forms of government? ________
F. Decide what should be done to improve public transportation. _____

If you labelled any of these N, go back and review your mistakes. Only questions B, C, and F should have been labelled with the letter E for evaluative. Question B directs the student to make a best choice between alternatives, while C and F seek an opinion. The only cognitive-memory question was D. Pupils must make a series of comparisons in Question E, which is one of the thought operations called for in convergent questions. Question A should be labelled divergent because the student is asked to hypothesize. If you labelled these six questions correctly, you are doing excellent work. Recognizing the different levels of questions is not easy. It takes time to recognize the key words that indicate the levels of thought. You may need to continue to review the four levels of questions until you can actually question and, in fact, think at those different levels.

Key words when writing evaluative questions are as follows:

Judge	Select
Value	Opinion
Defend	Rank

Other key words are as follows:

Assess	Recommend
Decide	Criticize
Rate	Justify
Choose	Evaluate
Grade	

(For additional key words, see the "Evaluation" level list in the cognitive domain taxonomy from chapter 7.)

Writing Practice

Writing good evaluative questions is not an easy task. Using the key words for this level question, on the lines provided below, demonstrate your ability to write three evaluative questions. Take notice of the key words as you write evaluative questions.

1. ______________________________
2. ______________________________
3. ______________________________

Where have we been?

Cognitive memory: Recall, Identify, Yes, No, Define, Name, Designate.

Convergent: Explain, Describe, Compare, Contrast, Why, How.

Divergent: Predict, Hypothesize, Originate, Create, Formulate.

Evaluative: Judge, Value, Defend, Select, Opinion, Rank.

Paying attention to the wording of questions is very important. By simply changing a word or phrase, questions can require a very different level of thinking. The sets of questions that follow illustrate this point. Notice how the questions change and evolve as they are re-worded.

Cognitive-Memory Questions

A. What is the average birth rate in Caribbean countries?
B. Give the infant mortality rate in the Eastern Caribbean.
C. State how many degrees north of the equator Barbados is.
D. Was the whole Caribbean ever colonized by Spain?

Convergent Questions

A. How does the birth rate of the Caribbean compare to that of Mexico?
B. Explain why the Caribbean mortality rate is high in comparison to Canada.
C. Describe the location of the following cities: Plymouth, Basseterre, and St Johns.
D. Why was the Caribbean never colonized by Japan?

Divergent Questions

A. Imagine what would happen to the standard of living in the Caribbean if the birth rate increased to 4.0.
B. How might the Eastern Caribbean be different if the infant mortality rate were lower?
C. Predict what might happen to Nevis in the event of a violent hurricane.
D. Suppose the Caribbean had been colonized by Japan, how might that have changed its history?

Evaluative Questions

A. Recommend what action you think the government should take to reduce family size and the birth rate.
B. Decide whether birth control would be beneficial to economic development in the Caribbean.
C. Judge whether or not the Caribbean should develop nuclear energy.
D. Justify your reasons for thinking that the Caribbean islands should become one self-reliant, interdependent nation.

Writing Practice

It is your turn again. Try taking a single topic and writing one question at each level on the topic. For example, topics might be: environment, development, crime, living standards, health – or you may select your own topic. Refer to the key words for help in writing your questions.

1. Cognitive-memory: ______________________________
2. Convergent: ______________________________
3. Divergent: ______________________________
4. Evaluative: ______________________________

Self-Test

This is a final check on how well you classify questions using the four levels you have just learned. Label all twelve questions below. If you are unsure about any of them, refer to the key words for each level. Place *CM* for cognitive-memory, *C* for convergent, *D* for divergent, or *E* for evaluative on the line provided before each of the questions (see answer key at the end of the chapter).

1. Imagine what might happen to Grenada's economy if the price of spices were to increase by 100 per cent. ________
2. What do you predict about the growth of the Eastern Caribbean region in this twenty-first century? ________
3. In your judgement, who makes the greatest contribution to society, a doctor or a lawyer? ________
4. What are the similarities and differences between the Leeward and Windward Islands? ________
5. When did Trinidad gain independence? ________
6. What are the similarities and differences between the population of Guyana and Barbados? ________
7. How do the capitals of St George's in Grenada and St John's in Antigua compare and contrast? ________
8. What is the best way to combat inflation? ________
9. As the minister of education in Barbados, how do you ensure that everyone receives an education? ________
10. What is the relationship between the production of goods and the standard of living? ________
11. Who was the last British governor before independence in Dominica? ________
12. Plan the steps you would take to ensure that adequate medical facilities are provided in rural areas. ________

Using All Four Levels

What questioning strategy will encourage all levels of thinking? The answer to this question is very simple and direct. Discussion is stimulated by the use of all four levels of questions. Teachers cannot get students to give thoughtful responses by asking them just to recall, waiting three seconds, and then asking another question. Nor are teachers likely to generate thoughtful responses just by asking evaluative questions. It is equally important to speculate (divergent thinking) as it is to recall information in one's own words (convergent thinking). It is the accumulated effect of having students evaluate, speculate, recall, and recite that is most likely to excite the students' imagination. Some teachers choose to start a discussion with cognitive-memory questions and proceed methodically to convergent, divergent, and evaluative questions in that order. Others choose to start with the evaluative level. Frankly, the evidence suggests that there is no one best way that questions should be sequenced. How questions are best sequenced depends on the class. Each class is different, thus needing a different approach.

Motivation

We must discuss a very practical problem. Many teachers say that they cannot get their students to answer questions. The students just won't talk, and under special conditions, this obviously is true. Think a minute about the levels of questions teachers and textbooks usually ask. You might agree that there is a considerable amount of monotony in asking, 95 per cent of the time, only lower-level cognitive-memory and convergent questions. There is an appearance of sameness if, day after day, all questions are pitched at a lower level. Asking the same level of questions may lead to student apathy; they just do not want to volunteer responses anymore. And, finally, what is there to discuss about a recall answer? From the students' point of view the teacher lectures or gives information as an addition to the students' responses. This teaching strategy (recitation, lecture), as research studies show, does not stimulate students to think for themselves. The recitation and lecture - which seems to be popular with many teachers - tends to discourage discussion and the willingness to participate. That is hard to accept, but it is true.

Applying Questioning Skills to the Problem-Solving Method

A questioning strategy is an absolute necessity if teachers are going to apply the problem-solving method. That strategy is not terribly difficult; it merely requires asking all four levels of questions. The pattern of questioning is governed primarily by the class. It is not required that more evaluative questions than cognitive-memory questions be asked. Nor should all levels be asked equally so that a quarter of class time is devoted to each. One level of questions should lead to another. For example, an evaluative question should lead to some call for evidence - cognitive-memory or convergent questions. It is important that a line of thinking be pursued that follows the steps of the problem-solving method. Different students respond to different levels of questions. It is the teacher's task to discover which questions stimulate responses from their students. It is the students' responsibility, in a democracy, to be effective problem solvers and decision makers.

Human beings by their very nature are inquirers. Students, being human, come to school anticipating the use of their total faculties, but soon learn that their expectations are different from those of the school. Asked only to use lower levels of questioning, students soon develop a split personality, operating at one level in school and both levels in the real world.

Looking Ahead

How can you prepare lesson plans that include effective teaching skills that make use of the taxonomy guides to classroom teaching? By looking ahead to the next chapter, you will learn how to write complete behavioural objectives that describe what you will actually practise in class.

Answer key: 1. D; 2. D; 3. E; 4. C; 5. CM; 6. C; 7. C; 8. E; 9. D; 10. C; 11. CM; 12. D

Scoring:

11–12 *Excellent.* You have mastered all levels. You are ready to practise all four levels in teaching.

8–10 *Good.* Although you missed a few, your working knowledge is above average, and you are ready to use all four levels of questions in teaching.

7–8 *Fair only.* Take a close look at those you missed. It may be that you are slightly confused on one of the levels.

0–6 *Weak.* Check the description of each level carefully, and try to determine exactly why you made so many mistakes. Do not proceed; questioning is a basic teaching skill, and you must try again to learn the four levels of questions.

A score of "Good" is the minimum expected.

9

Identifying and Writing Complete Behavioural Objectives

Theory for, and Practice of, Writing Objectives

Behavioural objectives deal with how students perform; and writing these objectives is a learned skill. This chapter will prepare you to practise that skill. You would have completed chapter 7, and thus know that the three taxonomies - cognitive/affective/psychomotor - are guides to developing specific learning behaviours, from low-performance to high-performance behaviours. The taxonomy's guides to teaching are in the form of action words that state what students should do, such as: define, describe, apply, classify, predict and judge, to achieve a desired behavioural objective. The three taxonomies offer a general guide to behaviour, whereas behavioural objectives offer a specific statement on how the desired student behaviour (to define, describe, etc.) will be practised in the classroom. In short, objectives describe how the growth and development of children, expressed as learning outcomes ("Students will be able to read a map, make a model, analyse reasons"), will help teachers to plan effective instruction.

In summary, you should be asking "How do I plan to use the statement of objectives to teach students?" The answer is, Use behavioural objectives because those objectives reflect the taxonomic levels (class activities) that you want your students to practise.

What Are the Purposes of Having Objectives for Any Activity? Why Objectives?

The answer to "why objectives?", beyond those of just a taxonomic guide to instruction, is that objectives identify what method, techniques, and strategy are to be followed. Why are objectives necessary? A teacher should think about how to organize instruction in order to maximize learning in the classroom, thus helping students to become effective learners. Having no objective or no expected student performance means the teacher is planning poorly. In short, if you, as the teacher, do not know what you want from the lesson, you cannot plan what the class is to achieve.

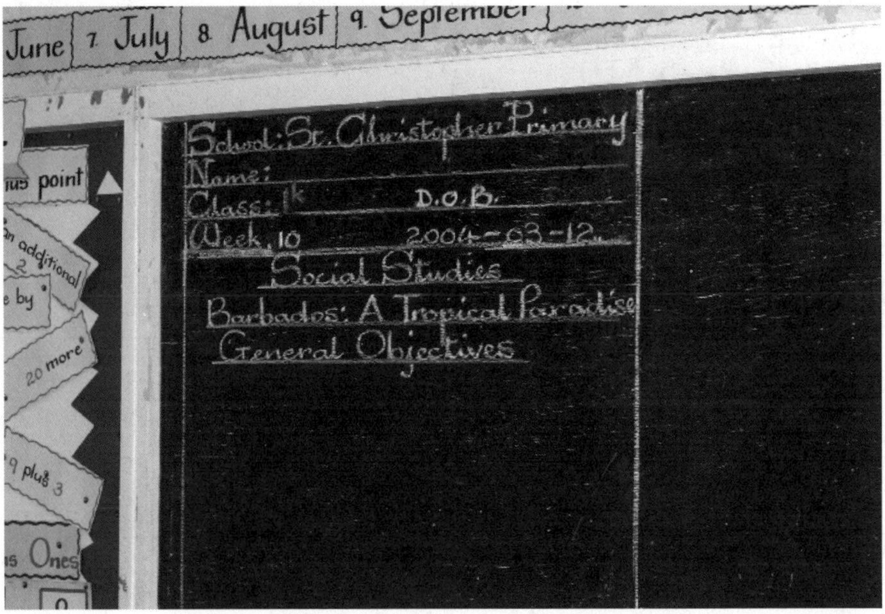

Why does a teacher need objectives, for surely there are experienced teachers in past generations who found no value in writing objectives? You could also argue that teachers have gone two million years without behavioural objectives, so why now? The answer is previous generations of teachers did not know classifications of learning, because the levels of growth and development and the three taxonomies, all of which helped to classify stages of learning, had not yet evolved. But now, you are able to take advantage of what is known about (1) children's stages of learning, (2) their growth and development, and (3) the three taxonomies, and apply what is known to the writing of behavioural objectives.

The effective teacher thinks about objectives before teaching a lesson. Many teachers, for example, consider the development of "good citizenship" as an objective. An objective could also be: "I'd like my students to understand and appreciate living in a democratic country." Do the words "understand" and "appreciate", as used here, have a precise meaning? No. If I said, "You should understand and appreciate complete behavioural objectives", would you know precisely what was expected of you? That is, would you know (1) what knowledge you should have, (2) what skills you should practise, and (3) what attitudes you should demonstrate? To "know" and "appreciate" are general objectives, but give no direction on what or how to teach. The point is, writing behaviour objectives that reflect levels of growth and development is a learned skill for a contemporary teacher. You will need to practise in order to develop that skill.

General Objectives versus Specific Behavioural Objectives

Teachers usually have objectives for teaching their courses, though often those objectives are neither spoken nor written down. Teachers' objectives are often also general (for example: understand, appreciate), and at times these objectives are in conflict with each other. Suppose the general objective is to "develop good citizens". This general objective provides the teacher with no specific guide as to what content to select, what students should learn, what methods or activities to use, what assignments to give the students, or how to evaluate the students. A teacher might spend the school year wandering all around the general objective "good citizenship" without defining what is to be done by both teacher and students in order to define and demonstrate "good citizenship". In the following summaries, note the difference between general and specific behavioural objectives. You will need to identify the difference if you are to think about writing complete behavioural objectives.

In summary, general objectives would be stated as follows:

> "In this course, students will learn to appreciate living in a democratic country."
>
> *or*
>
> "One of the major objectives of this course will be to develop the students' positive attitudes towards social justice."
>
> *or*
>
> "As part of this course, students will improve their reading comprehension using the course textbook."

But none of the above three general objectives gives guidance to what the teacher and students will actually do. Now, note the difference in wording of behavioural objectives on the same topics below.

Specific behavioural objectives might be stated as follows:

"Having *read the assignment in chapter 4* of the course text [*condition*], students will be able to *identify in a class discussion* [*observable behaviour*] the *three reasons* why a democratic form of government was adopted." [*acceptable performance*]

or

"After *reading Chapter 4* in the course text [*condition*], students *will demonstrate* on a post-attitude survey [*observable behaviour*], a *positive attitude* towards the aim of social justice." [*acceptable performance*]

or

"While *doing their reading assignment* [*condition*], students will *apply a reading strategy* [*observable behaviour*] to improve their reading comprehension which will be evaluated in class through *an oral reading survey*." [*acceptable performance*]

These objectives give specific guidance to planning and evaluation. In short, both teacher and students know specifically what behaviour is to be practised and how they are to be evaluated.

Turning Growth, Development, and the Three Taxonomies into Behavioural Objectives

The characteristics of complete behavioural objectives are as follows:

1. They should give both the teacher and the students a sense of direction.
2. They should guide the teacher in selecting materials, activities and strategies of teaching.
3. They should provide guides for teaching behaviour.
4. They should not be in conflict with one another.
5. There is a fifth characteristic. In order to determine whether the students have reached the objective or not, the objective should be stated in such a way that the teacher can objectively measure student behaviour. Objectives of this type are called "specific behavioural objectives", which means that the student's performance or activity can be evaluated. Remember the general objective, "good citizen", now turn this objective into a complete behavioural objective that a teacher can evaluate. That objective might look like this:

   "Having *read the unit on democracy* [*conditions*], the student will practise good citizenship, in small task-oriented groups, by *practising the attitudes of open-mindedness and cooperation* [*action word-observable behaviour*] to be evaluated by both an attitude *survey form and teacher observation*." [*acceptable performance*]

Writing Your Own Behavioural Objectives

Perhaps you already know how to write a complete behavioural objective. It is possible, of course, to write an objective which is not complete, which means it does not meet at least one of the three listed below. If you do know how to write a complete behavioural objective, demonstrate your knowledge and skill by writing an objective in the box below.

If you have attempted to write a complete behavioural objective, then check your objective against the three criteria listed below. Any complete behavioural objective fulfils these three criteria. Check each criterion if you have fulfilled it in your written objective above.

1. Are the conditions for behaviour specified? (Such as, "Having read the chapter . . .")
2. Is there an observable behaviour? (Such as, ". . . in an oral report . . .", or some action that can be seen)
3. Is there acceptable performance included? (Such as, ". . . evaluated on an oral report checklist"). For example, the following is a complete behavioural objective with the three criteria: Having *viewed* the film-strip "Caribbean Schools" and *read* chapter 4 of the text [conditions for behaviour], students will be able to identify, in small discussion groups [action word-observable behaviour], two or three reasons for the educational development in the Caribbean [acceptable performance].

Did you write a behavioural objective in the box? If you have not included all three criteria - conditions, observable behaviour, and acceptable performance - then your objective is not complete. If you have not written a complete objective, what you should do now is review the following explanation of each of the three criteria. Keep in mind that you are learning the skill of writing a complete behavioural objective; and learning the skill will take practice. It is important that you learn to write behavioural objectives that specify student performance, and finally act by using behavioural objectives to prepare units and daily lesson plans. If you have read chapter 7, you will recall the list of action words in the three domains: cognitive (thinking levels), affective (emotional levels), and psychomotor (physical levels). These action words will be used in writing behavioural objectives, and will thus reflect the different taxonomic levels at which students are expected to perform.

Criterion 1: Conditions

Does your behavioural objective include the conditions under which the student is expected to perform the desired behaviour? For example:

- *After listening in class to the audio-tape* with statements by the Court . . . [*this is a condition*]
- *Having completed one of the selected readings* in the class list . . . [*this is a condition*]
- *As a result of reading chapter 4* in the text . . . [*this is a condition*]

Instructions: Try your skill at writing out in the box below some conditions under which the students are expected to perform.

Criterion 2: Observable Behaviour

Does your objective include a behaviour you want to observe when the students have completed the lesson? For example:

- After listening in class to the audio-tape with statements by the Court, the students *will be able to identify* through discussion . . . [*this is observable behaviour*]
- Having completed one of the selected readings in the class list, the students *will be able to write* . . . [*this is observable behaviour*]
- As a result of reading chapter 4 in the text, the students *will be able to summarize* reasons for democracy developing in their nation . . . [*this is observable behaviour*]

Action words for observable behaviour other than identify, write, and summarize are as follows:

- analyse
- hypothesize
- support
- describe
- discover
- classify
- suggest
- define
- explain
- reject
- examine
- defend
- list
- name
- recall
- survey
- evaluate
- locate
- apply
- organize
- construct
- justify
- illustrate

For other words to use in writing behavioural objectives, see the six levels of thinking in the cognitive domain in chapter 7.

Instruction: Try your skill at writing out some observable behaviours in the box below using some of the suggested action words above.

Criterion 3: Acceptable Performance

Finally, does your objective specify an acceptable performance? For example:

- After listening in class to the audio-tape with statements by the Court, the students will be able to explain in a written report, *three of the four Court's opinions* [*this is acceptable performance*] concerning property rights.
- Having completed one of the selected readings on the class list, the students will be able to write a one-page paper noting *at least two reasons that justify* [*this is acceptable performance*] the national concern for social justice.
- As a result of reading chapter 4 in the text, the students will be able to summarize reasons for democracy developing in their nation, and in a small group *select two reasons* [*this is acceptable performance*] to be discussed in class.

Instructions: Try your skill at writing a complete performance objective in the box below.

What You Have Learned

Behavioural objectives are said to be complete when three criteria are met:

1. There are *conditions* under which the student is to perform ("After reading . . ., watching . . ., listening . . .").
2. There is an *observable behaviour* (such as, list . . ., locate . . ., recall . . .).
3. There is specified *acceptable performance* (for example, by writing a summary paragraph . . ., by doing a project . . ., by taking a test . . .).

What You Are About to Learn

There are three categories of behavioural objectives:

1. *Thinking,* which is logical, intellectual activities (for example, evaluate, describe, identify).
2. *Skill,* which is acquiring an ability through experience or training (for example, research, writing, practice).
3. *Attitude,* which is one's opinion, feelings or emotions as demonstrated by one's actions (such as, maintain an open mind, show self-respect, demonstrate cooperativeness).

▶ **Figure 9.1:** Characteristics of Behavioural Objectives

The Three Categories of Objectives: Thinking (Cognitive), Skill (Psychomotor), Attitude (Affective)

If you have mastered the skill of writing complete behavioural objectives, then you ought to feel a sense of accomplishment, for now you are almost ready to write good developmental lesson plans and test questions. You are almost ready because you still must master the skill of identifying and writing the three different *categories* of behavioural objectives. The three categories are closely linked to the three taxonomies in chapter 7. Thus, thinking objectives deal with the six levels of the cognitive domain, skill objectives deal with the five levels of the psychomotor domain, and attitude objectives deal with the five levels of the affective domain. In this final section of the chapter, you are expected to identify and write objectives that are classified within one of the three categories.

1. Thinking objective: Having read chapter 3 [*condition*] in the history text, students will *identify and list* [*observable behaviour-action words*] on a class quiz three of the five generals [*acceptable performance*] named. This objective calls for recall of knowledge, which is the lowest level in the cognitive taxonomy domain.
2. Skill objective: *Having selected an individual topic* [*condition*], students *will demonstrate research skills* [*observable behaviour-action words*] by *completing the required* [*acceptable performance*] written topic outline. This objective calls for the practice of research skills, which is level 4 of the psychomotor taxonomy domain.
3. Attitude objective: Students, *having studied the colonial period* [*condition*], will *display a critical, open-minded attitude* [*observable behaviour-action words*] towards that period on a *self-evaluation checklist* [*acceptable performance*]. This objective calls for an open-minded attitude, which is level 3 in the affective taxonomy domain.

You would have noticed how the three categories of objectives differ from each other. All three categories meet the criteria of complete behavioural objectives, but they differ on the specific behaviour called for: whether *thinking, skills,* or *attitudes.*

Thinking Behavioural Objectives

Thinking objectives call for logical thinking activities at any of the six levels of the cognitive domain taxonomy: knowledge, comprehension, application, analysis, synthesis, and evaluation.

For an explanation of these levels, and the action words for each level, see chapter 7. Examples of *thinking* behavioural objectives at each of the six levels are as follows:

1. After reading the article "Caribbean Hurricanes", in the *Daily News,* the students will be able to cite from the article two reasons for the continued concern about hurricanes, in a class recitation [*cognitive taxonomy, level 1 – knowledge*].
2. Having read chapter 7 in the textbook, students will be able to describe, in a written paragraph, daily life during the colonial period [*cognitive taxonomy, level 2 – comprehension*].
3. After listening to a story read by the teacher, students, in task-oriented small groups, will role-play the action described in the story. The effectiveness of the dramatization will be evaluated by the teacher [*cognitive taxonomy, level 3 – application*].
4. After seeing the film *History of Hurricanes in the Caribbean,* the students will be able to identify weather characteristics of hurricanes and com-

pare them with the characteristics of earthquakes in a brief written paragraph [*cognitive taxonomy, level 4 – analysis*].

5. Having completed a unit on economic development, students will compose a one-page written statement predicting what industries will develop and flourish in the future [*cognitive taxonomy, level 5 – synthesis*].
6. Having listened to speeches of candidates running for elected office, students, in small groups, will choose by consensus the candidate they wish to defend, and present their choice to the class [*cognitive taxonomy, level 6 – evaluation*].

Instructions: Pick one of the six levels, and try writing a complete *cognitive* behavioural objective in the box below.

Skill Behavioural Objectives

The taxonomy for the psychomotor domain in chapter 7 describes five levels of skill development and the key words for each level. Once a skill has been introduced (level 1), the levels of preparation (level 2), orientation (level 3), and pattern (level 4), where students attempt the skill and practise it, are the most often cited in skill behavioural objectives. For example, if you ask the student to read a paragraph and identify the main idea, you are literally asking the student to practise (level 4) the skill of reading comprehension. Other skills that have been traditionally practised are writing (which includes note taking, papers, essays), researching, speaking, studying, and grouping. Some examples of *skill* behavioural objectives are as follows:

1. At the beginning of class, the teacher asks the students to attentively listen to instructions on how to take notes [*psychomotor taxonomy, level 1 – perception*].
2. Before a lecture on the chapter assigned, students will prepare to take notes on the lecture, which will be handed to the teacher for evaluation [*psychomotor taxonomy, level 2 – preparation*].
3. Using the library, the students will apply, for the first time, research

skills learned earlier by selecting three sources and writing a two-hundred-word theme noting two environmental problems in the Caribbean region [*psychomotor taxonomy, level 3 – orientation*].

4. Having reviewed a reading strategy, students will practise reading-comprehension skills by orally reading in class [*psychomotor taxonomy, level 4 – pattern*].
5. Students will demonstrate proficiency in the skill of note taking by the end of the grading period, as evaluated by the teacher [*psychomotor taxonomy, level 5 – performance*].

Instructions: Pick one of the five levels above, and write a complete *skill* behavioural objective in the box below.

Attitude Behavioural Objectives

Your lessons call not only for thinking and skill development, but often call for students to acquire a particular attitude (level of maturity). For example, teachers often say, "I want my students to like social studies." In precise behavioural terms, the teacher in reality means, "I want my students to have a positive attitude towards social studies." In fact, one can measure whether students have a positive or negative attitude. The affective domain taxonomy in chapter 7 describes the five levels of attitude development and some key words for each level. Most attitude objectives are written at the levels of responding (level 2) and valuing (level 3). Attitudes that teachers wish their students to acquire and mature with are open-mindedness or critical thinking, self-respect, tolerance, cooperativeness, receptiveness, impartiality, and readiness. Some examples of *attitude* behavioural objectives are as follows:

1. At the teachers request, students will quietly receive instructions to get out their social studies books and turn to a map of the Caribbean [*affective taxonomy, level 1 – perception*].
2. Having been placed into small groups for the study of chapter 3, students will participate, in their small groups, with a cooperative attitude as measured on a small group self-evaluation checklist [*affective taxonomy, level 2 – responding*].

3. While a student is displaying an individual project to the class, students will show an attitude of respect for others by listening to the presentation. The attitude will be evaluated by teacher observation [*affective taxonomy, level 3 – valuing*].
4. In small groups, students will compare different types of maps to determine which type is considered most valuable by each group [*affective taxonomy, level 4 – organization*].
5. After studying conflicting historical evidence found in class readings, the students can be counted on to demonstrate, in class discussion, a critical attitude towards historical events as evaluated by the teacher through observing students' level of critical questions [*affective taxonomy, level 5 – characterization*].

Instruction: Pick one of the five levels, and write a complete *attitude* behavioural objective in the box below.

Some Behavioural Objectives Contain More Than One Category of Thinking, Skill, and Attitude

If you have successfully written a complete behavioural objective and then been able to advance to writing behavioural objectives for the three different categories, you are to be congratulated for accomplishing what, for many, are difficult tasks. As one last challenge, consider the following. You may have discovered by now that one complete behavioural objective may contain more than one category of behaviour. It is not uncommon to find the thinking category linked with skill or attitude, or to find skill and attitude linked in a single objective.

▸ Example 1

Students will name, in a class discussion, the three important points from a lecture after following the proper note-taking form.

"Name" indicates the cognitive category, while "note-taking" is a skill.

▶ Example 2

While working in small groups, the students will demonstrate an attitude of respect for others by adopting a cooperative attitude as evaluated on a post-attitude survey.

"Working in small groups" indicates a skill, while "respect" and "cooperative" are attitude categories.

So what should you conclude? You should conclude that the three categories of objectives – *thinking, skill,* and *attitude* – can be stated separately, or they can be combined in a single objective. For example, the following is a complete thinking, skill, and attitude behavioural objective, while applying the three criteria of condition, acceptable performance, and observable behaviour. "Having *watched* a TV programme and *read* several articles on the United Nations, students will *recall* in a short paragraph *two benefits of the United Nations* organization, and will *practise research and oral presentation skills* by *preparing* a brief in-class presentation and in that presentation will *demonstrate an open-minded attitude* towards the United Nations as *evaluated through teacher observation.*"

For practice, you may wish to try writing your own complete behavioural objective that fulfils all the criteria and contains thinking, skill, and attitude categories. However, you will probably never be asked to write such a complex objective. We merely presented an example to demonstrate that one could be successfully written. But you may wish to always bear the above in mind when writing your own lesson objectives, since such *behavioural objectives* encapsulate all of the important objectives which should drive your social studies lessons.

The Final Check on Your Skills at Identifying Complete Behavioural Objectives

Listed below are eight objectives on the topic "Developing Good Citizenship". Mark each one by writing "Complete" or "Incomplete" above the line after of the objective. (If the objective is incomplete, rewrite it to make the objective complete.) Also, circle the appropriate category or categories: *T* for thinking, *S* for skill, *A* for attitude. For example:

Having *studied the map of the Caribbean* in their class atlas [*condition*], students will *locate and name* on the outline map [*action words – observable behaviour*] three of the islands in the Caribbean [*acceptable performance*]. <u>Complete</u> <u>T</u> <u>S</u> A

1. Having studied the government, students will know the duties of the prime minister. _______________ T S A
2. Having studied the government, students will demonstrate, in their personal relations with others, the attitude of respect, and the demonstration of this attitude in class will be evaluated through observation by the teacher. _______________ T S A
3. Students, from their study of democracy, will demonstrate their research skills by listing a brief bibliography on the subject for an in-class exercise. _______________ T S A
4. Students will learn to appreciate religious freedom. ________ T S A
5. The values of a democratic system will become known as students think about the benefits they have come to enjoy. ________ T S A
6. Students in small groups, while studying the government, will show, by their rating on an evaluation form, their positive attitude towards group cooperation. _______________ T S A
7. From chapter 7 of the class text, students will identify and explain two of the three major concepts as part of a unit test ____________ T S A
8. Students, having studied the government, should really understand, fully appreciate, and finally have faith in the wisdom of those who fought for independence. _______________ T S A

Check your responses against the answers at the end of the chapter below.

Summary and Conclusion

Congratulations if you have successfully finished this chapter on writing objectives. You now know how to turn the levels of growth and development expressed as taxonomies into clear behavioural objectives. In short, you know how to express clear thoughts about how to teach. The task ahead is to apply that skill of writing behavioural objectives to the chapters on evaluation and planning.

However, please keep in mind that learning to write complete objectives is difficult. Writing objectives is a skill, and just because one can recall the three criteria and the three taxonomic categories (thinking-cognitive, skill-psychomotor, and attitude- affective) does not mean that one has mastery of that writing skill. You may need to read over this chapter a number of times. The only way you can improve your ability to write objectives is to practise until finally you have disciplined yourself to think in specific terms about objectives.

Looking Ahead

All of the research on how we learn best and teach, and on which this book relies, was completed in the twentieth century. The hope, of course, is that the reader will apply this knowledge in the twenty-first century. It is difficult to predict what our children will need from our schools in the twenty-first century, but surely, there are strong indications they will need to live effective lives. The authors believe that the twenty-first century will require people who are able to create knowledge and not just consume it, and a people who are dedicated to problem solving for themselves, for their country, and for the world.

Answer key:

1. Incomplete (T) because criterion 2 (observable behaviour) is improperly stated. What does "know" mean? Also, criterion 3 (acceptable performance) is not stated. Rewrite this objective so that it is a complete behavioural objective.
2. Complete (A)
3. Complete (S)
4. Incomplete (A) because criterion 2 (observable behaviour) is improperly stated. "To appreciate" cannot be measured or observed. Criterion 1 (conditions) and criterion 3 (acceptable performance) are missing. Rewrite this as a complete behavioural objective.
5. Incomplete (A) because criterion 2 (observable behaviour) is improperly stated. "Become known" cannot be measured or observed. Criterion 1 (conditions) and criterion 3 (acceptable performance) are missing. Rewrite this as a complete behavioural objective.
6. Complete (A)
7. Complete (T)
8. Incomplete (T, A) because criterion 2 (observable behaviour) is improperly stated. "Really understand, fully appreciate", and "have faith" cannot be measured or observed. Criterion 3 (acceptable performance) is missing. Rewrite this so that it is a complete behavioural objective.

10

How Facts, Concepts, and Generalizations Become Knowledge

Creating knowledge is one of the most effective ways to help students understand – that is, it gives meaning to what they are learning, so that learning is not just consuming, it is creating.

Introduction and Rationale

Have you ever thought of this before: that knowledge is created, is part of the process of thinking? It does not just exist, someone has to create it, organize it. Knowledge is simply inventions of the human mind, a way of ordering chaos. Education, in part, has to do with both gaining knowledge and creating knowledge. You know what it means to gain knowledge, but what does "creating knowledge" mean? Each individual is both different from, and alike, every other human being. You have a unique set of experiences, and it is from your experiences that you create a unique perspective on what knowledge means. It is from the sense of having a different perspective that you create knowledge. Has it ever occurred to you that you and your students should be creating knowledge? You have probably been led to believe that your task, as a student, is to gain and not create knowledge, and that your task, as a teacher, might be to gain and transmit knowledge, but not to help children create it.

Learning Is Both Gaining and Creating Knowledge

You have entered the twenty-first century where education will be the process of both gaining and creating. It would be fair if you felt confused because you may not know how to create knowledge, you may not know how knowledge is created. You may say, "I don't create knowledge; all I know is what I am told." But that is not true. Every day you create new knowledge. You are unique, meaning you are one of a kind. You are different from anyone else in the world, and also your experience with living is different from that of anyone else. No one has the same exact experience as you have had. No two people will see and feel exactly the same way. Your uniqueness, your experience, gives you a perspective for creating. Each of us is capable of creating knowledge just because we are unique.

Teach a Man to Fish

The thought "students should be taught that they are capable of creating knowledge" is as old as mankind. Remember this ancient proverb, or thought: "Give a man a fish and he eats a meal, teach the man to fish and he eats for a lifetime."

To teach students the process of creating knowledge is to help them to "think for a lifetime". In short, the task of a teacher is to help students become their own teachers, thus preparing them for lifelong learning. This chapter will centre on the topics of (1) identifying how knowledge is created out of the building blocks of facts, concepts, and generalizations, (2) how that knowledge is organized, and (3) your role, as a teacher, in the process of creating knowledge.

The Twenty-first Century Will Be a Different World: A New Universe of Teaching and Learning

Why not just continue what you very well understand, that is, the transmitting, memorizing, and consuming of information from an educational system that designates some people as creators of knowledge and others as only consumers? This memorizing and consuming system, at least three million years old, is not possible in the new electronic world. Teachers in the twentieth century were skilled in handling words. Teachers in future centuries must be skilled in handling experiences. You know about the technology of computers and software. You have heard about the information superhighway, the Internet, interactive multimedia with CD-ROMs, you have seen fax machines, tried cellular phones, and have seen advertised all the other electronic devices that connect the world and promise to change the twentieth century. Yet, technology is not about tools, it deals with how we work. You are, therefore, part of a new history, a new universe of work that is built upon an information revolution that even now sends forth so much information to be learned in so many different ways that teaching and learning will be fundamentally changed in the twenty-first century.

Students will need to organize and make sense of information, rather than become just storage bins for it. However, to organize and make sense of information, there must be some system for organizing it. Fact piled upon fact does not yield meaning. Our job as educated, creative, human beings is to find meaning in the chaotic pile of facts. In many cases, schooling in the past has meant learning the pile of facts and information in textbooks, the kind of thing a computer does in the twenty-first century. School in the future will assign facts and information to the memory chips of some electronic devices, and to humans, assign the task of finding and organizing meaning from the mass of bits and pieces that flow electronically on the information superhighway.

Information Revolution and Concept-Based Instruction

In practical terms, what is meant by "information revolution"? The world is doubling its information about every eight to ten years. This means that all of the knowledge created up to now will be doubled eight years from now. Every minute of the day, four thousand pages of books, newspapers, and reports are published somewhere in the world, enough to fill a two-thousand-foot-long bookshelf every day. Consider the effect of having a worldwide Internet, a system that allows computers to communicate with one another. People on the Internet are creating knowledge. They research term papers, make new friends, communicate with astronauts in space, and if they are also tied into the Netbook, they are connected with libraries around the world. Even now, kindergarten and first-year students in some developed nations receive laptop computers from the school. Thus, at the age of five and six, they are communicating with other students around the world. The twenty-first century will be a different world of teaching and learning.

What does this information revolution mean to you? Imagine a child entering the first year of school and for the next eleven years being taught by a fact-oriented, single-subject-centred social science course. At the current rate that new knowledge is generated, little that the child has learned will be true as fact at the time of leaving school. The child's school life, in a sense, has been wasted if that child just memorizes and consumes. The

child has only been "given a fish". Information is being created faster than we can distribute it. We increase knowledge at electronic speed, but distribute it in school with the traditional lecture and textbook.

On the other hand, imagine a twenty-first-century child taught in a contemporary curriculum based on how to create knowledge, which includes both the new electronic universe and the building blocks of knowledge: facts, concepts, and generalizations. That curriculum is called concept-based instruction. That instruction prepares students to think in higher-order concepts that help to summarize and organize the chaotic pile of facts into meaning. That "teaches the student to fish".

For the second child, upon completing school, the facts may have changed, but the building blocks that contain major social studies concepts, such as nation, scarcity, values, family, interdependence, and time, will remain relatively true summaries and organizers of information. Nations, for example, may have changed over time, or their leaders, their borders or their traditions may have changed, but the concept of "nation" will remain valid for quite a while and still serve students as they attempt to understand their own culture and the world.

Concepts Summarize and Interpret

Concepts, over time, remain stable and relevant, and are valuable for interpreting a changing world. They are part of the system for creating knowledge. The past and present school curriculum that depends on memorized facts and events has historically already passed. In summary, the information electronic revolution has already happened, but educators are still working on how to effectively organize and give meaning to the increasing flow of information. The recommended way to organize materials and instruction is by a concept and generalization-based curriculum, which summarizes and interprets information. It is from these concepts that you and I create knowledge.

If concept-based instruction is the curriculum design for the future, then the questions you should ask are, (1) "How do I use concepts to create knowledge with my class?", and (2) "After the class has created knowledge, how is that creation to be used as part of a lesson?" This chapter will help answer those questions. The answer lies in a series of complex ideas. The series of ideas are that (1) words are symbols, (2) symbols are used for thinking and reasoning, (3) symbols are categorized into facts, concepts and generalizations, and finally (4) facts, concepts, and generalizations are organized according to a problem-solving, concept approach.

The Process of Creating Knowledge: Words Are Symbols

The ideas sound complex but, in reality, all of the hundreds of textbooks and other instructional materials you have read, and all of the knowledge you have learned, were created and organized by a simple process. The process starts with symbols. You know very well that words are symbols, meaning, simply, inventions of the human mind. We think and have thoughts using symbols (words); thus manipulating words helps mankind to organize the chaotic pile of facts into meaning. If there are no words, then there are no thoughts, there are just images. Images cannot be translated (communicated) easily without words. Our ancestors three million years ago had images, but probably not words to talk about the past and the future. Words hold complex societies together. Words are the tools we use to store and pass on information to make sense of our world. They are the fuel that generates the electronic flow on the information superhighway. They are the change agencies of the twenty-first century.

Attaching words to things is a relatively new event in the history of humankind. Words are easily manipulated, images are not. Suppose you imagined the concept "change" but had no word for it. If you wanted to tell someone else about the concept "change" but had no words, only images in your mind, how would you translate (communicate) the meaning of "change"? Perhaps you could draw a picture as our ancestors did. The process of mentally manipulating symbols, whether words or numbers, is what we normally refer to as thinking. Symbols can be categorized into (1) facts, (2) concepts, and (3) generalizations, and it is these categorized symbols that we use in order to think and also to reason. Educators use these three categories to create knowledge for curriculum materials, textbooks, and lectures. The process is simple; the hard part is developing useful concepts.

Thinking Requires Symbols: Words Become Facts, Concepts, and Generalizations

Examine the following series of word symbols that represent facts, concepts, and generalizations. This is an example of how we create knowledge by using facts, concepts, and generalizations.

1. Facts = concrete symbols Below are facts:	**2. Concepts** = abstract symbols Below are concepts drawn from the facts:	**3. Generalizations** = the highest abstract symbols Below is a generalization drawn from the concepts:
Some women are wives. Some men are husbands. Some women are mothers. Some men are fathers. Some women and men are teachers or doctors or lawyers or farmers.	Men and women have family roles as partners. Men and women have family roles as parents. Men and women have occupational roles.	All men and women are expected to fulfil a variety of roles that will identify their place in society.

▶ **Figure 10.1:** From Facts to Concepts and Generalizations

When thinking about husbands and wives, you can group these facts and summarize them to mean that husbands and wives make a *family*. *Family* is a higher abstraction than *men* and *women* because *family* is a summary of a married relationship. Suppose you are looking at the house next door. In the house are seven persons, a husband, a wife, and five children (*facts*). Or you could summarize the seven persons next door and interpret them as a family (*concept*). You could look down the street at your community and imagine that your community has (1) families, (2) a culture, (3) tradition and (4) a social structure. These four are also concepts. Summarizing the four concepts, you could generalize that "each individual is born into a society (community) which has a certain social organization and structure" (*generalization*). This process of thinking starts with facts, and from summarized facts emerge concepts, and from summarized concepts emerges a generalization. This is the process of creating knowledge. The process is simple, you unconsciously follow it every day. The process is problem solving, making decisions. The hard part in the process is creating concepts and generalizations which offer meanings which are true interpretations that yield accurate ideas.

Defining Fact, Concept, and Generalization

What is a fact? Of course, we know what a fact is. "St Vincent and St Kitts are Caribbean countries." This is a fact. We have memorized, repeated, researched, and analysed facts throughout our education. A *fact* is concrete, has been objectively verified (is real, actual, concrete, proven to be true) and known as a certainty such as, "The sun rises in the east and sets in the west."

What is a concept? A *concept* is a main (abstract) idea represented by a word or statement standing for a category of related facts, and therefore a bit more difficult to imagine than concrete facts. For example, when thinking about the West Indies, an island called Barbados is a concrete fact. However, Barbados is also a democracy. "Democracy" is a higher-order, abstract concept that is a bit more difficult to imagine than a country that can actually be seen. Concepts are a grouping of facts that have been summarized (briefly stated, main points) and interpreted (explained the meaning) as a main idea or understanding. In short, they are a group of facts that have similarities, and resemble each other in some point, feature, or instance.

Lower- and Higher-Order Concepts

Just as all facts are not equally complex, so are concepts not all of the same complexity. "Complex" refers to the degree of order that is imposed on facts and concepts. As you can imagine, there are *higher-order* and *lower-order concepts,* which means that higher-order concepts summarize many facts, while lower-order concepts summarize only a few facts. For example, a geographer might think about higher-order concepts, such as movement, place, and environment, which summarize many complex facts. Suppose you were to watch primary school children, teachers, and a visiting education officer after lunch in the schoolyard. *A lower-order* concept might be, "This is a group of children at different age levels." You might also consider a *higher-order* concept such as, "What I am looking at are *educational roles,* which students, teachers, and an educational officer play in a school setting." For example:

Facts	Concept
(One can observe that these educational roles objectively exist.) 1. Teacher 2. Student 3. Advisor 4. Inspector 5. Administrator	(Statement about the similarities of these roles.) "Educational roles" is a concept: All of these roles, when summarized and interpreted, have similarities. The concept that explains these similarities is "educational roles".

▶ **Figure 10.2** Facts Become Concepts

Now in the box below, make a list of two different groups of related facts and, in each case, label the main idea (concept) that these facts represent.

Facts	Concepts
1.	1.
2.	2.

Obviously here we are not going to make a long list of facts, because there are billions. But what we can do is encourage you to know that there are higher and lower concepts, and that we encourage you to think at both levels. For example, some of the major universal higher-order concepts that organize thinking in the different social sciences might be:

Social Science	**Concepts**
Anthropology	- social control, family, language
Sociology	- culture, groups, social interaction
History	- change and time, diversity, interpretation
Political Science	- interdependence, political system, power and authority
Geography	- movement, place and location, environment

Higher-order concepts exist for each of the social sciences. These concepts are the major organizing ideas around which content is developed in textbooks and other curriculum materials. If curriculum development and instruction in the twenty-first century is organized according to the major concepts, then it is of some importance that you have some idea what those concepts are. Thus, in this chapter, major concepts in each of the social sciences are listed and explained in an appendix. The concepts listed are, of course, the building blocks of a social studies programme. We therefore encourage you to examine carefully the major concepts listed at the end of the chapter.

What is a generalization? A generalization – a broad, overall statement of conclusion – is a higher abstraction than a concept, and also more complex than a concept or fact. The conclusion drawn from a group of related, interpreted concepts is known as a generalization. A *generalization* can be defined as an idea – an invention of the human mind – in the form of a statement or conclusion drawn from related facts and concepts, that interprets the relationship between concepts. Both universal concepts and generalizations are transferable from one setting to another. In short, if a generalization is true in the Caribbean, then it is true also in Japan and everywhere else. Generalizations apply the same everywhere, that is, the idea is universally applicable everywhere, but concepts are not always universal, thus may not necessarily apply everywhere. For example, it is true that some Caribbean countries have local, regional, and national governments. If you summarize and interpret the governmental structure, you might identify the three concepts of leadership, institutions, and government. If you summarize and interpret the meaning of those three concepts, you could reach a number of generalizations. For example, one generalization based on the three concepts might be: "Every known society has some sort of authority structure that is granted power." If this generalization is true in Caribbean countries, then it is true elsewhere in the world. In short, the generalization is transferable. However, while the concept of "a democracy" may apply to most Caribbean countries, it may not necessarily apply to all countries universally.

To illustrate some social science generalizations, note the following examples: Do each of these generalizations apply in both the Caribbean and Japan and are they thus applicable and transferable everywhere?

Anthropology: The family is the basic social group.

Sociology: Humans learn social behaviour from groups with which they interact.

History: Space and time form a framework within which all events can be placed.

Civics: A principle underlying all systems of government is a willingness to sacrifice for the general good of the group.

Geography: The extent of natural resources is related to human desires and the level of technology.

Economics: While all members of a family are consumers, only some are producers.

The point is, you and your students can very well collect a series of facts, create concepts, and from concepts create generalizations which potentially can be used to study social studies course content. You do not have to wait until some authority identifies concepts and generalizations, as those examples cited above or those found in the appendix at the end of this chapter. You and your students, from their experiences and perspectives, can very well create the class' own concepts and generalizations, which means creating knowledge.

Instructions

In the box below, (1) identify a number of concepts related to any one topic in social studies, and (2) summarize, or interpret, the meaning and relationship between those concepts in order to create a generalization. *Remember:* a generalization is *not* a definition; and it *must* contain two or more concepts in a statement that is universally true.

Concepts	**Generalization**

Remember, knowledge does not just exist, it does not just belong to a few people. Someone has to create it and organize it. That is, the process of creating gives meaning to what students are learning. Learning is not just consuming. Learning is creating, and if it is an accurate creation of concepts and generalizations, then they can be universal and equally true in Caribbean countries, Japan, and elsewhere in the world.

Perhaps you are convinced that facts, concepts, and generalizations are the building blocks of knowledge and thinking, but you say to yourself, "How is this useful in planning a lesson for the classroom?" In chapter 4, the point was made that there are actually only two methods of teaching. One is the traditional transmission of knowledge, and the other is problem solving. What follows are two illustrations of methods: one is a problem-solving method where the class identifies facts and interprets concepts and generalizations. The second illustration shows how knowledge in social studies is created and transmitted.

Illustration of How to Create Knowledge in the Classroom by a Problem-Solving Method

The teacher wants the students to reflect on how their lives are different from the lives of their grandparents when they were the students' age. They are studying the changes in their community and country over the last several generations, and the class is trying to understand how their lives are changing. The teacher divides the class into task-oriented small groups. The task of each group is to prepare a list of ten items that the students know, have seen, can do, or experience, which were unknown, impossible, or, unimaginable for their grandparents when they were the students' present age. After the lists are complete, the groups report their choice of items to the class. These choices are written on the board, for example, heart transplant, man on the moon, cable TV. Once the list is on the board, the teacher asks the class, "Are there similarities between items?" The students develop categories of similar items, identifying and naming the categories. For example, the following might be the class categories and items listed on the board:

Medical	Space/Science	Electronic	Food
transplants heart kidney liver pacemakers new therapy chemo-radiation	man on moon living in space solar power satellite transmission genetic engineering artificial limbs that can move antibiotic drugs synthetic fibres	cable TV cellular phones lasers microwave ovens calculators VCRs compact discs fax machines dishwasher washer and dryer	fast-food restaurants packaged foods foods for microwave Coca Cola and Pepsi plastic bottles supermarkets frozen food

The teacher then asks the class to examine the categories (facts) to see if there are any interpretations they might make about the difference between their life experiences, given the items listed on the board, and their grandparents' experiences. The class identifies that their lives are rapidly changing, particularly because of electronic devices, and they are more dependent on a technological world than were their grandparents when they were the students' age. What have the students discovered? They have discovered and defined the concepts "change" and "dependence". The teacher then asks the class to summarize and interpret the two concepts of change and dependence, in short, to generalize about their lives, given the two concepts identified by the class. The class suggests a number of generalizations but eventually agrees upon the following generalization: "As the class becomes more dependent on the items listed on the board, the more rapid will be the change, and part of that change is greater dependence on others." This generalization, the class believes, helps them explain the difference between their experiences and those of their grandparents. The class also thinks this generalization will help explain the difference between themselves and future generations.

Did the class, by following the problem-solving process of inductive thinking, create knowledge? Yes, because they identified a "pile of facts", put them on the board, categorized them, and turned those facts into an interpretation identifying concepts of change and dependence which explained how they are different from previous generations. Did the class summarize and interpret the concepts to reach a class consensus on a generalization? Yes, the class created new knowledge, a generalization based upon their contemporary experiences, which were unique to this particular class.

Illustration of How Social Scientists Organize Facts, Concepts, and Generalizations to Create and Transmit Knowledge

Practise your understanding of how social science knowledge is organized. Start with a generalization that is normally found in a textbook. In this case, the generalization, concepts, and facts are identified *for* the students. A generalization may be: "A country's climate is determined by a number of geographic factors." How did geographers arrive at this generalization? In other words, how did geographers create this bit of summarized knowledge?

The word "climate" means the generalized weather conditions of a particular region. Climate is itself determined by concepts that include

(1) sunlight, (2) temperature, (3) humidity, (4) precipitation, (5) atmospheric pressure, (6) winds, (7) unequal rates of heating and cooling of land and water surfaces, (8) irregular shape and distribution of land and sea, (9) ocean currents, and (10) mountain systems. Moreover, each of the concepts has specific facts associated with it that give the concept meaning. These facts are objective, meaning they can be accurately measured. For example: for "sunlight", some facts are known because it is possible to record variation, intensity, and composition, all of which are facts that make up the meaning of the concept "sunlight". For the concept "temperature", some facts are established by noting variation, change, and effects; while for the concept "wind", facts are recorded by watching directions, patterns, and speed; and for "humidity", facts are recorded on degree of moisture, dampness, and effect on comfort. So how does a geographer, for example, establish generalizations that are true everywhere in the world, given certain facts and concepts? Figure 10.3 illustrates the process.

Generalization (summary of concepts)	**Concepts** (summary of facts)	**Known Facts** (gathered from measurement of these)
	sunlight	variation intensity composition
A country's climate is determined by a number of geographic factors.	temperature	variation change effects
	winds	direction patterns speed
	humidity	degree of moisture dampness effect on comfort

▶ **Figure 10.3:** Deductive Reasoning

Keep in mind that Figure 10.3 is an example of how textbook and curriculum materials are written. Authors start with a generalization, eventually arrive at concepts, supported eventually by facts. Authors usually do not start with facts. A chapter is usually a summary of what the author believes to be true, supported by interpretation (concepts) and facts. The text becomes a justification of the author's organization and interpretation, of which this chapter is no exception.

In summary, then, the first illustration on the generation gap, with the class discovering and defining concepts and generalizations, was an example of the problem-solving method. The geographical illustration is a traditional transmission method, if the student is asked to know only the geographer's concepts and generalizations. In the first illustration, the class is learning *"how to fish"* for a lifetime, they are creating knowledge. In the second illustration, the class is *"given a fish"*, and is eating only one meal because they only memorize knowledge created by others.

Inductive and Deductive Reasoning

The point of the above illustration in Figure 10.3 is that we manipulate facts, concepts, and generalizations in a disciplined, organized process. Why? Because the concepts and generalizations, if they are to be accurate, valid (meaning precise, well defined), and reliable (meaning trustworthy, dependable) summaries, must be based on accurate information. Manipulating facts, and creating concepts and generalizations, is the logical process by which we learn to think and reason. Reasoning is the way we create ideas, and this can be from the particular - that is, facts - to the general, which is called *inductive* reasoning. The reverse reasoning, from the general to the particular, is called *deductive.*

Look at the illustrations on the previous pages in this chapter. The first two (Figure 10.1 and Figure 10.2) are examples of inductive reasoning, starting from facts to concepts to generalization. Each example of inductive reasoning started with a collection of facts that were summarized to make concepts, which in turn were summarized to make a generalization. The problem-solving method used on the example of the generation gap above, is a good illustration of the class practising inductive reasoning. Figure 10.3, the geography illustration, is deductive reasoning, starting with a generalization, and moving then to concepts and finally to facts. The geography illustration above demonstrates how social scientists transmit knowledge through a deductive reasoning process.

You may have heard historians say that each generation tends to reinterpret history. Usually, the reinterpretation results from a set of concepts different from those used by earlier generations of historians. In short, different generations tend to emphasize different facts and concepts. Thus, history is continuously being reinterpreted. So what should you conclude? The process of thinking, either inductively or deductively, is useful in establishing what we believe to be knowledge. However, that knowledge which depends upon interpretation is transitory, meaning that knowledge depends on which facts and concepts are chosen and emphasized. The point is, no matter if reasoning is inductive or deductive, the reasoning is simply a preference to reason in a particular way. The purpose for reasoning is the same for both ways: categorize, summarize, and interpret such that knowledge can be remembered and used in the future.

Organizing Social Studies by a Concept-Based Instruction Approach

The following is a concept-wheel illustration of a concept-based instruction approach. A concept wheel visually shows the relationship between facts, concepts, and a generalization. The concept-based approach can be either inductive, starting with facts and proceeding to a generalization, or it can be deductive, moving from generalization to facts. Note that the arrows between facts, concepts, and generalizations are pointing both ways. This means that a study on the topic could start with an abstract generalization and proceed *deductively* from the general to the specific, as illustrated by the geography lesson, or it could start with concrete facts and proceed *inductively* from the specific to the abstract, as was illustrated in the lesson on the generation gap. The topic, stated as a generalization for Figure 10.4, is "Emerging nations all tend to have development problems."

Note on the concept wheel how the known concrete facts such as "purification", "storage", "form of government", and "mining industries" are summarized and interpreted to mean concepts such as "natural resources", "government", and "economic system", which in turn lead to the highest abstraction, the generalization. Can you identify how this concept wheel is an illustration of a concept-based instruction approach? The following topic may help to answer the question.

Concept-Based Instruction Organized According to an Interdisciplinary or Integration Approach

Social studies could be defined as the "interdisciplinary integration of the social sciences for the purpose of citizenship education". The integration mentioned in the definition refers to the universal concepts, for example, change or interdependence, that are held in common, meaning that all the social science fields recognize these ideas as shared concepts. (Review the major social science concepts in the appendix at the end of the chapter for

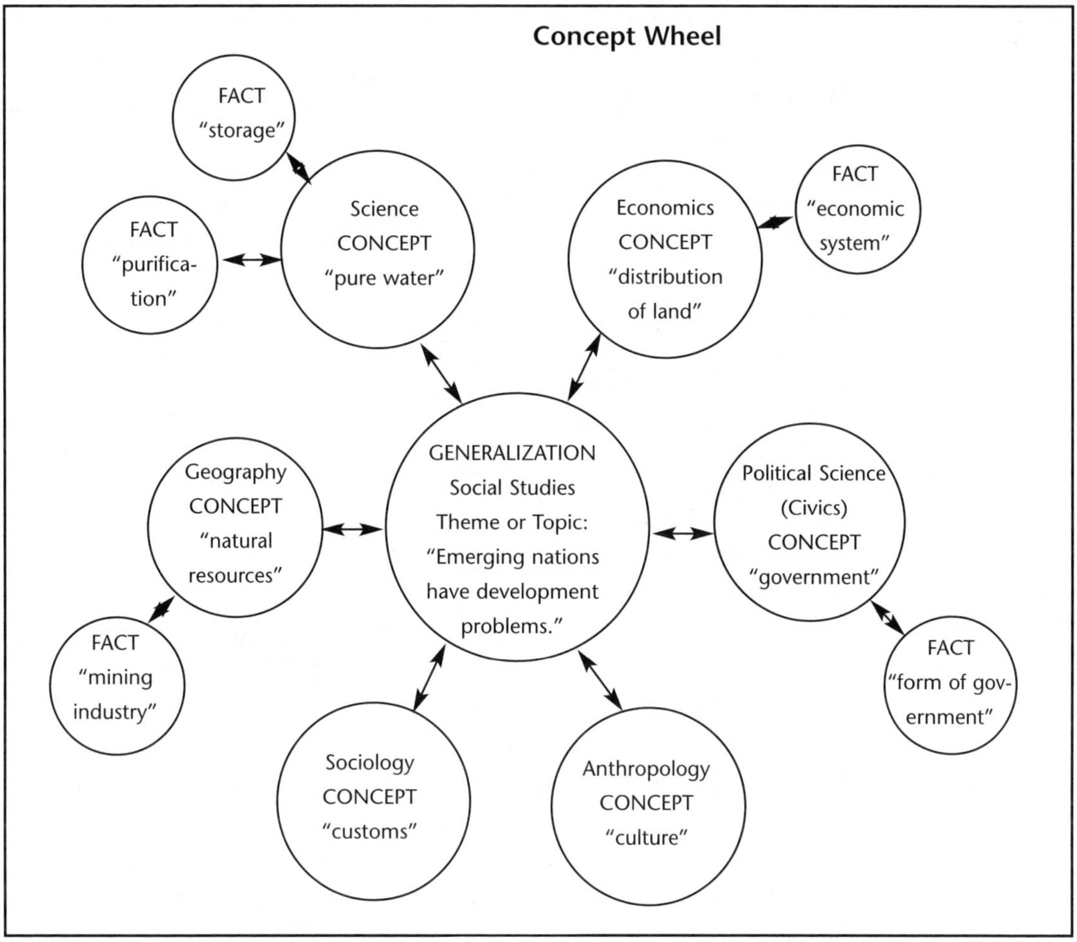

Figure 10.4: Either Inductive or Deductive Reasoning

examples of shared concepts.) "Interdisciplinary" refers to how the social science subject-fields – for example, history, geography, and civics – relate to each other. Each social science field has facts, concepts, and generalizations that contribute to a study of the topic "Emerging Nations". In short, every social science field contributes facts, concepts, and generalizations to a study of the topic, "Emerging nations all tend to have development problems."

Do you recall the social studies curriculum scope and sequence in chapter 2? The scope and sequence integrates facts, concepts, and generalizations from all relevant social science fields into themes at each year level, demonstrating how the interdisciplinary integration concept approach is applied in social studies. The scope and sequence describes how the curriculum develops citizenship education: starting with self, family, and school, then expanding and spiralling through each succeeding year to the local, national and regional community, and to the world. At each year level, facts and concepts focus on a generalization. For example, at the third-year level, a generalization, or theme, or topic might be "I am a citizen of my city (or village) and country", supported by a deductive study of concepts from the general to the specific, such as government, change, location. The facts to support the concepts are derived from questions such as: "Where is the city located in Grenada?" (geography question); "What are the characteristics of the regional culture that make up the city?" (economics, sociology, civics question); "How has the city changed over the last two generations?" (sociology, anthropology, history question).

Learning to Think and Reason Based on Ten Universal Concepts or Themes

Suppose Caribbean countries wished to adopt an interdisciplinary, integrated developmental social studies curriculum from infant through to the secondary level. Such a curriculum should be organized according to concept-based instruction. The major concepts that would be considered important to the development of curriculum materials are listed and explained in an appendix at the end of this chapter. But as can be seen in the appendix, there are many major concepts. Thus the question, "How can these major concepts be organized in the effective social studies school programme when there is too much content but not enough time?"

The concept-based instruction would be developed on an expanding environment spiral that encourages the accumulation of knowledge from concrete experiences to abstract ideas, from year to year. The objective of a primary to secondary school curriculum would be that each student should be able to think and reason using the following ten universal interdisciplinary concepts or themes as ideas around which to summarize and interpret information. The following concepts are basic to an integrated, developmental social studies programme.

The Ten Universal Interdisciplinary Concepts or Themes

1. *Culture:* Human beings create, learn, and adapt culture. Although each human culture is unique, all cultures have systems of beliefs, knowledge, values, and traditions. Students need to examine different cultures in order to relate to other people in the world.
2. *Time, continuity, and change:* Human beings seek to understand their history and place themselves in time. Such understanding involves

knowing what things were like in the past and how things change and develop.

3. *People, places, and environments:* The study of people, places, and interactions of human environment assist students to create their space and geographic perspectives of the world. Such study will help students make informed decisions about the relationship between human beings and their environment.
4. *Individual development and identity:* Personal identity is shaped by one's culture, by groups, and by institutional influences. Examination of various forms of human behaviour will lead to understanding the relationships of social norms and personal identities, the social processes that influence identity formation, and ethical principles underlying individual action.
5. *Individuals, groups, and institutions:* Institutions such as schools, families, government agencies, and courts all exert influence in our lives. Students need to know how institutions are formed, what controls and influences them, how they control and influence individuals and culture, and how institutions can be maintained or changed.
6. *Power, authority, and governance:* Understanding the historical development of structures of power, authority, and governance, and their evolving functions in contemporary West Indian society as well as other parts of the world, is essential for developing effective citizens. After studying various forms of governance, and the rights of individuals and groups, students become more effective problem solvers when faced with the persistent issues and social problems found in adult life.
7. *Production, distribution, and consumption:* People have wants and needs that exceed resources available to them. Unequal distribution of resources necessitates systems of exchange and trade, increasingly global in scope, requiring study in world economy and the role of technology in economic decision making.
8. *Science, technology, and society:* Modern life, as we know it, would be impossible without technology and the science that supports it, but new technology is the basis for some of our more difficult social choices. Students need to acquire a knowledge base for considering responses to social issues related to science and technology.
9. *Global connections:* The realities of global interdependence requires understanding the increasingly important and diverse global connections among world societies. Analysing patterns and relationships within and among world cultures will help students understand policy alternatives that have both national and global implications.
10. *Civic ideals and practices:* An understanding of civic ideals and prac-

tices of citizenship is critical to full participation in society. Students need to study civic ideals across time and in diverse societies as well as their own in order to ensure the practice of the ideals upon which our democratic society is based.

Practice on the Concept Wheel

Assuming you were a teacher assigned to teach the topics Self, Family, and Home in kindergarten or first year, how might you apply the interdisciplinary integration, concept-based instruction approach to a concept wheel? As you examine the inductive reasoning on the following wheel, note how facts in the outer circles lead to concepts which eventually lead to the generalization in the inner circle, the point being that all concepts found in the appendix are integrated in an interdisciplinary approach according to the ten social studies universal interdisciplinary concepts or themes.

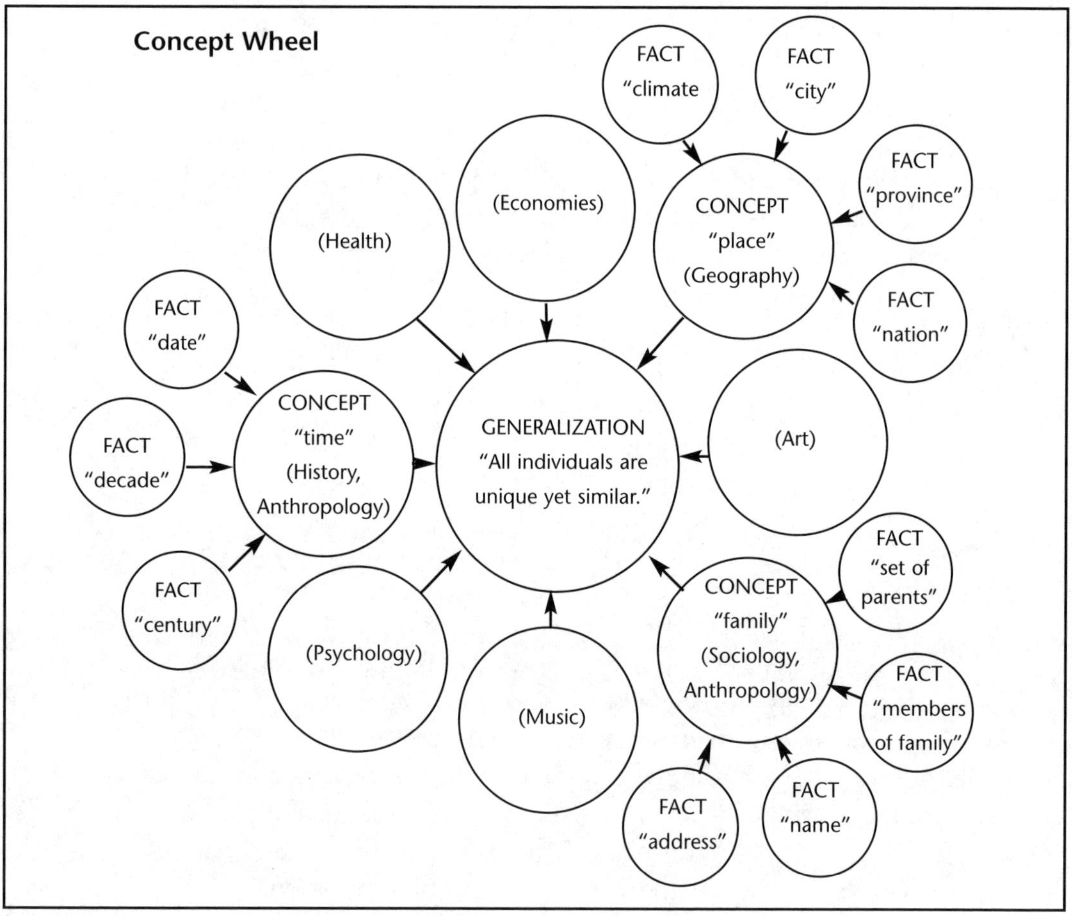

Figure 10.5: Inductive Reasoning

The concept wheel demonstrates the different fact, concept, and generalization levels of creating knowledge, using inductive reasoning from fact to generalization. These different levels of reasoning are extremely important to the practice of social studies because citizens face the problems of life not as philosophers, historians, or anthropologists, but rather as Caribbean citizens who should know how to integrate relevant concepts from history, geography, and civics so that they might make more effective decisions about life. In short, you teach students facts, concepts, generalizations, skills, and attitudes, but also you teach them to integrate, that is, to reason, deductively or inductively, in a rational, logical, problem-solving process. After all, is that not what is required of a thoughtful citizen who lives in the new world of the information revolution, and also participates in a democracy? Is it not the major goal of the Ministry of Education to educate citizens to live effective lives?

Summary

You could conclude that as concrete ideas become more generalized, they also become more abstract, and thus, for many students passing through school, ideas become more difficult to understand. Facts, as we know, are usually concrete and can be personally verified, but concepts and generalizations require higher cognitive thinking skills such as asking and answering divergent and evaluative questions. Higher levels of thinking also require mature attitudes (affective) and accomplished skills (psychomotor). Teaching students the thinking process represents a special challenge. The challenge is to clearly demonstrate in class the process by which concepts and generalizations are drawn from facts. Students will need to practise how ideas are summarized, interpreted, and expressed so that they themselves can participate in the process of creating knowledge, a process that will be required for effective citizenship in the information revolution of the twenty-first century.

A Practical Application of What You Have Learned

As a final check and a help in clarifying your thoughts on the process of creating knowledge, fill out the concept wheel in Figure 10.6 using any geography or history text. Why? Because it is time you prove *to yourself* that the process by which almost anything is organized and written, including textbooks, newspapers, and most other publications, can be easily identified. A more important reason is that, as a classroom teacher, you will be encouraging students to practise the process. In short, you need to know how the process of reasoning works either inductively or deductively. By knowing how the world of learning organizes ideas, you and your students can take charge of creating knowledge by using the building blocks of knowledge: facts, concepts, and generalizations. As often repeated, what is most important is the *creation of knowledge,* for it is through this process that students understand, and give meaning to, their thinking, so that thinking is not just repeating answers; it becomes the art of creating.

Instructions

Select a chapter of a textbook, then find the generalization, the concepts, along with the supporting facts. Though not always true, normally the title of the chapter will be a generalization such as, for example, the title of this chapter could be stated as a generalization: "Facts, Concepts, and Generalizations Become Knowledge". The headings in the chapter or book are usually concepts; facts will be in the body of the text. Your task is to identify what facts, concepts, and generalizations the authors have used to write the chapter. Fill out the concept wheel by reasoning from the general to the specific facts (deductive) or from the specific facts or factors to the general (inductive), whichever best fits your style of learning. Now fill in the wheel.

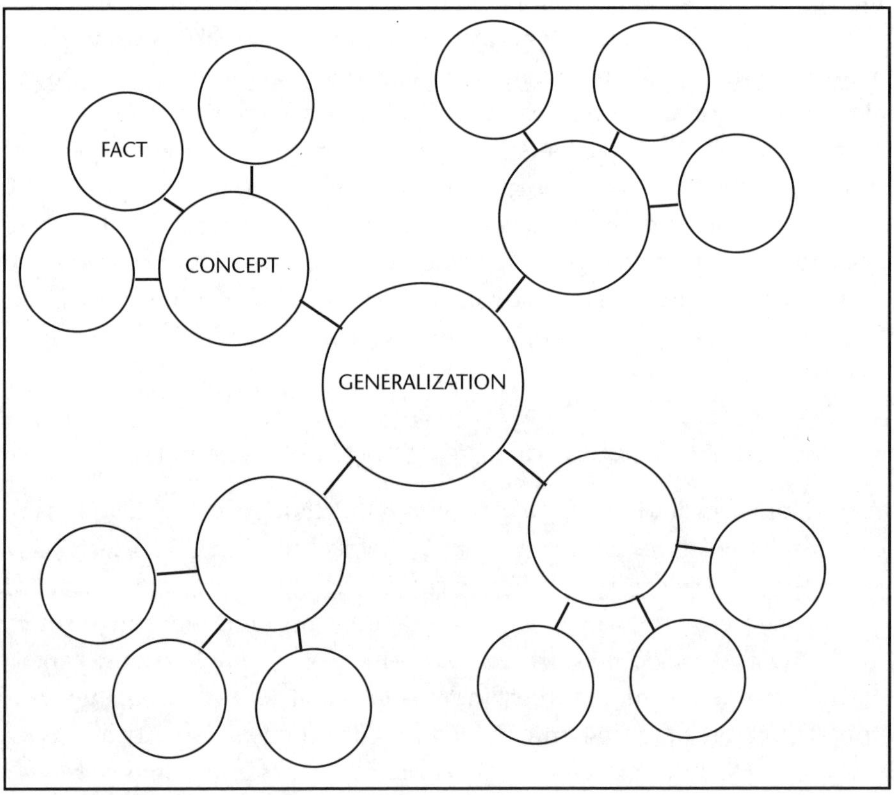

▶ **Figure 10.6:** Concept Wheel Format

Conclusion

This chapter has introduced a series of complex relationships, and one could be forgiven if all the relationships were not clearly understood at this point. The following review should be carefully read with the purpose of gaining a clear idea about your changing universe of work. That work requires knowing the process of creating knowledge.

On 14 February 1996, the world's first working electronic digital computer was fifty years old. The imagination that helped to create this machine has changed your universe. A whole new vocabulary from electronic technology - cyberspace, Internet, information superhighways, Worldwide Web - has changed the way we communicate. A new world of ideas means, for education, a new world of information. It means different methods of teaching, it means different curriculum materials, and most of all, it means different educational tools. But technology is not about tools; it deals with how we work.

The major point addressed to you in this chapter is that a teacher's task includes helping the students create knowledge. But how can you carry out this task if you do not know the formal process by which knowledge is created and organized for instruction? That is, if you are unfamiliar with the process, how can you participate in effective teaching? Another point is that students need to know how content is created because they should be learning content, skills, and attitudes, integrating them, and using them to reason. In a democracy, one of the key citizenship skills is gathering and creating knowledge. If the government is the sole agency of creating knowledge, democracy and freedom are not expected to survive.

The discussion on the thinking process focused, first, on the capacity of humans to attach symbols to reality, and then to associate and manipulate those symbols to the thoughts. However, all symbols are not equal. Some symbols represent concrete reality (facts), whereas other symbols represent higher-order abstractions (concepts and generalizations). In short, we usually think and reason by following a formal process that requires manipulation of facts, concepts, and generalizations. The two ways of manipulating information are *inductive,* which is reasoning from the specific to the general, and *deductive,* which is reasoning from the general to the specific. The twentieth-century school was usually based on deductive reasoning. That reasoning encouraged teachers to emphasize the transmission of content. In contrast, the twenty-first-century school will emphasize inductive reasoning. That reasoning will feature problem solving supported by the electronic superhighway.

Pause for a moment and ask yourself, "Why is the above of any particular importance? What have symbols, abstractions, thinking, and reasoning processes to do with the task of primary school teachers?" The answer is, teachers are in the symbol-creating, thinking, and reasoning business, and all the curriculum materials (content) that you will use in class will have been organized according to a formal process. You have just reviewed that process. If it is your task to organize, develop, and educate children, then knowing the process by which curriculum materials are developed is important. In practical terms, you will be asked to plan teaching units, which is one way of determining what and how to teach. Why is the process of thinking important? Because almost everything you do as a teacher illustrates how "you think and reason using facts, concepts, and generalizations". If this is true for you, it is also true for your students.

Now, to continue to review. We have said above that thinking and reasoning follow a formal process. Every subject field applies its own unique approach to that formal process, which means that history, geography, and civics are distinct from each other, yet related by the concepts that they share. To identify some of those shared major concepts, please see the appendix at the end of this chapter. Social studies also applies an approach to the formal process. The name of that approach is concept-based interdisciplinary integration of universal concepts or themes through an expanding environment spiral. "Interdisciplinary" requires the integration of at least the ten identified universal concepts or themes. The development of citizenship education through an integration approach is demonstrated in a social studies curriculum scope and sequence where themes, concepts, and facts are spiralled through an expanding horizons environment at each year level (see chapter 2).

How does knowing the social studies approach to organizing and presenting curriculum materials help a teacher to think about the new world of the twenty-first century? We have said that the following points are important when considering citizenship education in the twenty-first century: the building blocks of knowledge and thinking are facts, concepts, and generalizations. We have talked about inductive and deductive reasoning. We have said that "Creating knowledge is one of the most effective ways to help students understand. That is, it gives meaning to what they are learning, so that learning is not just consuming, it is creating", and creating knowledge and meaning is important in a democratic society. As a citizen, if you cannot think by gathering information, if you cannot make judgements on the validity of information, and thus cannot make rational decisions, then expect the democracy to fail.

Looking Ahead

We suggest that the appropriate method of teaching that integrates the building blocks of knowledge, as discussed in this chapter, and that helps children create knowledge for the twenty-first century is the problem-solving method. This is the topic of the next chapter.

▸ Appendix

Social studies shares and draws on all the concepts below, as and when they can be applied to help understand issues in the ten interdisciplinary themes noted above. These, therefore, represent some of the major concepts that you should utilize, focus, on and reinforce in your unit plans, daily lesson plans, and your classroom teaching. These are some major concepts that your students need to use together with the related facts and generalizations, as the building blocks to create knowledge.

Major Concepts in Geography

Because classroom teachers are assigned to teach geography, geographers and educators designed the following concepts to establish major strands of geography for instruction in the social studies curriculum. These concepts provide windows through which teachers can view geographic content. Thus, the five concepts serve as an instructional framework for organizing ideas in the teaching of geography. The five major concepts are (1) location, (2) place, (3) human/environment interaction, (4) movement, and (5) regions.

1. *Location* refers to the absolute location, usually determined by use of latitude and longitude coordinates, of places and people on Earth. Location also refers to relative location determined by associating a particular place with other places (near to . . ., for example, or a short drive from . . .). Before any geographic analysis or higher-order thinking can take place, it is essential to know the location of the place one is trying to understand.
2. *Place* refers to the describable physical and human characteristics of places. All places on Earth have distinctive tangible and intangible characteristics that give them meaning and character and distinguish them from other places. Using observation and description, the concepts of location and place set the stage for further geographic analysis.
3. *Human/environment interaction* refers to how people interact with and within particular places. All places on Earth have advantages and disadvantages for human settlement. This concept encourages the study of the modification and transformation of environments by human and physical causes and the effects of physical features on the lives of people.
4. *Movement* refers to people interacting with each other and other places on Earth. Humans occupy places unevenly on Earth, but they

interact with each other through the transportation of commodities and through travel, trade, information flows, and political events. This concept also concentrates on the patterns of human migration and the movement of ideas from one place to another.

5. *Region* refers to a basic unit of geographic study. A region is an area that displays a coherent unity in terms of specific criteria, such as a governmental unit, a language group, or a landform type. Regions are human constructs, and they can be mapped and analysed.

Major Concepts in History

Contemporary history is both science and art: science, in that the historian, like a scientist, develops imaginative, speculative, intuitive hypotheses and then, using a scientific approach to evidence, tests those hypotheses against the evidence; art, in that the historian aspires to a craftsmanship where evidence is carefully weighed. The point is that history is important because it gives us the background, helps us to understand present problems, and offers a perspective. The major concepts are (1) change and time, (2) human experience, (3) response to change, (4) consequences, (5) diversity, (6) interpretation.

1. *Change and time.* History is a record of peoples and groups seen over periods of time. Institutions and civilizations undergo modifications. Sometimes, through evolution, at other times by revolutionary methods.
2. *Human experience* is a continuous and interrelated web. Events are dependent on previous situations, and ideas come from earlier ones. Man is to a degree dependent on the past, but can free himself from it.
3. *Response to change.* History is a record of man's answers to the challenges of each period in his history. The successful accomplishment of each response leads to further problems.
4. *Consequences.* Actions and ideas result in other activities, some of which can be foreseen, many of which are unpredictable. Analogies between past and present give valuable insight into social change.
5. *Diversity.* Individual cultures and subcultures have evolved different values and beliefs. Although it is difficult and improper to use the same yardstick to measure other cultures, each individual culture historically has done so.
6. *Interpretation.* Although individuals and groups see problems in relation to their own experiences, the historian tries to interpret history as he sees it from the evidence available.

Major Concepts in Sociology

Sociology is concerned with the study of people living together in groups. Group behaviours, group characteristics, and social institutions are included in sociology. The major concepts are (1) social interaction (interaction, groups), (2) culture (culture, social norms), (3) social organization (population, social classes, human ecology, institutions), (4) social dynamics (social change, social disorganization).

1. *Social interaction*
   Interaction: People learn all characteristically human behaviours through group interaction.
   Groups: Humans are by nature gregarious creatures. To understand human beings, one must understand the various groups with which they associate.
2. *Culture*
   Culture: Every society develops a culture of its own, even though some of the ideas are borrowed from other cultures.
   Social norms: The culture provides the norms, "the rules of the game", by which social life is structured.
3. *Social organization*
   Population: Individual lives are affected by a population size, rate, growth, and age and sex distribution changes.
   Social classes: All members of a society are ranked into levels of prestige and power, which are called social classes.
   Human ecology: Human beings' social relationships and behaviour are affected by their distribution in geographic space.
   Institutions: All societies develop social institutions which may be defined as complex sets of folkways, mores, and laws which are integrated around the major functions (or needs) of the society.
4. *Social dynamics*
   Social change: All societies are in constant change.
   Social disorganization: No society is completely harmonious; some form of social disorganization is present in all societies.

Major Concepts in Political Science (Civics)

Political science examines the process of governance and types of governments. In most primary schools, content from political science is integrated into citizenship education. The concepts are (1) interdependence, (2) emergence of politics, (3) the political system, (4) power and authority, (5) change and stability, (6) interacting systems, (7) political ethics, (8) rights, liberties and obligations.

1. *Interdependence.* People are interdependent.
2. *Emergence of politics.* Political action emerges when men make binding decisions on the whole of society.
3. *The political system* is part of the society that makes such binding decisions.
4. *Power and authority.* Power is the energy of the political system; authority is legitimate power.
5. *Change and stability.* Political systems change and try to remain stable.
6. *Interacting systems.* Political systems interact in conflict, cooperation, or indifference.
7. *Political ethics.* Ethical standards undergird political systems.
8. *Rights, liberties, and obligations* define the individual in relation to the political system.

Major Concepts in Economics

Economics is concerned with the manner in which goods and services are produced, distributed, and consumed. Economics also examines the nature and distribution of wealth. Many elementary social studies programmes integrate economic topics such as needs, wants, goods, and services. The concepts are (1) interdependence, (2) scarcity, wants, and decision making, (3) money, income and wealth, (4) the market economy, (5) economic stability, (6) economic growth, change, and adaptation.

1. *Interdependence.* People are interdependent, and dependence has been increased.
2. *Scarcity, wants and decision making.* A conflict between unlimited wants and limited resources creates the need for decision making.
3. *Money, income and wealth. Money* is an institution to facilitate the operation of an exchange economy; *income* is earned by producing goods and services; and *wealth* takes many different forms.
4. *The market economy.* Free enterprise assumes freedom to seek economic gain.
5. *Economic stability* is a goal towards which all sectors of an economy strive, that is, to moderate the upswings and downturns in the economy.
6. *Economic growth, change, and adaptation.* Economic prosperity and change are related to the prosperity of, and change in, the rest of the world.

Major Concepts in Anthropology

Anthropology is a discipline in which human beings and their origins and customs are studied. Anthropology examines aspects of culture that include lifestyles, artefacts, rituals, art, tools, and ideas. The major concepts are (1) man and culture, (2) the family, (3) tools, (4) language, (5) curing illness, (6) quieting fears, (7) environmental adjustment, (8) acquiring, (9) social control.

1. *Man and culture.* As an animal, man occupies a unique place among living things.
2. *The family* is the basic unit of society in the transmission of culture.
3. *Tools.* Culture includes tools.
4. *Language.* Culture includes language.
5. *Curing illness.* Culture is the means for curing illness.
6. *Quieting fears.* Culture provides the means for quieting fears.
7. *Environmental adjustment.* Culture is the means of adjusting to and changing the environment.
8. *Acquiring.* Culture is acquiring food, shelter, and clothing.
9. *Social control.* Culture is social control.

11

Teaching by the Problem-Solving Method

Introduction

In chapter 10, it was proposed that the most effective way to help students learn was by encouraging them to create knowledge. The twenty-first century will be a new electronic world that functions as an information revolution. In that revolution, learning is not just traditional consuming, it is the creating of information that will be valued. The problem-solving method is believed to be the most effective approach to education in the twenty-first century, because the method is related to a logical, decision-making process, to creating knowledge, and to the practice of democracy. Decision-making skills are essential to the process of change and to the maintenance and strengthening of democratic foundations.

Problem Solving: A Part of the "Age of Reason" Century

We are compelled by curiosity, the need to explore, and the experience of rapid change, all of which is part of living in the "Age of Reason". The twenty-first century could well be called the "age of problem solving" because what characterizes the century is the attempt of mankind to solve problems in such a way that there is positive development. Even though the century may be characterized as problem solving, the educational system, as in most countries, remains more related to the twentieth century.

Thus, although in our everyday lives we are required to be problem solvers and decision makers, our educational system does not provide experiences in being effective in that real problem-solving world. It does seem strange that we live in a world that requires certain habits of personal decision making, yet we are not educated in the skills of that method. You can now identify why most contemporary educators believe that citizens should be educated by the problem-solving methods because that is the world they live in. But we should not accept the twenty-first century's problems, questions, and answers without first considering the past and the future. All of the evidence about learning and remembering suggests that students learn best when they are actively seeking answers to relevant problems and questions. And all levels of the three taxonomies - cognitive, affective, and psychomotor domains - are emphasized as part of the problem-solving method.

Applying the problem-solving method is not easy, in part, because you have probably been brought up under the transmission method, and thus your school experience is not helpful in thinking about applying problem solving. Just as the century you live in is significantly more complex than the preceding centuries, so is the problem-solving method much more complex than the transmission method. In fact, to apply the problem-solving method, you will need special training, and that is what this chapter is all about.

What Is Problem Solving?

Problem solving is a rational (being able to reason) process. The method of problem solving is just applying this reasoning process. The term problem solving refers to a category of rational thinking processes that include such names as scientific method, discovery, critical thinking, decision making, reflective thinking, enquiry, and reflective enquiry. Though these terms for a rational thinking process are all forms of problem solving, they do differ somewhat from each other in how they describe the process.

The problem-solving process may be well known to you, having been introduced under one of the terms above, probably as a scientific method. But, in brief, the process evolves through the following steps:

1. *Define,* determine, or bring into focus any problem, issue, or event to be considered.
2. *Gather information* that will help define the problem.
3. *Hypothesize,* generate, or offer tentative explanations, solutions, or conclusions.

4. *Acquire* as much *evidence* as is necessary to validate, reject, or modify the hypothesis or tentative answer.
5. *Synthesize* the findings, information, and insights into warranted conclusions, or generalizations.

Applying the Problem-Solving Method

If you know what problem solving is, then the next question is, How do you apply the process as a teaching method? Do you need special training? Or is applying problem solving just as natural as breathing and eating? It is certainly not natural. It has taken humans approximately two million years to arrive at the Age of Reason and to develop the problem-solving skills. And it takes training to apply the method to teaching. What might that training include? If you have already learned the skill of questioning, then you have already begun the training. The following is a brief list of the skills and attitudes, both cognitive and affective domains, which are thought to be necessary to the training of both yourself and, of course, your students, in using the problem-solving method.

Training List in Attitudes and Skills

1. The *skill* of sensing and identifying a problem.
2. An *attitude* that encourages critical thinking, which means a question-raising attitude about problems and issues.
3. The *attitude* of open-mindedness to alternative points of view.
4. Questioning, a *skill* basic to critical thinking, requiring knowledge of lower and higher levels of questions.
5. A *receptive attitude,* a *willingness* to test or verify conclusions.

The training list, as you have noted, includes at least three important attitudes: critical thinking, open-mindedness, and receptiveness. Do you begin to see the differences between traditional teaching, which relies on the transmission method of assign-study-recite-test, and the problem-solving method that includes: define, gather information, hypothesize, acquire evidence, and synthesize? Under both methods, the students learn. But under the problem-solving method, students are to develop the cognitive thinking and affective skills and attitudes that enable them to know how to both use and create knowledge in order to solve future problems. And this is what a citizen is expected to do in the twenty-first century.

Problem solving is a systematic, rational, some say logical or consistent reasoning process of studying a problem. Those who have written about problem solving are substantially in agreement about the definition and meaning of problem solving. They differ usually on the theoretical description of how the method should be applied. It is important, at this point, not to become immersed in arguments over the number and exact labels placed on each of the steps of the problem-solving process. Rather, in the following pages, an attempt will be made to describe and illustrate the problem-solving method, including the necessary training in skills and attitudes, and the six steps of the problem-solving process.

Introduction to the Six Steps of the Problem-Solving Process

- Step 1: *Experience* – The process of problem solving starts with an experience and a willingness to create knowledge.
- Step 2: *State of uncertainty and doubt* – The heart of problem solving is not fact. It is uncertainty. It is not the established, symmetrical "givens" that generate problem solving. It is that which does not fit, the irregular, the confusing, the dissonant.
- Step 3: *Framing the problem* – This sensing of the problem may lead to framing that which is not known, and it is that frame that becomes the statement of the problem, the new knowledge. The statement of the problem prescribes the boundaries within which the conflict, in the form of new knowledge, is seen and the tension created.
- Step 4: *Formulating hypotheses* – When framing a hypothesis, one is brainstorming the possibilities. The framing of the problem gives the limits within which to hypothesize.
- Step 5: *Exploring and evidencing* – The title of this step almost explains itself. At this step, one gathers and evaluates sources of evidence, attempting to find evidence to support or reject the hypothesis.
- Step 6: *Generalization or warranted conclusion* – The final step in the problem-solving process is reporting warranted conclusions, or verified knowledge, which is a statement about how well the hypothesis has given meaning to the understanding of the problem.

Explanation of the Problem-Solving Steps

The following explanation will help to clarify what are the steps of the process and how the steps are applied in the classroom. However, before proceeding to further explanations of the steps, it is important to consider the teacher's attitude towards problem solving.

Although the problem-solving approach is encouraged among teachers by educators, it is not usually achieved in practice. This discrepancy between encouragement and achievement exists primarily because the method of problem solving has not been understood by the classroom teachers. Classroom teachers, for example, have not always understood that problems belong to people. A problem is felt by someone. It belongs to someone. Many of the problems presented by teachers are not *felt as problems* by most students.

To feel a problem is to be aroused to the point where one wants to learn enough about it to do something about it. This feeling has two components: doubt and concern. Any attempt by a teacher to create a problem without arousing students emotionally (affective domain) can result only in pseudo-problems. When students are disturbed, upset, perhaps even angry, they are coming closer to *personally owning* the problem because they are actively involved, they are interacting, they are willing to create knowledge to solve the problems. If there is to be true problem solving, *students should own the problem*; that is, students should identify, emotionally feel, and want to do something about the problem.

Now let us turn to a full explanation of each step and an illustration of how it is applied in the classroom.

Step 1: Experience

The process of problem solving starts with an experience. An experience is defined as an interaction which students have with their environment, talking with a friend, eating lunch, watching a soccer game, shopping, planting crops, or living in their neighbourhood, that sort of thing. Not all experiences will or should require problem solving. However, some experiences confront students with a conflict between what the students think they know - their values, beliefs, knowledge - and what is encountered in the experience. An experience challenges preconceived ideas, perhaps stimulates curiosity, encouraging students to question their knowledge and beliefs. An experience makes students feel uneasy and promotes a sense of inadequate understanding or even concern and worry, all of which will eventually encourage students to create relevant knowledge to solve the problem.

Brief Classroom Illustration of Step 1: Experience

The teacher has introduced a general scheme of work on ecology with special attention to environmental issues. The teacher's school is in a small village that is threatened by drought and encroachment of erosion. This village has survived for many generations and its members have a deep and abiding attachment to their land.

As an opening experience, the teacher leads the students on a field trip to the forest or wooded area which is adjacent to the village. The students are instructed during the field trip to note the conditions of the wood and to sample the soil in the forest as well as the areas surrounding the forest. These primary students are asked to bring samples back to the classroom and, having returned from the field trip, are asked to draw a picture from memory of how the forest appeared to them or perhaps a mural to show the village, forest, hills and valleys. This picture or mural is the students' first attempt to "create knowledge" about the world they see and understand.

The teacher has carefully planned a concrete experience in such a way that the students may begin to sense, to *feel* that *their environment* is changing and that change needs to be understood. In this way, they are beginning the problem-solving process from learning, to thinking, to acting.

Step 2: Doubt and Uncertainty

To have an experience is not synonymous with having experienced problem solving. Problems may start when the experience raises doubt and uncertainty as to what is known. In other words, if the experience does not create a "sense of a problem", a conflict, an absence of certainty, a felt need to know, or a question, then the student is probably not ready to continue the process of problem solving, and the teacher should be alert to provide additional experiences and more training in the skill of sensing and identifying problems. Refer to chapter 10 in which students are taught to create knowledge. *Identifying problems is a form of creating knowledge.* This state of sensing a problem is the essential step in the process.

In summary, the experience means that the students must try to own the problem if it is to be relevant or personally meaningful. Think carefully about what you have just read. Students must try to *own* that problem in order for the examination of the problem to be effective problem solving. In short, you cannot solve a problem if you do not see a problem. Suppose the teacher presents some issues as a problem which the class is to study, is that problem solving? Yes, it could be practised as problem solving, but the problem may not be meaningful to the students. It is effective problem solving only if the students internalize, or identify, the problem - which is a form of creating knowledge - as their own.

Brief Classroom Illustration of Step 2: Doubt and Uncertainty

The teacher wants to find out if students sense an environmental problem, given the experience they have just had in the field trip to the forest or wooded area. Though these students have known this forest throughout their entire lives, they have not perceived the environmental changes that have taken place. The teacher encourages the students to reflect on their field experience using the pictures and mural they have drawn, the examples of soil they have brought back to the class, and their observations on the conditions of the forest and wood.

The teacher asks them, "What did you see? What do the pictures you drew tell you?" (The teacher is applying questioning skills by asking for personal opinion, thus the teacher's questions are at the evaluative question level.) The students begin to describe what they saw and what they drew. Many of the trees had been partially destroyed for firewood, some of the village animals had cropped the vegetation on the floor of the forest and had eaten some of the lower parts of the trees. And they observed that the soil in the forest was becoming much like the dry and sandy soil at the edge of the forest.

The teacher then asked, "Is there a reason why we should be concerned about the forest?" (This is also an evaluative question, asking for personal judgement). Some students answered that the forest just seemed to be changing. Some others said they did not know if there was a problem. Still others think there might be a problem for they observed that the forest seems to be disappearing. The teacher, by asking evaluative questions, has encouraged the students' doubt and uncertainty about what they know and emotionally feel concerned about. They are doubting what they know and are beginning to think for themselves by creating knowledge which is relevant to their environment.

Step 3: Framing the Problem

To begin the process of responding to a sense of doubt and feeling of concern, students attempt to frame the problem, that is, to create a statement of the problem. The statement of the problem describes the boundaries, or context, within which the problem is seen and the tension, meaning worry and concern, that is created. The reason for this is that it is impossible to explore every aspect of a complex and unclear situation simultaneously. Therefore, different elements of the problem are marked off from each other. And a person begins to take stock, that is, to assess both the situation and his or her understanding of the situation. To do this, an individual begins to ask him or herself a series of convergent, divergent, and evaluative questions. These questions might include the following:

- *What do I know?* That is, what knowledge am I fairly sure I possess? (A convergent question.)
- *What do I think I know?* That is, in essence, a matter of examining one's

own assumptions. Students begin to make a distinction between what they are fairly sure they know and what they believe to be true. (An evaluative question.)

- *What do I not know?* Often raising a question about what is known and what is unknown is an important prerequisite to solving a problem. By simply identifying and naming the unknown elements, students can at least begin to define the nature of the problem. (The question is divergent, and the answer to the question will need the creating of new knowledge, because the answers are not written anywhere.)
- *What do I understand?* That is, having identified the boundaries that frame the problem, students question whether or not these boundaries make sense. (The question calls for an inference, a speculation, a prediction, which makes the question divergent.)

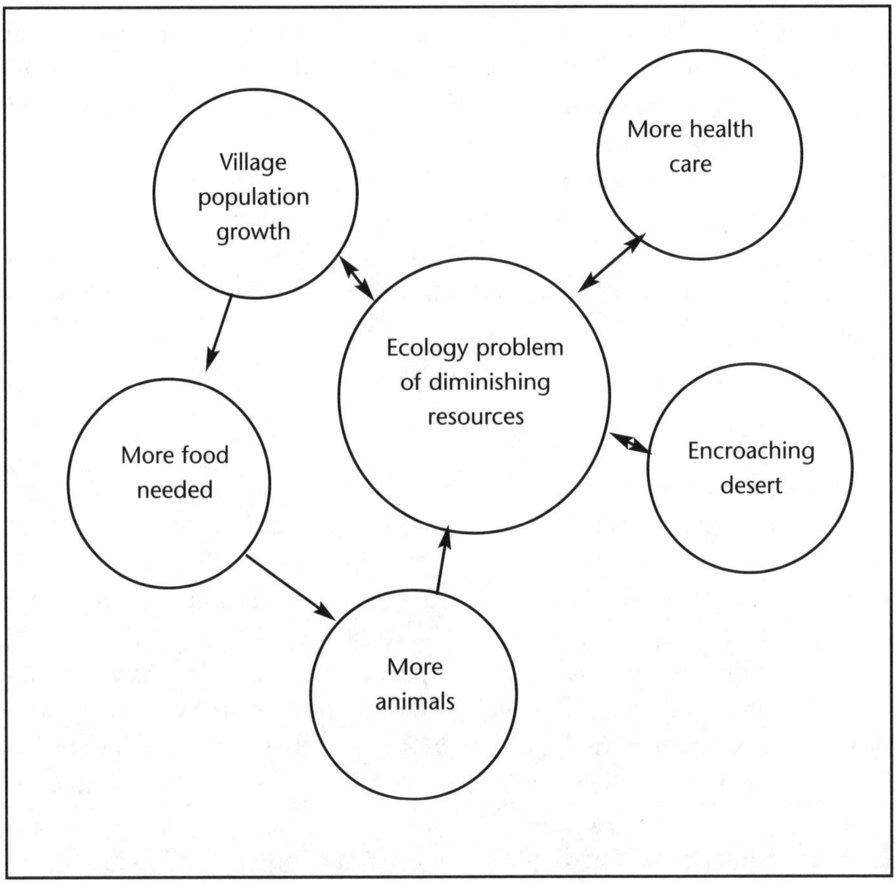

▶ **Figure 11.1** Framing the Problem

Brief Classroom Illustration of Step 3: Framing the Problem

The teacher is now ready to assist the class in trying to create a statement of the problem if, in fact, there is one. Obviously the class is experiencing a complex and unclear situation. Therefore, it is the teacher's role to help the students identify what they know and what they do not know. The teacher begins the discussion by asking: (1) *"What do you know?* What facts are you sure of about your village forest?" Students volunteer that there has been change in the forest in their lifetime. That change could be called deterioration. The forest no longer provides the wood necessary for the village needs because, they note, their families have to travel further to find adequate firewood. The teacher continues the questioning by asking: (2) *"What do you believe is happening to your forest?* Do you have some opinions on what you think is happening?" The students give many different personal opinions which, when discussed, seem to cluster into two categories. These opinions and categories are noted on the chalkboard. The teacher continues the discussion by asking: "Are these categories the things that you don't know but need to test, question and verify? (3) *Are there other things that you don't know* that you think are important to know in understanding what is happening to your forest?" The class identifies three other questions about the forest that they just do not know how to answer and for which they would need to create answers. As a final part of this third step, the teacher asks: "Now that you have identified (1) what you know, (2) what you think you know, and (3) what you don't know, the remaining task is to put it all together and think about (4) *What you think you understand* about the changes that are happening in the forest area. In other words, make some guesses, some hypotheses (inferences, speculations, predictions) based upon what we have discussed, and what you have experienced."

Step 4: Formulating Hypotheses

When framing a hypothesis, one is brainstorming the possibilities. The framing of a problem defines the limits within which to hypothesize. A hypothesis is an explanation of the known extrapolated into statements, or educated guesses, about that which is unknown. In other words, the students have an experience which causes them to doubt or question what the experience means. Students then frame a problem that contains within its dimensions the conflicting opinions. From this frame of reference, students generate hypotheses that are proposed explanations which, if valid, will resolve or explain the doubt.

Brief Classroom Illustration of Step 4: Formulating Hypotheses

The students offer a number of hypotheses, or guesses, but most of them centre on three statements that they think can be studied: (1) There is a relationship between the forest and the increased population of the village. (2) That there is a relationship between technological progress, such as roads, electrification, water, and the deterioration of the forest. (3) That there has been a climate change over the past fifty years that might be directly affecting the forest (These statements may also be stated as "research questions". For example: "Is there a relationship between . . .?")

Step 5: Exploration and Evidencing

The title of this step almost explains itself. At this step, students gather and evaluate sources of evidence. This step describes what students do in demonstrating the validity, the testing, of a hypothesis. Students explore the sources of possible information. Students then evaluate the adequacy of these sources. This step may be driven by the question: What do I need to know, or find out, in order to test the hypothesis?

Brief Classroom Illustration of Step 5: Exploring and Evidencing

Given the students' hypotheses, the teacher asks: "How shall we proceed to determine if your guesses, the knowledge you have created, is accurate?" The class suggests a number of ways, some of which have to do with identifying helpful sources of information on environmental problems. Some students suggest interviewing grandparents on what the forest was like when they were children and then asking their parents and older brothers and sisters, so that there could be some evidence of change. One student suggests interviewing the staff at the village clinic about changes in health care that would result in longer life expectancy. Another suggestion is to invite, as a resource person, someone knowledgeable in agriculture from the local technical school. Another student suggests sending away for materials on population growth in the district or for environmental educational materials that deal with their part of the country.

Step 6: Generalization of Warranted Conclusion

The final step in the problem-solving process is creating a generalization from facts and concepts. The generalization is a *statement about how well the hypothesis (facts and concepts) has given meaning to the understanding of the problem.* Clearly, the generalization is more than a mere restating of the hypothesis, but rather a statement of how the hypothesis provides a valid, or tested, explanation. Recall in step 3 the example of how a problem is defined. There were four questions, starting with (1), What do I know? and ending with (4), What do I understand? What a generalization does is provide continuity and explains the relationship between the four questions that frame the problem.

Brief Classroom Illustration of Step 6: Generalization

The class by now has listened to a resource person from the local technical school, and received and read materials on population and environmental studies. They have listened to reports from class task-oriented small groups who had visited the village clinic, doctor, and village elders. By class consensus on facts and concepts, they have come to a generalization about what has been happening to their village forest. The generalizations went something like this: "There is a direct relationship between the deterioration of the village forest and the population of the village." The reasons cited for this generalization were that ten years ago, with the introduction of the clinic, the new water supply, and a paved road (technological development), the forest began to deteriorate because the population of the village doubled, thus requiring more firewood, animals, and crops. If the forest is not to continue to deteriorate, solutions will need to be found to the growing pressure from an increased population on an overused resource, the forest.

Following the consensus generalization by the class, what do you believe the teacher will do next, if he is following the problem-solving process from *learning* to *thinking and creating ideas,* which the class has been doing, to *acting?* Do you think the teacher will try to identify, with the class, what are the specific actions the village might take to restore or protect its forest?

Do you remember that the problem solving starts with a question? Students became involved in identifying just what was the right question to ask, and finally arrived at the generalization based upon the evidence in the form of facts and concepts that they were able to gather. Do you understand why questions are important and why students should be encouraged to ask questions at all four levels and to follow a logical system of problem solving and decision making.

Other Illustrations of the Problem-Solving Method

As you may have gathered from the illustration above, the classroom teacher was concerned that his students become problem solvers with the hope of saving the village from a growing environmental problem. One easy way to think about the problem-solving method is to see it as essentially an attitude towards knowledge, skill, and values. A problem-solving teacher believes that contemporary problems, issues, and crises call for contemporary, relevant information, new skills, and probably new attitudes.

We know as educators and as teachers that we cannot just give students skills and attitudes. The students must be willing and able to develop skills and evolve attitudes – no one can do it for them. To merely know and repeat information, as well as skills and attitudes from the past, will not be adequate for a contemporary, twenty-first-century developing society.

To illustrate the point that problem solving is a state of mind, you are asked to read the two following examples. However, we caution you that no attempt is made in these illustrations to exhaustively examine the issues raised. The intent is merely to show how a teacher might plan to follow a problem-solving method. At the end of this chapter, be sure to note the discussion on authentic teaching and reasoning, a contemporary way of describing problem solving, and to see the problem-solving form which the teacher may use to introduce and practise the problem-solving method in class.

Illustration 1: Introduction to a Problem-Solving Discovery Lesson for Social Studies

This illustration of problem solving as a discovery lesson is meant for teachers in training, and concerns the topic of pollution and the questions: "What is pollution? Is it a problem in our community?" Very often, teachers will spend the entire lesson time on the first two steps of problem solving: (1) experience, and (2) uncertainty. Thus they do not allow sufficient time to complete the remaining four steps in the problem-solving method. In the following lesson, the instructor for the teachers in training sets forth, in a specific way, the objectives for teaching this topic and provides a number of opportunities for teachers in training to experiment with the effects of pollution. This is followed by activities that call for (3) identifying problems, (4) hypothesizing, (5) gathering data, and (6) generalizing. Many of these activities are done as individual or group projects, and are not described in detail in this illustration.

Rationale for the Lesson on Pollution

The instructor explains the rationale for applying the problem-solving method and why she has planned the lesson to accomplish certain goals she thinks are important for the students, in this case, the teachers in training.

> Just because I say to you, as teachers in training, that I think pollution is a problem, that does not make it a problem for you. You may not really identify pollution as a problem. My job is to set up discovery experiences that your students can really think about, talk about, and in the end, reason out for themselves. Your job is to learn, then to think, and then to act – in short, to create knowledge about problems that are relevant to you. This is just a simple recognition that the problems I understand are not necessarily the problems you know and accept. My task is not to convince you of what I perceive as problems, or of my values or beliefs, but rather to help you identify, from your experience, the problems you have come to know. My rationale for this lesson is that you, as teachers in training, should be encouraged to think critically for yourselves. You will have the opportunity to take part in a series of experiments that are in the form of activities. I am following a problem-solving process from learning to thinking to acting. This process, of course, includes training in the skills and attitudes that are important for practising problem-solving and creating answers. I have named the lesson "What Is Pollution? Is It a Problem in Our Community?"

General Objectives for the Lesson

Teachers in training should

1. Begin to identify problems that affect their lives and learn that, as citizens in a democracy, they can do something about these problems, which is to act on their convictions.
2. Be able to practise the skills of observation, reading, and discussing, and should identify resources that bear on the problem.
3. Be able to think critically when identifying problems. An open-minded, receptive, and willing attitude is a necessary part of performing the activity.

Specific Objectives for the Lesson on what Teachers in Training Should Create

1. *Knowledge objectives:* After you, as teachers in training, perform four experiments and choose one activity, you should be able to list three ways to conserve water, name at least three different kinds of pollution problems, and list at least two examples of appropriate responses to the problems in a pre-test as part of the activities.
2. *Skill objectives:* After completing the activities in this lesson, teachers in training should be able to do the following:
   a. Given three pollutants in an experimental situation, you will

demonstrate research skills by (i) forming hypotheses, (ii) writing observations of the interaction, (iii) recording the results, and (iv) drawing a conclusion.

b. Apply the problem-solving method in such a way that problems may be identified as well as sources of information and a possible solution to those problems.

3. *Attitude objectives:* After completing this lesson, you should be able to demonstrate an enquiring (questioning, critical) attitude about the environment in which you live by identifying environmental problems, other than the one studied in the lesson, as measured by a pre- and post-evaluation attitude survey.

Pre-Evaluation Directions for Teachers in Training

Please take this evaluation before starting your activities. If you can answer all the questions in the evaluation correctly, you may not need to perform the four experiments, but you will need to select an activity.

Pre-Evaluation Survey

1. Name three non-wasteful products, and explain why the are non-wasteful.
2. Name three wasteful products, and explain why they are wasteful.
3. List two things you can do to save and keep water clean.
4. Summarize, in writing, a current pollution problem you have identified in your environment. Be sure to include why you think it is a problem and what you think the best response to the problem would be.
5. Attitude survey:
   Circle the word below the statement that best expresses your feeling on the following:
   I am concerned about whether my environment is polluted.
   always sometimes neutral almost never never

Experiments and Activities

For this lesson, the instructor has set up activities in a "learning centre" in one corner of the classroom. In this particular lesson, she is having the teachers work individually or in small groups in the learning centre. The following experiments may be done in the learning centres individually or in small task-oriented groups, or the instructor may perform the first three experiments in front of the entire class.

Experiment 1

Instructions for teachers in training in the learning centre: "In front of you are three different kinds of paper: newspaper, toilet paper, writing paper. (Wax paper, wrapping paper, facial tissues, for example, can also be used.) Describe each kind of paper using your five senses: touch, taste, smell, sight, and hearing. Notice the differences and similarities."

"Now, think about this: What would happen to each of the papers if it was dropped into water? Write what you think would happen, your hypothesis."

"Next, fill three jars with water. Put a different kind of paper in each jar, and shake the jar. Let the jars stand for a while and observe them. What happens to each paper in the water? Does this agree with what your hypothesis stated? Which type of paper dissolves fastest? Why? Draw a conclusion. What does this experiment tell you about using paper?"

Experiment 2

"Using the jars provided, fill each with water. Add a cupful of detergent to each. What happens to the soap (detergent) when it is put in water? Make a guess (hypothesis). Now, empty the same jars, and fill with water again. Pour a capful of *different* detergent into each jar. Shake each jar vigorously with the lid on! What happens? (convergent question, there is a right answer). How could this affect a river? (convergent question). Which soap would be the least polluting?" (convergent question).

Experiment 3

"Read the booklet *Ways to Curb Pollution.* Can you think of some other ways not mentioned in the booklet? (a divergent question: which asks teachers to originate, to imagine other ways). What could we do in our classroom? (divergent question). After reading this, complete the brief question and answer quiz (which the instructor has prepared) to check your understanding of the main ideas in the booklet."

Experiment 4

"Tonight when you go home, gather information by asking someone in your family or in the neighbourhood, whom you believe might know about environmental pollution, what they think are local problems. As an alternative, look for articles about pollution in the newspaper or magazines, or listen for news about environmental problems on radio, TV, or on the Internet. Bring to school a short written report on what you have discussed, seen, or heard."

Project Activities

Select one of the activities below.

Activity 1

Using paper and available materials (for example, tempera paints, water-colours, sand, mosaic, collage, crayons - anything!) Make a picture or poster of what pollution means to you.

Activity 2

With two or three classmates, develop an experiment on noise pollution. Record sounds you hear, for example, at an airport, market, a sports event, or road noise.

Activity 3

As a follow-up to activity two, ask yourself how noise affects us. To find out, the class of teachers in training will divide in half. One half of the class should read a passage under usual classroom conditions, and the other half should read the same thing while a tape of loud noise or music is being played. Develop a quiz on the content of the reading and give to each half. Compare their results. Which half did better? Draw a conclusion.

Activity 4

With one or two classmates, find out how dangerous motor vehicle exhaust fumes are. Place live beetles, earthworms, or other insects in clear plastic bags. Fill the bags with exhaust fumes by holding them over the exhaust pipe of a car with its motor running. After they are filled, tie them shut. What did you think would happen before the experiment? What actually happened? (The fumes produced by the car exhaust is called carbon monoxide. Carbon monoxide is a gas produced by anything burning, including wood or charcoal fires).

Activity 5

Keep a daily record of things you can do to stop pollution, or observe and look for signs of pollution in your community. Keep a record of what the pollution is and where it comes from.

Activity 6

Plan an activity of your own. Before proceeding, check your proposed activity with your instructor.

Summary

You will have noted that the instructor provided many different experiences, all of which require the teachers to perform (learn, think, and act) by the problem-solving method. One final thought: The instructor did not necessarily follow the six problem-solving steps consecutively in all activities. However, if you, as a teacher, completed all of the required activities and projects, you will have experienced all of the six steps, but not necessarily in the exact sequence described in the previous illustration about the effect of pollution.

Note: You are advised that, when you have finished your teacher training and are a classroom teacher, this lesson on pollution can effectively be adapted for third- and fourth-year primary school students.

Illustration 2: A Lesson for Upper Primary or Lower Secondary School

Mr Marshall Louis is a social studies teacher. His lesson is based on the idea that students need to examine contemporary, relevant issues in their own and neighbouring countries. In particular, the issues surrounding population growth are pertinent to all of the students because, during their lifetime, they will be called upon to make judgements about how their society should respond to the issues. Now and in the future, students need to know how to learn, think, and act by questioning their own basic assumptions and knowledge about society. If they learn to be critical about their own knowledge, they are more likely to become effective decision makers. In this illustration, Mr Louis will follow the steps of the problem-solving method using the problem-solving process form found at the end of this chapter.

Step 1: Setting Up an Experience

Mr Louis has decided to introduce the lesson, on "Population: Problem Solving", by showing the film *Tragedy of the Commons,* by Garrett Hardin. The film portrays the world as a common pasture in which each herdsman increases his herd for personal gain. Eventually, the pasture is ruined for all. The implication is that, if population is not restricted, the world will be ruined. The film argues that there should be some restriction on the freedom to have families. Other similar films or video cassettes of other materials such as pamphlets or booklets may be available from national or local population study associations. Mr Louis instructs the students to reflect on the film and also upon their own personal experience and knowledge about population growth, in short, to think for themselves. He asks them a divergent question, "Is population growth a problem?"

Step 2: Creating a State of Uncertainty and Doubt

A number of students respond to the teacher.

First student: "I don't think there is a problem. I can't think what the problem would be. There's no problem in our community."

Second student: "As the film said, there is a problem, but it's in the future. We don't have a population problem in our country right now."

In response, Mr Louis asks, "You suggest there is a problem, but what is the problem? Can you define it? Because if you can't define it, you don't know whether it is a problem or not."

Third student: "There's too rapid a population growth and simply too many people."

Using a tone of agreement but wanting clarification, Mr Louis replies, "Is this an accurate definition of the problem? Is it possible that the problem is just a myth? Can someone state more precisely what population growth has to do with problems of social living? Can you explain why it might be a problem?" At this point, the teacher has asked the class to begin the process of creating knowledge upon which they will make decisions.

During the ensuing discussion, the students make the following points: (1) survival of the Earth, perhaps even the continuation of human life, may depend upon slowing population growth; (2) quality of human life will be in jeopardy without some management of population; (3) problems such as pollution, destruction, and consumption of natural resources and perhaps starvation can be controlled by restricting the population; and (4) the overcrowding of cities, traffic congestion, and social pressures are all the apparent result of too many people.

Step 3: Framing the Problem

Mr Louis at this point tries to bring order out of the various suggestions from the class by attempting to help the class frame the problem from which hypotheses about the population problem ought to emerge. He asks, "What do we know, what valid information do we have on population growth? Can we verify that knowledge and know that it is true?" Students suggest the following as testable knowledge: "Some countries, like China, are attempting to restrict population growth. Other countries, like Egypt and Nigeria, relate population growth to development." Mr Louis continues, "What do you think you know about population growth?"

One student responds: "There is a relationship between technological development and population growth. To decrease the population, have an industrial revolution." "Isn't it true," another student asks, "that the traditional society had much larger families than do the contemporary technologically developed societies? Isn't it true that our families are smaller now than they were before independence?"

Another student: "I think that pollution or deterioration is directly related to overpopulation."

Another student: "I believe that the poor of the world produce the overpopulation. If you can keep the poor from having children, the problem would be solved."

Mr Louis continues, "If those replies reflect what you think you know, then what is it that you don't know?" The general consensus from the class is that they are not sure they understand the problem, or they do not have much evidence to support their speculations about population. They just have their own feelings about what they have heard.

Mr Louis asks the final question, "What is it that you think you understand?" A class discussion leads to the conclusion that they think there is a potential problem, but having listened to each other, they are beginning to feel that they do not know enough about the situation. They do not even know if population is a problem.

Step 4: Formulating Hypotheses

Mr Louis asks, "How can we study population growth? What assumptions can we try to explore? Think about what you said during the framing of the problem. Based on what was said, state the hypotheses that you would wish to examine as precisely as possible. Can you now identify several hypotheses that the class could build its study around? I'm ready to write them on the chalkboard."

The class agrees on three hypotheses:

1. The poor and underdeveloped countries are responsible for overpopulation.
2. Controlling population will control pollution, environmental deterioration, and starvation.
3. Post-industrial societies such as France, Sweden, and Japan, have smaller families; this means less-developed countries have a population problem, but the developed nations do not.

Step 5: Exploring and Gathering Evidence

Based on the three hypotheses agreed upon by the class, Mr Louis divides the class into three large cooperative learning, task-oriented groups, giving each group one hypothesis to explore. Each member of the group is asked to research an aspect of the group's hypothesis. During their investigation, the students turn to a number of sources including books, pamphlets, films and a guest speaker. Mr Louis plays an important role by acting as a resource person and suggesting where students can look for the data they need. He has asked that each group prepare a group project paper and be prepared to report their findings to the class orally during the next three weeks.

Step 6: Making a Generalization

After researching their hypothesis for a period of time and discussing their findings in their three separate groups, the students are called to a general discussion. Mr Louis asks each group, "Were you able to verify, that is, support, the hypothesis suggested by the class?"

In each case, the hypothesis proved invalid (not true):

1. There was no evidence that the poor are more responsible for overpopulation than the non-poor. Also, the group faced the problem of defining what is meant by poor people. The group asks, "Is being considered poor or underdeveloped partly in the eye of the beholder?"
2. There was no evidence to suggest that overpopulation is necessarily the cause of pollution. Many authorities on population talk about resource management and say that improper management of resources as well as waste and pollution is perhaps a greater problem

than overpopulation. There continues to be disagreement among authorities on the role population plays in environmental deterioration.

3. The third group identified research studies that denied their hypothesis. In fact, the studies showed that family size in pre- and post-industrial countries was approximately the same. Furthermore, if overpopulation is a problem, it exists equally in developed and newly developed nations.

The class also discovered that there is considerable disagreement among authorities on just how to define the problem. Students are now convinced that it is a complex issue which requires complicated answers, but they are not sure that it is a crisis.

Having received the written and oral reports, Mr Louis now asks the question, "Do you think that we have properly framed the problem, given the hypothesis that the class eventually developed?" The class readily admits that they did not know what they were talking about when they first began to discuss their knowledge of population and overpopulation. In conclusion, Mr Louis says to the class, "Overpopulation may be a problem for our country as well as an individual problem. It is something that one should consider when planning one's own family. So if there were problems with our first study, how should we rewrite the study so that each of us will gain useful information? What can we do to find information that will help each class member arrive at some personal, rational decision on how to approach questions about population?"

The students suggest that before conducting any additional research, they must try to reframe the problem. Their hope is that in developing new hypotheses, they will be better able to explain what is happening with population growth around the world, as well as in their own country. To help the class start to reframe the problem, Mr Louis asks the class, "Do you remember the film *Tragedy of the Commons* and how you individually reacted to that film? The film concluded that in the absence of birth control, the ultimate result is one totally miserable world. What do you now think of the film's conclusion?"

Summary

In this illustration, Mr Louis closely followed the steps of the process because the issue was extremely complex. Therefore, he used the sequenced steps of the problem-solving method to structure the discussion.

However, the major source of instruction took the form of the teacher's and students' questions. The questions the class raised called for many different levels of thinking. Some of the questions called for cognitive-memory facts, some called for convergent-level questions which required describing or explaining, some called for divergent hypothesis and inferences, and some asked for evaluation, such as "What do you think?" All of these different levels of questions are an essential part of a problem-solving questioning strategy and are intended to increase learning, thinking, and acting in a rational, logical way.

Authentic Teaching and Learning

Within the last decade, an educational movement has developed called "Authentic Teaching and Learning" and "Authentic Evaluation". This movement is directly related to the problem-solving method and represents a particular way that contemporary educators discuss the relevance of problem solving. The authentic, meaning genuine or real-life, strategies of instruction are defined as those that require students to (1) produce (not reproduce) knowledge that is relevant to their lives outside of the classroom through a problem-solving method, and (2) achieve in ways that are of value to them and the society. Through these strategies, it is hoped that students not only learn, but begin to develop skills that enable them to know how to create knowledge and also to solve future problems.

The three problem-solving illustrations about the forest, pollution, and population that you have just read are examples of authentic learning. These illustrations focus attention on the students and demand that they define the issues at hand. In this fourth illustration, a first or second form in secondary school is instructed to simulate the role of citizens in a fictional community. Students encounter various perspectives and evaluate many alternatives to the environmental problem of waste disposal. The city or village council members or the local government, as role-played by class members, are required to choose an alternative waste-control programme by weighing costs, environmental impact, practicality, and other considerations. Then all students in the class are required to write reactions to, and evaluations of, the process and outcome of the simulation. The result of student effort must be an understanding of how to use and create knowledge as the basis for making decisions.

Authentic strategies, such as role-playing and simulation techniques as illustrated above, engage students in class work that is valuable in a realistic setting. The strategies also raise the expectations of students, and challenge them to learn, think, and act as decision makers. According to the authentic teaching and learning strategies, students who learn, think, and act will achieve gains in all the cognitive and affective skill levels necessary to succeed in the new world information age of the twenty-first century.

Looking Ahead

You have been reviewing, in the preceding chapters, how to apply the methods and techniques of teaching. But this application would be incomplete without consideration of how you and your students will effectively evaluate their progress. The next chapter will focus on evaluating growth and development.

Note: The following problem-solving process form may help to guide the study of problems.

Problem Solving Process Form

1. Experience: What experience have you had with the problem you have chosen that has caused you to be interested in or curious about that problem?

   ---

2. State of uncertainty and doubt: The problem can become a personal as well as a social problem if you feel the need to know. Express as best you can the uncertainty you feel about the problem. What confuses you?

   ---

3. Framing the problem: What do you know about the problem?

   What do you think you know about the problem?

   What is it you do not know about the problem?

   What do I understand about the problem?

   ---

4. Formulating hypotheses: The hypothesis is a proposed point of view on the problem. That view needs to be proved or disproved.

   ---

5. Exploring and evidencing: Gather and evaluate sources of evidence on the problem. Circle and then name the sources you will use in finding information about your hypothesis.

   books pictures newspapers filmstrips magazines
   interviews personal observations other

   List specific pieces of information that deal with your hypothesis.

   ---

6. Generalization: How does your information prove or disprove your hypothesis?

Evaluating the problem-solving process: What have you learned? Has the problem solving method provided you with an accurate point of view on the problem? Explain:

12

Evaluating Growth and Development

Learning, Thinking, and Performance

Introduction

Evaluation is often misinterpreted as merely testing. Thus, the assumption might be that this chapter will discuss only the writing of test items. This assumption is wrong. Evaluation has a broader meaning than testing. Evaluation in school means obtaining information the teacher wants about the students that will allow the teacher and students to appraise, assess, judge, estimate, and finally, evaluate performance. The process of collecting this information on both how well the student has grown and developed over a period of time and how well the school curriculum has worked, is called evaluation.

Testing Is a Limited View of Evaluation

Traditional testing is often on low-level cognitive learning (knowledge, comprehension, application), but what about higher-level thinking (analysis, synthesis, evaluation), and the domains of the affective and psychomotor? Only one conclusion can be drawn from the way schooling and learning are tied to testing, and that is that satisfactorily passing low-level thinking examinations (tests) becomes the path to continuing education and future opportunity.

When students' growth and development is tied to tests that are essentially an examination only of content often committed to memory, then it is reasonable to assume that low-level cognitive content examinations are what teachers and other authorities value as important. Though recognizing the dominant role still played by traditional content examinations, the suggestion, as found in chapter 7, is still valid, for a social studies curriculum, that low-level content testing is merely one small part of the process of evaluating a student's developing sense of citizenship. Evaluation in social studies citizenship education includes the *cognitive domain* (name, define, recall), but equally so the *affective* (adopt, accept, reply), and *psychomotor* (prepare, imitate, practise) domains. Evaluation over all three domains will be illustrated in this chapter.

Active Learning Requires Complex Evaluation

You will recall from chapter 3 that the key to a student's learning and remembering is spending quality time on a task, which refers to how well a student concentrates on the task. Further, we suggested that concentrating a student's attention on a task, in many instances, is best performed by active involvement in what is to be learned. This was illustrated by the percentages on learning and remembering, from the low 10 per cent of what we hear, up to 90 per cent of what we attempt to teach others. From an evaluator's point of view, it is much easier to test what students should be hearing in a lecture than it is to evaluate higher-level thinking, as when students discuss with others in small groups, experience directly through a project, or attempt to teach others as in peer teaching. In other words, as a teacher increasingly uses learning activities that require the students' active participation, the more complex becomes the evaluation of performance. The task of evaluation is no longer the traditional asking of students to just recall, cite, or repeat information. Given what we know about growth and development and the three taxonomy levels of development, then how should a teacher view the complex process of evaluating, at each age level, the development of a student's maturing citizenship education? Notice in the following story how an education officer, whom we will call Stanley Marshall, evaluates a nine- to ten-year-old primary class.

The Education Officer Visits a School

Stanley Marshall, an officer from the Ministry of Education, was observing a social studies class of nine- to ten-year-olds. He watched the class of thirty students working in small task-oriented groups, each group seated in a circle at five various locations in the room. During the class period, the teacher moved from group to group observing each group's progress. The students were using a wide variety of teaching aids: periodicals, maps, a globe, and dictionary. One member of each group was acting in the role of leader, while the rest of the group members were taking notes while organizing their particular parts of the project. The officer, Mr Marshall, observed the students discussing how their particular topics were integrated into the whole project and how the group critically evaluated the contribution of each topic. At the end of the class period, each member of the group filled out a "Self and Group Evaluation" form, noting his or her progress and contribution. In short, what the officer, Mr Marshall, observed was students practising a variety of teaching and learning skills.

He had observed most of these students four years ago in a junior social studies lesson and noted that they could not then proficiently use the cooperative skills which he observed today. They were unable to read, understand maps, to grasp abstract ideas or participate as skilled team members in group work. They were dependent, in the five- to six-year-old class, essentially on the teacher for direction and social control. Mr Marshall was sure that the students he now observed four years later did not develop their skills just by maturing or just by attendance in school. What he saw now was the result of *good teaching* that *emphasized* learning *skills* and appropriate *attitudes* and *psychomotor* skills which contribute to the development of a sense of mature responsible citizenship. He thought to himself: "These students should be able to do well on national examinations because they know how to use information." But he was also convinced that an equally important part of their education was the development of the appropriate skills of problem solving, and cooperative attitudes about shared responsibilities that would help them to be effective citizens throughout their lifetimes.

The officer believes that the success of a social studies citizenship curriculum should be evaluated not only by immediate objective test results, but also by evaluating the affective and psychomotor domains in the development of mature behaviour among students. "A citizenship curriculum," Mr Marshall said, "is intended to help students develop a cognitive knowledge base, skills of problem solving, and affective attitudes about shared responsibilities – all these are essential to the student's performance as a maturing citizen. The most reliable evidence about effective teaching and learning in social studies is the students' future performance as mature citizens."

Three Categories of Evaluation

The three categories of evaluation are cognitive thinking, psychomotor skills, and affective attitudes.

Category 1: Cognitive Thinking

Cognitive thinking comprises knowledge, comprehension, application, analysis, synthesis, and evaluation.

Measuring How Well Pupils Learn What the Teacher Thinks They Should Learn

The cognitive thinking domain comes to mind when most teachers, students, and parents think about evaluation. The traditional cognitive evaluation is the most used in schools, almost to the exclusion of the other (affective and psychomotor) domains. Cognitive evaluation includes two sections: objective testing, and subjective essay testing. Though you may not have experienced in your own schooling all the following forms of objective evaluation, you undoubtedly are familiar with them. The most familiar are written objective testing and essay examinations. The following seven different types of objective testing are the most frequently used in the classroom. But before proceeding to examine these different types of questions, it is well to keep in mind the following general rules when constructing such items.

Rules for Constructing Evaluation Questions

1. Be sure to give instructions, including point value, at the beginning of each different type of question so there will be no misunderstanding as to how the test is to be answered or how much time to spend on any one section. For example, when using true-false questions, instructions should read: "If any question is not entirely true or false, then mark the question as false."
2. Authorities on test design recommend that no more than four different types of test questions be used in any one test, for example, (a) true-false, (b) multiple choice, (c) matching, and (d) essay. Including more than four types of test questions tends to confuse students.
3. The test should sample all of the content that was studied. Any emphasis in the test should be a reflection of what was emphasized in class.

4. Have something for everyone in the class and begin with the easiest questions. A test is a real threat to many students. It helps to ease the tension if the first questions are easy, and this ensures that everyone will achieve some degree of success.
5. When you have completed constructing the questions, put them aside for a day or so, then take the test yourself. Errors in construction or wording are best detected by you, the teacher.

Different Types of Cognitive Objective Questions

The different types of objective questions are as follows:

1. True-false
2. Fill-in
3. Short answer
4. Matching
5. Sequencing
6. Labelling
7. Multiple choice

Identifying the Weaknesses of Objective Questions

One of the major weaknesses of objective testing is that the student may be able to answer the examination successfully without interpreting, or clarifying the meaning of, the content being tested. It can be a weakness of all objective questions that a student may memorize words and phrases from a lesson and respond only to these when answering test questions. Thus the student may be skilful in taking the examination and yet escape learning the lesson. Given that the objective of evaluation is determining the students' learning from the lesson, it is important that the questions, as much as possible, measure how well the student thinks, using what has been learned. The following discussion, on the seven types of objective questions, includes some basic rules for writing the questions in order to avoid some of the weaknesses of objective tests. For action words to use in writing questions on different cognitive levels of thinking, see the cognitive domain taxonomy in chapter 7.

Illustrations of the Seven Objective Type Questions

1.1. Objective evaluation by the use of true-false questions

True-false is most deservedly criticized as the weakest type of test questions, because the question encourages guessing. There is a fifty-fifty chance of guessing the right answer and, of course, it is difficult to determine if the student just recognizes and responds to familiar words, or whether the student did learn and think about the content being tested. However, true-false questions are useful when measuring learning, if a few basic rules are followed.

a. The question should be entirely true or entirely false. If the questions are not entirely true or false, then in the instructions you should state, "If any question is not entirely true or false, then mark the question as false."
b. The answer to the question should not depend on some trivial or meaningless detail.
c. Do not quote from the textbook. Change the wording to avoid questions that encourage guessing without learning.
d. Avoid a pattern of answers. One useful way to do this is to arrange the order of true-false questions on the flip of a coin.

The following is an example of a true-false quiz based on a stated behavioural objective.

> Having studied the map of the West Indies in a geography lesson, *[condition]*
>
> students will be able to recall on a test *[observable behaviour]* the location of land and
>
> water forms and areas of population density with 100 per cent accuracy *[acceptable performance].*

Instructions: Circle *T* for true or *F* for false. If any question is not entirely true or false, then mark that question as false.

1. Grand Etang is in the eastern part of Grenada and is therefore east of the capital, St George's. T F

2. Most of the population in Grenada lives in the city of St George's. T F

1.2. Objective evaluation by the use of fill-in questions

A properly constructed fill-in, or completion, question can prevent guessing, unlike true-false and multiple-choice questions. Fill-in questions call for cognitive-memory level thinking in recalling one right answer. The following are some basic rules for constructing "fill in the blank" test questions.

a. Omit only significant words, but do not omit too many. A chopped-up sentence may only confuse students.
b. Keep the blanks uniform in length. This lessens the possibility of guessing, and allows an equal amount of credit for each blank.
c. Ideally, there is only one possible right answer to any fill-in question.
d. Avoid quotes from the text for reasons given previously; it encourages empty word memorization.

The following is an example of a fill-in quiz based on a stated behavioural objective.

> Having listened to a lecture on Anguilla *[conditions]*, students will be able to
>
> recall the year when it became a Crown Colony, and
>
> the length and width of the island *[observable behaviour]* on a quiz *[acceptable performance]*.

Instructions: Fill in the blanks to complete the sentence.

a. Anguilla became a Crown Colony in the year _______.
b. The approximate length of Anguilla is _____ and the width is ______.

1.3. Objective evaluation by the use of short answer questions

Short answer is a popular type of test question for many teachers. It is easier to grade than an essay, yet it establishes whether the student did learn, think about and remember the required information. This type of question calls for convergent-level thinking, a correct answer, but in the student's own words. The following are some basic rules for constructing brief, written short-answer-response questions.

a. Be sure to tell students in the instructions whether they are to write their answers in sentence or paragraph form. Often students write short written response answers in fragmented sentences. Be sure to suggest how you want the answers written.
b. Does spelling and punctuation count? Students ought to know ahead of time if they will be penalized for spelling or punctuation.

The following is an example of a brief, written short-answer-response test item based on a stated behavioural objective.

Having read chapter 6 in the text, students will describe the aim of commercial development in St Vincent and identify positive and negative reasons for that development in a brief, written response.

Instructions: Construct a paragraph for each of the statements below. The first statement requires a description of St Vincent's aims. The second statement requires a summary of reasons. Mistakes in spelling and punctuation will not be counted off. The statements are as follows:

a. The aim of St Vincent's commercial development.
b. The positive and negative reasons for that development.

1.4. Objective evaluation by the use of matching questions

The matching form of examination questions is frequently used by teachers to measure recognition and recall. Properly constructed, this type of question makes guessing difficult. Remember that the question should be written to measure the students' thinking about relationships as much as possible, eliminating guessing based just on recognition of words. There are some basic rules to remember when writing this type of examination question.

a. Do not use more than fifteen items or less than five items. More than fifteen tends to confuse students. Less than five encourages guessing. If you want to use more than fifteen in your question, break them up into two or more sections.
b. All items in any one section should be on the same page. Do not let the question itself be a handicap.
c. Arrange the premises (statements) on the left-hand side of the examination page and responses on the right. Number or letter these chronologically or alphabetically. If you are using an answer sheet, both numbers and letters are necessary.
d. Include more responses than premises, or have one response match more than one premise. This cuts down on guessing.
e. Avoid patterns in the location of your responses.

The following is an example of a matching quiz based on a stated behavioural objective.

Having read about the geography of the Eastern Caribbean in their textbook, students will be able to identify the capital cities of selected countries on an objective test.

Instructions: Match by writing the letter for the correct response from the right column, next to the correct statement number on the left.

Countries	Capitals
_____ 1. Barbados	a. St George's
_____ 2. Antigua	b. Plymouth
_____ 3. Grenada	c. Kingstown
_____ 4. St Vincent	d. Castries
_____ 5. St Kitts	e. St John's
_____ 6. Montserrat	f. Fort-de-France
_____ 7. Dominica	g. Bridgetown
_____ 8. St Lucia	h. Roseau
	i. Basseterre

1.5. Objective evaluation by the use of sequencing questions

Sequencing is quite a popular type of teacher-made examination question. But it is also one of the most disliked by the students because if they miss one item by sequencing a response in the wrong place, then surely there is a second error. Sequencing is particularly good for evaluating students' sense of time and place. There are certain basic rules to remember when writing this type of evaluation question.

a. Make sure that the instructions state how the items are to be sequenced, for example, by time (chronologically), by importance, according to some authority, or as stated in the text. Sequenced according to what . . .?
b. Sequencing encourages guessing. Suppose there are five items to sequence. If three items are known, the other two items' placement can often be accurately guessed. Keep this in mind when thinking about using sequencing, for there is no way to cut down on guessing on this type of question.
c. Be careful of creating long lists of items to sequence. It is best to divide a long list (say fifteen items) into two sections and, as in matching, place all items to be sequenced on one page.

The following is an example of a sequencing quiz based on a stated behavioural objective.

> Having studied the problem-solving method in the chapter "Teaching by the Problem-Solving Method", students will be able to construct the sequential steps of the process with 100 per cent accuracy on an objective test.

Instructions: Sequence the steps of the problem-solving method according to the chapter "Teaching by the Problem-Solving Method" by placing numbers from 1 to 6 in the brackets ( ), 1 for the first step and so on up to 6 for the last step.

( ) formulating hypotheses
( ) state of uncertainty
( ) generalization
( ) exploring and evidencing
( ) experiencing
( ) framing the problem

1.6. *Objective evaluation by the use of labelling questions*

You are familiar with labelling. Remember, in primary school, the blank map of the Eastern Caribbean with instructions to locate and name the capital cities of each country. Labelling is a favourite technique for a limited number of topics. What can be labelled? Maps, pictures, diagrams, graphs, charts, timelines. This type of question calls for cognitive-memory level thinking, with key words such as: label, find, locate, name.

The following is an example of a labelling quiz based on a stated behavioural objective.

> Having studied an atlas with the Eastern Caribbean region, students will be able to locate and label the capital cities of at least the five largest Caribbean nations on an outline map with 100 per cent accuracy.

Instruction: On the outline map of the Caribbean, locate and label the capital cities of the five largest countries.

1.7. *Objective evaluation by the use of multiple-choice questions*

The multiple-choice question has significant weaknesses, yet is generally considered to be the most versatile type of objective question. It is also the most difficult to construct properly, for it can be written to measure different levels of student response. Special training is required to successfully write those levels. There are six thinking levels in the cognitive domain taxonomy from which multiple-choice questions can be written. Needless to say, learning to incorporate the six levels in multiple-choice questions requires considerable test construction sophistication. Most teachers, when writing multiple-choice tests, use the lower levels of the cognitive domain – knowledge, comprehension, and application.

However, multiple-choice questions can also be used to objectively evaluate higher-level problem-solving skills such as analysis, synthesis, and evaluation. Both lower-level and higher-level multiple-choice questions are illustrated in this unit.

A multiple-choice question consists of two parts: a stem and the responses. The stem is the statement at the beginning of the question. The responses are the choices that follow the statement. (For primary students, three is the recommended number of responses for each question). As an example:

Stem: English belongs to which of the following language groups?
Responses:

a. Ural-Altaic
b. Finno-Hungarian
*c. English-German

The composition of both stem and responses is crucial for effective use of this kind of question. The following are some basic rules on constructing multiple-choice questions:

1. The question should be written in a way that justifies only one best answer.
2. The choices should be as brief as possible, and all should be about the same length.
3. Make the chances as plausible as possible. The students should have to consider all the choices.
4. It is suggested practice that primary students be given three responses to choose from, secondary students four responses, and higher education students five responses.
5. When giving instructions, be sure to say, "the answer that best fits the statement" (stem). The reason for this instruction is that all or part of the responses to a statement could be true, but there is only one best response. You will save yourself from students arguing that all the responses are correct.

The following is an example of a multiple-choice quiz based on a lower-level behavioural objective.

> Having read about and discussed a nation's constitution, students will be able to identify the important points discussed on a unit test.

Instructions: Circle the letter representing the answer that best fits the statement.

1. Which of the following is not included in the Dominican Constitution?
    a. The Parliament
    b. The Supreme Court
    c. The name of each parish
2. Which country in the following list is considered part of the Eastern Caribbean region?
    a. Tortola
    b. Jamaica
    c. Cuba

1.7.1. Measurement of higher-level problem-solving skills by multiple choice

For most teachers, measuring the development of thinking skills in problem solving is a relatively new idea. Evaluations have been devised to measure the development of problem-solving skills. Just what do tests of problem-solving skills measure? At least four types of skills are measurable: (1) the students' skill in identifying the central issue or problem; (2) the students' skill in recognizing basic assumptions; (3) the students' skill in evaluating evidence; and (4) the students' skill in determining whether or not conclusions are warranted, or follow from the evidence. Identifying a problem, recognizing assumptions, evaluating evidence, and determining warranted conclusions are all basic, not only to problem solving but also to democratic decision making. Decision making and the higher-level thinking skills are what is required in a democratic society. All primary students, as citizens, will be called upon to effectively think and act in that democracy, which means they should mature through practising the four types of problem-solving skills.

There are a number of ways of measuring these four types of problem-solving skills. One is by using the problem-solving process form at the end of chapter 11. A second way is to ask students to write papers that identify central issues, demonstrate assumptions, evaluate evidence, and draw conclusions. Also, objective evaluation exercises can be written such that a variety of multiple-choice questions may be used to measure the skills of thinking.

1.7.2. Measuring the skill of identifying a central issue

The process of problem solving requires the skill of identifying a central issue. In other words, "What is the point of the reading, or the speech, or the commercial advertisement?" An exercise to determine the students' skill in identifying a central issue or problem might have the students read a short paragraph and choose a main idea.

The following is a behavioural objective from which the multiple-choice question has been drawn.

> Having read a passage, the student will be able to choose the main idea on a multiple-choice evaluation no less than three-quarters of the time.

I'm not complaining. Teaching is the most rewarding and important career in the world, but I hope in my lifetime that the teaching profession will be elevated to the respectable position now given medicine and law. Believe it or not, every doctor and lawyer was once in primary school.

Choose the main idea from the paragraph above:

a. The teacher is dissatisfied with her work.
b. A teaching career is inferior to other careers.
*c. The teaching profession should be equal to other professions.

1.7.3. Measuring the skill of recognizing basic assumptions

A second skill is recognizing basic assumptions. This skill may be tested by an exercise that presents a problem in which the student is required to compare and contrast, or analyse, information as a way of recognizing basic assumptions.

The following is a behavioural objective from which the matching question has been drawn.

> Given a compare and contrast matching question, the student will recognize basic assumptions at least three-quarters of the time.

With respect to political philosophy, match the word or phrase that best fits the assumptions.

Words and phrases

A. liberal democracy
B. communism
C. fascism
D. both communism and fascism
E. both liberal democracy and communism

Assumptions

1. There should be respect for individual personality in both ends and means of government.

2. The ultimate goal is freedom and equality for all.
3. The right to and value of a political opposition are denied.

[The correct answers are 1, A; 2, E; and 3, D.]

1.7.4. Measuring the skill of evaluating evidence

The third skill calls for evaluating evidence. Often this skill is measured by asking students to distinguish between statements of fact and statements of opinion.

The following is a behavioural objective from which the classifying question has been drawn.

> Given a list of statements, the student will correctly categorize and classify those statements as either fact or opinion three-quarters of the time.

Instructions: In the list that follows, some of the sentences are statements of fact, and others are statements of opinion. Indicate to which class you think each statement belongs by placing the letter *F* (for fact), or *O* (for opinion) in the space provided at the end of the statement. Do not try to decide if each statement is true or false but only whether it should be classified as a statement of fact or as an opinion.

1. Dictators are never happy men. ( )
2. Man is basically good. ( )
3. A high degree of artistic skill was developed in ancient Greece. ( )
4. All men have natural rights of life, liberty, and property. ( )
5. Barbados is to the windward in the Caribbean Sea. ( )
6. An excellent kind of education for boys is military training. ( )

[The correct answers are 1, O; 2, O; 3, F; 4, O; 5, F; 6, O.]

1.7.5. Measuring the skill of determining warranted conclusions

The fourth skill calls for determining whether or not conclusions are warranted, in other words, follow from the evidence. Just a reminder: Notice that measuring the students' skill to draw warranted conclusions is being objectively tested by a multiple-choice question.

The following is a behavioural objective from which the multiple-choice question has been drawn.

> Given a list of items, the student shall inspect that list to determine, or identify, which item is a warranted conclusion.

Instructions: In each of the following questions, there is one of the five items which would be more difficult to prove than the other four. Place the number of that item in the space provided at the end of each question.

1. Which of the following would be most difficult to prove whether true or false? (1) Many plans have been proposed in the past to provide for some sort of international law or government; (2) The United Nations owns only a part of the property in New York City on which its buildings are located; (3) The adding of new members to the United Nations, such as new countries in Africa, will weaken the influence of the Security Council; (4) The United Nations has been unable to settle some cases of quarrels between countries; (5) Difficulties in Central Africa caused much trouble for the United Nations. ( )
2. Which of the following would be most difficult to prove whether true or false? (1) Nearly every large city has rich and poor people; (2) Race and nationality are sometimes confused; (3) Most nations have a national language; (4) We have always had war, but it is not inevitable; (5) For many centuries, women in China were denied the right to receive an education. ( )

[The correct answers are 1, 3; 2, 4.]

Objective and Subjective Type Questions

Objective questions deal with knowledge, that is, those things outside the mind that are real and true. Subjective questions deal with judgement, that is, cognitive evaluation or affective attitudes preceding from a person's emotions or mind. For example, an objective question might be:

Is St John's the capital of Antigua?
[*The answer requires recall of one right answer.*]

A subjective question might be:

What is the best place to live in the Leeward Islands?
[*The answer requires personal evaluation and judgement.*]

Often, test questions are categorized as either objective or subjective. Objective questions are those that we have already discussed: true-false, fill-in, short answer, matching, sequencing, labelling, and multiple choice, while subjective questions are often thought to be essay questions where a degree of speculation and judgement is usually called for. However, not all essay questions are subjective. It is possible, of course, to construct essay questions that call for an objective answer. So it is not always true that all essay questions are necessarily subjective. For example, you could be asked to identify and describe the steps of the problem-solving method in an essay exam, and the correct written answer could be graded objectively.

Objective and essay tests have advantages and disadvantages. Below are listed some strengths and some weaknesses of essay and objective examinations. See if you can match them with the category of test they *best fit*. Put *O* if you think the statement best fits objective tests, and *E* if you believe the statement is most characteristic of an essay question. Write *O* or *E* on the line after each statement.

Strengths

1. Gives an extensive test sample. ___________
2. Is easy to construct. ___________
3. Promotes more intensive and comprehensive-type study. _________
4. Can be made highly reliable. ___________
5. Can be graded objectively. ___________
6. Measures writing, organizational ability, and creativeness. _________
7. Can be subjected to item analysis and further refinement. _________
8. Can be made highly valid. (Does it measure what it is supposed to measure? Is it precise, well-defined, accurate?) ___________

Weaknesses

1. Encourages guessing. _________
2. Is difficult to prepare (construct). _________
3. Gives limited test sample. _________
4. Is difficult to grade. _________
5. Favours the verbally inclined student. _________
6. Has low reliability. (Reliability means trustworthy, in short, how well a test measures what it is supposed to measure.) _________
7. Encourages bluffing. _________
8. Frequently neglects measurement of higher-level thought processes. _________

Check your responses with the correct answers on the following page.

Validity and Reliability

You can check your responses in a moment, but before you do, consider two terms: validity and reliability. These are important terms because they reflect the *quality* of the test. Validity refers to whether a test measures what it is supposed to measure. In other words, is it precise, well-defined, accurate, well-written, based on the relevant content? Reliability refers to how well a test measures what it is supposed to measure. In other words, is it trustworthy and dependable? Did the test achieve its purpose? Were the answers consistent? What you should know is that objective tests such as multiple choice, true-false, fill-ins, sequencing, labelling, short answer, and matching can more easily be developed to ensure good validity (precision) and reliability (purpose) just because these types of questions tend to yield right answers or short correct responses that can be objectively analysed. Validity and reliability are much more difficult to establish with essay questions, which are more subjective, that is, evaluated at the grader's discretion.

Check Your Responses

Objective tests will give you a much more extensive test sample than will an essay exam. Unfortunately, well-written objective tests such as true-false, multiple choice, and matching are quite difficult to prepare because they encourage guessing, rely on rote memory, and frequently neglect the measurement of organizational ability and higher thought processes. Essay tests, on the other hand, are easy to construct and can measure writing, organizational ability, and higher-level thinking such as creativeness. But essay questions have liabilities, too. They give you a limited test sample, are difficult to grade objectively, favour the verbally inclined students, and encourage bluffing.

Key to Strengths and Weaknesses

Objective tests

Strengths – 1, 4, 5, 7, 8
Weaknesses – 1, 2, 8

Essay tests

Strengths – 2, 3, 6
Weaknesses – 3, 4, 5, 6, 7

Four Types of Essay Evaluation Questions

1. *Cognitive-memory* (recall or rote-memorized knowledge)
2. *Convergent* (summarize or restate answer in own words)
3. *Divergent* (formulate in a new way by organizing or inventing)
4. *Evaluative* (forming own opinion by criticizing or judging)

(For action words to use in asking different levels of essay questions see chapter 8, "Practising the Skill of Asking Questions".)

One advantage of the essay examination may appeal to the overworked primary teacher. The essay examination does take less time than any objective test to construct. One or a few essay questions could occupy students for an entire examination. Fifty to seventy-five objective questions might be needed for a similar time period. However, constructing essay questions does take time and careful thought, and of course, the grading time for essay questions is one of the major drawbacks for teachers with large classes. The following are considerations to keep in mind when constructing essay questions.

Is an essay evaluation appropriate for measurement of the course's stated objectives? Obviously it can be, even if you want students to demonstrate cognitive-memory and convergent levels of thinking that call for defining and citing of information. An essay question can require the recall of and proper sequence of events such as in: "Describe, in order, Columbus's four voyages, noting date and places visited." Probably we would suggest that this level of thinking (cognitive-memory and convergent) would be better evaluated by objective-type questions, for example, true-false, fill-in, matching, multiple choice. In short, if the objectives call for the lowest levels of thought, then think of using objective-type questions. However, if the objectives call for higher levels of thinking, such as analysis, synthesis, evaluation, and affective performance plus divergent evaluative questions that call for organizational ability, imagination, and criticism or appreciation, then essay-type questions should be used.

Constructing Essay Questions

What should you keep in mind when constructing essay questions? Consider two items of crucial importance: the content (what the question is about) and the structure (how the question is written). Content determines what you are going to measure, structure determines how well the question measures it. The following four rules are a guide to good essay test construction.

Guide to Constructing Essay Questions

1. Keep the language simple and precise. An essay question should tell the students exactly what is required for a good answer. Words like discuss, analyse, or react are confusing unless they are qualified by some kind of criteria. If students are asked to discuss something by illustrating, defending, comparing, outlining, or summarizing, they have a better idea how to answer the question.

2. Several short essay questions are better for evaluation purposes than one or two long ones. Shorter essays give teachers a more extensive sample of students' learning and thinking.
3. Let students know exactly how the essay is to be scored and how long they have to spend on the essay question. If some questions are to be given more credit than others, this should be made clear. The students should be aware if grammar or spelling are to be considered in the marking of the essay.
4. Do not assume that students know how to write an essay examination. Teacher expectations differ on just what ought to be included in a "good" essay. Be sure to review with students, during instruction, how to answer essay questions "successfully" if you intend to use essay questions in the examination.

Below are some essay questions illustrating the four different levels of questioning. (If you wish to review the four levels of questions, see chapter 8.)

- *Cognitive-memory objective essay question, lower level (cite, identify):* Name the principal agricultural crops of your country. Also cite where they are grown and identify the seasons in which the crops are grown.
- *Convergent objective essay question, lower level (find, describe, summarize):* Find, from the text reading, two important historical events, then describe those two events by summarizing how important each was in the development of your country.
- *Divergent subjective essay question, higher level (predict, change):* Predict what will change, from what now exists in your country, if most citizens were to live to be one hundred years old.
- *Evaluative subjective essay question, higher level (select, rank):* Select, rank, and justify what you believe to be the best answers to the educational problems in your country.

This completes the section on the evaluation in the cognitive domain, which includes objective and subjective testing on thinking and learning. We turn now to the second category of evaluation: for the psychomotor domain.

Category 2: The Psychomotor Domain

The psychomotor domain refers to motor behaviours involving mental or muscular coordination of eye/hand/body/mind in order to effectively speak, write, read, and exercise. Evaluation calls for the objective measurement of performance through oral evaluation and evaluation of student's responses through the creation of an object.

1.0. Oral evaluation: strengths and weaknesses

Strengths

1. Particularly effective with the affective domain (emotion).
2. Focuses attention.
3. Provides students with practice in orally presenting thoughts.
4. For special students who cannot take paper or pencil tests.

Weaknesses

1. Too time-consuming.
2. Provides limited sample unless students are tested individually.
3. Often difficult for teacher to comparatively judge students' responses.
4. Some students are orally gifted just as some students are good at taking written examinations.

Oral evaluation is often limited to students' responses to questions in class and oral reports, but this view is much too limited. Oral can include all domains: cognitive (learning and thinking), psychomotor (which includes physical movement), and affective (emotional). Oral examinations refer to speeches, debates, panels, discussions, participating in a dramatization, play, or simulation – that is, performing verbally before an audience – all of which are in the psychomotor domain, and may also call for levels of performance from the other domains. See chapter on "Applying Methods, Learning Activities, and Strategies", for an oral report checklist and descriptions and illustrations of how to organize and use debate, panel, and simulation activities.

On the next page is an example of an oral evaluation form for students to fill out.

2.0. Evaluation of students' responses through the creation of an object

This is an evaluation technique used to interpret how students' ideas are expressed through creation of an object. For example, the teacher, to evaluate students' psychomotor level of development, asks them to plan and construct audio-visual aids that the students will demonstrate and display during peer teaching or at a school open-house. Examples of those aids might be: maps and globes, posters, collages, pictures, diagrams, charts, graphs, mobiles, models, dioramas, and sand tables.

The creation of audio-visual aids requires psychomotor skills at level 3 (orientation) and level 4 (pattern) in the psychomotor domain. See

Oral Report Evaluation Form for Students					
____________ Student giving report ____________ Student evaluator Check the box that best fits your responses to the statement.					
	Very Weak	Fair	Good	Very Good	Superior
1. Introduction was interesting.					
2. Student related topic to what we are studying in class.					
3. Student was able to make report interesting with personal opinions, yet stuck basically to facts.					
4. Student summarized briefly.					
Comments					

"Audio-Visual Aids for Teaching Social Studies" in chapter 6 for descriptions of audio-visual aids and how they may be constructed by students using low-cost and free construction materials.

Of course, besides the oral presentation and creation of an object, psychomotor also assumes skill in writing and reading, the evaluation of which was covered earlier in the chapter in "Applying Methods, Techniques, and Strategies". We turn now to the third evaluation category, the domain of affective behaviour (attitudes, maturity).

Category 3: Affective Domain – Objective Measurement of Attitudes, Values, and Maturity

Affective questions deal with interests, attitudes, values and other maturity aspects of emotional behaviour. Questions about attitudes and values can be asked in order to have students consider their commitment to given values. For example: "How important is it to know the facts about pollution growth in the Windward Islands before giving your opinion on whether growth is a problem?" Or "Should we try to improve our community even if we know that many in the community will not help us?" Is it important for the teacher to know students' interests, what they think, how mature they are, what their attitudes may be? If so, then how should these affective behaviours be measured? Of course, subjective evaluation has traditionally been done by teachers, by noting students' behaviour and by inferring based on what students say and how they treat each other. Subjective evaluation and inferences about the meaning of students' behaviour is valuable. We now know that there are ways to measure attitudes, values, and maturity.

Evaluating the development of attitudes is undoubtedly the least-used form of objective evaluation in the classroom; yet the maturity of student attitudes and behaviour is often judged informally by the classroom teacher. Actually, maturing students' attitudes is one of the most important contributions that the school makes to the community. The school can properly expect its students to modify values, change attitudes, and develop maturity throughout their years of schooling. These attitudes are informally observed by teachers, but not objectively evaluated; and teachers are therefore often unsure of their success in developing the attitudes they wish students to demonstrate. Thus, educators strongly suggest, particularly when teaching social studies, that teachers be conscious of objectively observing progress that students are making in developing the proper attitudes and values necessary for successful future performance as mature citizens.

Many teachers believe they cannot objectively assess or measure attitudes. This, of course, is not true. The following are examples of means by which attitudes and values can be objectively measured: (1) Attitude Survey on Self-Concept; (2) Evaluation of Students Attitudes towards Small Group Participation; and (3) Evaluating Open-Mindedness. Good self-concept, cooperation, and open-mindedness are all values the school may wish to develop.

Attitude Survey on Self-Concept

The following is an example of a behavioural objective that includes the "Attitude Survey on Self-Concept".

> Having attended class and participated in citizenship activities, students will adopt a positive attitude towards their growth and development as measured by the "Attitude Survey on Self-Concept".

Attitude Survey on Self-Concept

Instructions: Circle the word or words that best fit your attitude about the following statements.

1. I feel good about myself.

   Always Sometimes Neutral Almost never Never

2. I feel good about myself in school.

   Always Sometimes Neutral Almost never Never

3. I feel good about myself when I am able to accomplish my own projects.

   Always Sometimes Neutral Almost never Never

4. I feel good about myself when I am working.

   Always Sometimes Neutral Almost never Never

Administer the above survey as a pre-test, then after several months, administer the survey as a post-test. (Pre-test means finding out what students know or how they feel about a topic before presenting the lesson. Post-test means administering evaluation to determine what the students know and how they feel after having had the lesson.) The difference between pre- and post- is the measured change. The change informs the teacher as to the success of the lesson objective on attitude. If an objective of the school is to improve the student's self-concept, then it would be possible, using the results of the pre- and post-test, to determine if there is a positive or negative change in the student's attitude of self-concept. Besides a self-concept attitude, the school might also wish to develop attitudes and values such as respect for others, tolerance, cooperation, and open-mindedness. All of these attitudes and values can also be objectively measured by pre- and post-evaluation.

Evaluation of Students' Attitudes towards Small Group Participation

The following is an example of a behavioural objective that includes "Evaluation of Students' Attitudes towards Small Group Participation".

Having completed the task-oriented small group project, students will demonstrate, on an attitude survey form (Evaluation of Students' Attitudes towards Small Group Participation), a positive attitude towards cooperative group participation.

Instructions for responding to the evaluation: The following statements are designed to provide information on how you, the student, feels. You may find yourself agreeing with some statements, disagreeing with others. Whatever your response, you can be certain that many other people feel the same way you do.

There are no right or wrong answers to these statements; rather your response simply indicates how *you* feel about each statement. Response to any statement should indicate how you usually feel.

Your response to each statement can range from "strongly agree" to "strongly disagree" as follows: 1, strongly agree; 2, mostly agree; 3, uncertain; 4, mostly disagree; 5, strongly disagree. Circle the number which best represents your feeling.

Evaluation of Students' Attitudes towards Small Group Participation

1. I feel that cooperation by participating in a small group is important.

   1 2 3 4 5

2. Students in my small group contributed to the group's effort.

   1 2 3 4 5

3. I believe that I should respect others in my small group.

   1 2 3 4 5

Evaluating Open-Mindedness

Can the teacher objectively measure whether students are open or close minded? In short, are students ready to consider alternative or new ideas? The answer is yes. Teachers can determine if students are open or closed minded. How? By the use of a survey.

The following is an example of a behavioural objective that includes the survey form, "Evaluating Open-Mindedness".

> Having studied the unit on democracy, students will display an open-minded attitude on an "Evaluating Open-Mindedness" survey.

In scoring items of this type, no attention is paid to the underscoring of any of the three middle words. The underscoring of either of the extremes, All or No, is counted as closed mindedness. This type of evaluation is used to measure open-mindedness, the willingness to accept that there may be another point of view.

Evaluating Open-Mindedness

Topic: "Citizenship in a Democracy"

1. Modern ways of doing things are better than those of the past.

   All Most Many Some No

2. People today are more highly civilized than people who have lived in the past ages.

   All Most Many Some No

3. Democratic governments are better than any other kind.

   All Most Many Some No

4. Citizenship duties in a democracy are good for everyone.

   All Most Many Some No

5. Economic development is best achieved in a democracy.

   All Most Many Some No

Developing Democratic Attitudes through Learning and Serving in the Community

One last suggestion concerns developing positive democratic citizenship attitudes, in the social studies curriculum, that can be measured through observing the students' participation. In this case, participation means learning and serving in the community. In chapter 2, there is a chart, titled "Summary of Developmental Perspective of Children and Youth", which suggests that at the end of stage 2 (age seven), a "child often develops a strong attachment to the country", and between ages eight and ten, a "child begins the internalization of symbols of national identity and the acceptance of positive national ideals".

Developing a sense of community and a shared sense of responsibility are, at times, best developed through a youth participation programme that is aimed at serving the needs of the community. In particular, the social studies curriculum should include some participation in the students' local community; for it is often through community service that students seem to develop cooperative attitudes that are closely related to effective citizenship in a democracy. Thus community service learning (CSL), or learning and serving in the community's programmes, when included in social studies, have resulted in students developing positive attitudes towards their own self-worth. Learning and serving often include projects such as developing a community garden, working as volunteers in hospitals, museums, and other institutions that serve the public. A popular programme has been peer tutoring where older students work with younger students both in and out of school. There is also a youth-elder programme where youth are paired with an older person for specific activities. In short, the attitudes of positive self-worth, cooperation, and open-mindedness that we want to encourage in social studies are often best developed by youth who learn to serve the community. Indeed, the most important lessons offered in a social studies class may not be found in the textbook, but can be found in the local community.

The following is an example of a behavioural objective that includes the "Evaluation of Student's Attitude and Performance on Community Service Projects."

> Students, having been assigned to a community service as part of a social studies programme, will demonstrate a positive and cooperative attitude in the performance of their duties as measured by the Community Service Representative on the form "Evaluation of Student's Attitude and Performance on Community Service Project".

Evaluation of Student's Attitude and Performance on Community Service Projects

____
Community service representative

Instructions: Circle the word or words that best fit your evaluation of the student.

1. The student demonstrated a cooperative attitude towards performing the service.
   Always Sometimes Neutral Almost Never Never

2. The student displayed a willingness to cooperate.
   Always Sometimes Neutral Almost Never Never

3. The student was open-minded as demonstrated by their willingness to learn.
   Always Sometimes Neutral Almost Never Never

4. The student demonstrated good work habits.
   Always Sometimes Neutral Almost Never Never

5. The student demonstrated initiative by going beyond the requirements of the service.
   Always Sometimes Neutral Almost Never Never

Summary and Conclusion

You have constantly heard the message that evaluation should flow from your lesson objectives; but we have emphasized in this chapter that evaluation should not flow only from general and behavioural objectives, but these objectives should also reflect the three taxonomic domains: cognitive, psychomotor, and affective. We have emphasized that there is good test construction and bad test construction. The guides on how to write good test items, as found in this chapter, have evolved from research and experience and from test construction authorities, and represent the best we know about how to organize teacher-made evaluations. Finally, we have made the point that all evaluation is not necessarily objective measurement. Evaluation is more inclusive than objective exams and measurement, and thus subjective evaluation - such as through the creation of an object, oral presentations, the writing of essays, and community service learning - is considered an important way of measuring the growth and development of children. In short, the process of collecting information on both (1) how well the student has grown and developed over a period of time, and (2) how well the school curriculum has helped students learn, is called evaluation.

Looking Ahead

We turn now to a chapter on "Planning to Teach Social Studies", where many of the ideas introduced over the previous chapters are applied to the actual planning of classroom lessons.

- One who hears forgets.
- One who sees remembers.
- One who does learns.

13

Planning to Teach Social Studies

The Planning Process: Annual Plan or Year Plan, Unit Plan, Daily Lesson Plan

A teacher's process of planning includes three interrelated parts: (1) an annual plan, (2) a unit plan, and (3) a daily lesson plan. The first, or annual plan, is the one recommended by the Ministry of Education, and is comprehensive, covering an entire school year. The second, or unit plan, is the teacher's planning based upon the annual plan and written to cover a week or month of teaching. The third plan is a daily lesson plan, usually planning for a single class lesson.

The Process of Planning Is Interrelated

Planning is actually a process, because the annual plan provides the content from which are drawn the unit plans, and the unit plans provide the content from which are drawn the daily lesson plans. The annual plan answers the long-term question: How and what am I going to teach at this age level this year? Unit plans answer the short-term question: What will I teach during the term or semester? And the daily lesson plan answers the question: What am I teaching today? In summary, the process of planning involves thinking long-term, short-term, and daily.

Planning Is Based on Effective Teaching Practices

Eleven effective teaching practices were noted in chapter 3. Of the eleven practices, perhaps six are the most helpful in thinking about how to plan:

1. Goal setting

2. Accommodating
3. Integrating
4. Challenging
5. Reinforcement
6. Providing feedback

Planning should include specific objectives because effective teaching results from a clear idea of what is to be accomplished (goal setting). Second, effective teaching requires consideration of students' needs and learning styles (accommodating). It is also obvious that students are growing and changing as they mature, and those changes should be accounted for in planning. Further, effective teaching integrates new information and knowledge with applied practice and performance (integrating), which means that planning implies the integration of new subject content with materials that were learned at an earlier time, linking the new with the old. Effective teaching also involves a challenging experience which calls for the planning of activities that generate high interest and stimulate the desire to learn (challenging), as well as the reinforcement of ideas by repeating the same idea in different forms of presentation (reinforcement). This repetition needs to be carefully planned through a series of learning activities. And finally, effective teaching provides an opportunity to practise on the basis of feedback or coaching, which means that planning should include an organized evaluation (feedback).

Planning Organizes the Complex Ideas That Need to Be Considered Before Instruction Takes Place

The effective teaching practices, along with other ideas from the preceding chapters, are brought together through planning - ideas such as: (1) growth and development; (2) methods, techniques, and strategies and how to apply those methods, techniques and strategies; (3) audio-visual aids; (4) the three taxonomies; (5) questioning skills; (6) behavioural objectives; (7) the creation of knowledge; (8) problem solving; and (9) evaluation. Teachers cannot carry all the important information about how children learn best in their heads - there is just too much to remember. The reason for unit and daily lesson plans is simply that planning organizes all the complex ideas that need to be considered before instruction takes place.

Keeping the reasons for effective planning in mind, let us turn now to a description of each of the three parts of the planning process: annual plan, unit plan, and daily lesson plan.

Sample Annual Plan Outline

1. *Statement of the general purposes*
   This statement is intended as an overview. In considering this overview, the Ministry of Education, colleagues, head teachers, and parents should be consulted to determine their thoughts on the needs of the children. The overview identifies how the teacher intends to approach the subject. For example, the statement would explain what the suggested method of teaching should be, either the assign-read-recite-test transmission approach or a problem-solving approach, to presenting the lesson content.

2. *Listing of broad topics*
   This is an enumeration of topics and questions to be addressed by the course. For suggestions on specific appropriate topics at specific grade levels, see chapter 2, "The Social Studies Curriculum According to Theories of Growth and Development".

3. *Methods, techniques, and strategies*
   The method would be identified with an extensive listing of possible alternative techniques. Often, it is in this category where a set of strategies is developed. As a reminder of the wide variety of suggested techniques that teachers can and are encouraged to use, see chapter 4, "Methods, Techniques, and Strategies for Teaching Social Studies".

4. *Audio-visual aids or media*
   All the audio-visual aids and media available for teaching this course are noted. These include all films, filmstrips, tapes, slides, maps, pictures, radio programmes, programmed lessons, and any other appropriate materials that could possibly add to the teaching of a lesson. In particular, suggestions would be made on audio-visual teaching aids that could be produced by students and teachers from local resources: posters, collages, mobiles, and models, for example. To refresh your memory, note the many different types of audio-visual aids discussed in chapter 6, "Audio-Visual Aids for Teaching Social Studies".

5. *Bibliography and outside resources*
   A listing of all the appropriate reading materials: books, magazines, pamphlets, newspapers, and journals, as well as speakers or resource persons, and field trips.

6. *Evaluation*
   Suggestions for alternative types of teacher-made tests to evaluate how well content has been learned and remembered – for example

true-false, multiple choice, fill-in, short answer, matching items, essay, oral evaluation, testing through the creation of objects, evaluation of problem-solving skills, and evaluation of attitudes. Remember that a discussion on each of the different types of teacher-made tests is found in chapter 12, "Evaluating Growth and Development: Learning, Thinking, and Performance".

▶ **Remember, from the annual plan comes the unit plan.**

Sample Unit Plan Outline

Why organize teaching according to unit plans? There are good reasons that ministries of education usually require teachers to plan according to units of work. For example, so that teachers can

- plan for individual differences among the students;
- plan to help students develop themselves in the cognitive, affective, and psychomotor domains;
- plan to make content relevant to life experiences, since to acquire learning is of great significance for life;
- sequence planning of the unit so there will be continuity among subject content;
- select methods, techniques, and strategies for continuity;
- organize the unit to help fit method and content to the school environment; and
- plan good evaluation of teaching and of learning.

If you find some of the above reasons as reasonable arguments for planning units, then the following unit plan outline should be of interest.

1. Description title (including age and level for which the unit is planned)
2. Duration: Indicate the length of time needed to cover the unit.
3. Rationale: Briefly state how this unit fits into the annual plan and relates to other subjects and other course content.
4. Topical outline:
   a. the major subject matter content, or
   b. a statement of problems to be solved, or
   c. a series of projects to be completed.
5. Statement of specific objectives:
   a. Outline the specific knowledge (cognitive domain) which students are expected to master (for example, "Know the three major reasons for . . .", or "Originate a plan . . .", or "Summarize").

b. State the specific skills (psychomotor domain), which students will develop (for example: research, note taking, writing, creation of learning aids, oral presentation).
c. Outline the specific attitudes (affective domain) which students will develop (such as being cooperative, open-minded, critical, respectful, self-confident).

6. Teaching/learning activities: The actions in which students will engage to achieve objectives.
   a. Initiating activities (to spark interest, gain attention)
      i. Outline a series of activities in which students will engage to make a successful beginning. Indicate the sequence of these activities (strategy). Activities should be constructed to stimulate interest in, and call attention to, the topic.
      ii. Indicate the time anticipated for initiating the unit.
   b. Developmental activities (to encourage learning and remembering)
      i. Outline activities in which the students will engage to acquire knowledge, skills, and attitudes. Indicate the sequence of activities, or the strategy, in terms of how the knowledge, skills, and attitudes are to be learned.
   c. Concluding activities (to complete the unit): Outline a summarizing activity or group of activities towards which the whole class will direct effort throughout the major portion of the learning period, and which may serve as a basis for evaluating individual student achievement.
      (See chapters 4 and 5 for suggested techniques and their application and chapter 3 for the eleven effective teaching practices.)
7. Instructional materials, audio-visual aids, and resources
   a. Locate reading materials, teaching and learning aids, and materials for demonstration and experimentation which are needed to make the activities most worthwhile.
   b. Locate and outline types of facilities that will be used outside the classroom, in the school, and in the community.

   (See chapter 6, "Audio-Visual Aids for Teaching Social Studies".)

8. Evaluation procedures
   a. Outline the procedures that will be employed to determine where students are at the beginning – a pre-test or activity which measures the students' knowledge about the content and topics to be covered.
   b. Outline activities to be used in assisting students to measure their own progress.

c. Outline procedures to measure student growth in knowledge, skills, and attitudes throughout the unit.

(See chapter 12, "Evaluating Growth and Development: Learning, Thinking, and Performance".)

9. Vocabulary: A list of specific terms and symbols in the unit that will need to be defined or experienced.

▶ **From the unit plan, come daily lesson plans.**

Just as the ministry may have good reasons for requiring planning according to units, they have good reasons for asking teachers to think of planning according to daily lesson plans. Some of those reasons are suggested in the following list.

Things to keep in mind when planning to teach a lesson:

1. The needs of each child.
2. Act as a guide to enable student to be active in the classroom.
3. Should know method and activities for every single lesson.
4. Be flexible – try different methods and techniques (remain updated).
5. Demonstrate what is not being taught; lecturing is not enough.
6. Get necessary equipment ready.
7. Follow time constraints.
8. Get students to know themselves and respect differences between themselves and others.
9. Motivate students to take part (participate) in social activities (develop maturity).
10. Evaluation – focus on missing parts (what student did not understand or comprehend).

Sample Daily Lesson Plan Outline

Keep the ten suggestions above in mind. Each daily lesson plan should contain the following minimum requirements:

1. Objectives
2. Content, method, strategy of sequenced techniques
3. Summary and conclusion and evaluation

1. *Objectives.* A complete objective which is stated in the unit identifies (a) what content will be taught, (b) how it will be taught, and (c) what students should be able to do or know by the end of the class period.

There is a distinction between "general objectives" and "behavioural objectives". General objectives, or outcomes, are broad statements of aims or goals such as, "Students will demonstrate an understanding of how independence was achieved, and of the role of various groups and persons." Behavioural objectives are similar statements spelled out in specific behavioural terms, and suggesting what knowledge, skills, or attitudes are to be learned and evaluated. (See chapter 9 for examples of complete behavioural objectives.)

2. *Content.* Content is essential, but it is not the only part of planning. Content includes the facts, concepts, and generalizations that the teacher will present in class, in short, the topics to be covered that day.

Method. The teacher will make a choice of teaching, for example, either by the transmission method or the problem-solving method, and will specify which techniques are to be used.

Activities. There are an infinite number of techniques that could involve students in active learning, for example: grouping, role-playing, debates, panels, and any of the other 247 techniques listed in chapter 4. The method, technique, and the strategy should be included in the lesson plan.

3. *Summary/conclusion and evaluation.* Teachers frequently fail to "pull together" the major ideas discussed during the class period. Summarizing helps students understand where they have been and where they are going. Evaluation allows the teacher to examine what students have learned, how well the lesson progressed, what techniques worked well, and what needs adjustment or reinforcement at the next class meeting.

Putting Planning All Together

Do you believe that planning is important? All primary teachers are usually required by the school and Ministry of Education to develop a written plan before teaching a lesson. But this does not mean that unit and daily lesson planning are considered important by all teachers. Planning, however, should be important, if teachers believe in effective teaching as explained in the chapters on growth and development, methods, and audio-visual aids. The process of planning that has been discussed here focuses on planning to teach. If you have found yourself (1) agreeing with the purpose of teaching social studies, (2) accepting the results of research on learning, remembering, and effective teaching practices, and (3) reacting positively to the methods, learning activities, and strategies, then in order to pull all this together and to be able to apply all these ideas, you have *no choice but to plan*. You cannot carry all the information from these chapters in your head and try to keep ideas straight while trying to teach a class. Planning is not the only part of being an effective teacher. But surely, lack of planning can prevent you from becoming an effective teacher.

The remainder of this chapter will concentrate on examples of unit and daily lesson planning. The units and daily lesson plans follow the outline suggested above. The four examples of unit plans are based on topics found in most social studies programmes and are specifically targeted at different age levels.

Note: The generalizations and concepts in the following four sample units are found in chapter 10 under the heading "Universal Interdisciplinary Concepts or Themes" and "Appendix". The suggestion is to use these two sources as the place to begin identifying appropriate generalizations and concepts that will be covered when planning units of instruction in social studies.

Sample Unit Plan 1

Topic: Feelings and Attitudes

1. *Introductory statement:* This unit is designed for preschool or reception classes, and also for five- to six-year-olds and seven- to eight-year-olds. Discussing feelings and attitudes is appropriate with topics such as Self, Family, and Living in the Neighbourhood, topics that are usually found in the early primary social studies curriculum.
2. *Duration:* This unit will take five class periods to complete.
3. *Rationale:* Learning about feelings and attitudes can help children form positive attitudes about themselves and others. They need experiences where they can learn to express their feelings. At this age, children are more concerned about themselves, and thus need to learn to get along with other children, to practise sharing materials, and to learn the attitude of cooperation in completing tasks.

   Preschool covers topics on the self, home, and classroom. Topics on the self are Who am I? How am I like other children? How am I different? School topics deal with attitudes about working in groups, sharing classroom tools, and expressing feelings verbally and visually. Topics for the five to six and six to seven age group cover democratic life in the class, feelings and attitudes of love and respect, and feelings of joy for Independence Day.

   The unit *generalization* is "Personal identity is shaped by one's culture, by groups, and by institutional influences."

The *concepts* covered in the unit are culture, institutions, social norms, social interaction, and identity.

4. *Topical outline:* Content

- What are feelings and attitudes?
- How do I show or express my feelings and attitudes?
- Why do I feel that way?
- Who has feelings and attitudes?
- Is it all right to show or express your feelings and attitudes?

5. *Behavioural objectives*
   a. Knowledge
      i. The students will be able to distinguish between feelings by matching a picture of a feeling to the word. The words will be written on the board, and the students will display the picture in front of the correct feeling until they get it right.
      ii. Following a discussion on what feelings and attitudes are, the students will demonstrate brainstorming activities by adding some additional examples of feelings and attitudes to those already written on the board.
   b. Skills
      i. Students will demonstrate good listening skills and identify how feelings and attitudes are expressed by making their faces show the correct expression that is asked for (happy, sad).
      ii. After choosing a feeling, the children will demonstrate how that feeling relates to their lives by producing a visual aid that expresses the feeling. That aid may be in the form of a mobile, collage, drawing, puppets, marionettes, or a flannel-board display. They will display this aid to the class and describe the feeling or attitude.
      iii. Children will be placed in small groups to demonstrate role-playing by acting out various people's feelings.
   c. Attitudes
      i. Children will display a cooperative attitude while working in small groups as measured by teacher observation.
      ii. Children will display an attitude of respect while viewing the visual aids of other students as observed by the teacher.

6. *Activities to achieve objectives*
   a. Initiating activities
      i. Class discussion on what are feelings and attitudes. Students will give examples of feelings and list them on the board.

Students will brainstorm additional feelings to add to list on the board. (This will take one day to complete.)

b. Developmental activities
   i. Class discussion: How do I show or express my feelings and attitudes? Teacher should give some examples of expressions by face, body movement.
   ii. Class discussion: Why do I feel that way? Teacher will start the discussion on the various things that can cause emotion such as people, objects, situations, sounds, smells.
   iii. Students will choose and make visual aid of a feeling or attitude to display later to the class.
   iv. Class discussion: Who has feelings? Teacher will start the discussion on who has feelings, including family members, friends, teachers, and others.
   v. Students will be put into task-oriented small groups and be given pictures of people expressing different feelings and attitudes. These will be written on the board, and groups will decide to which feeling or attitude their picture belongs.
   vi. While in the small groups, students will be given a situation to role-play. For example, a situation might be a child breaking a window. How would the child, or the mother, or the father feel? (This part will take three days to complete.)

c. Concluding activities
   i. Students will display their visual aids on feelings and attitudes to the rest of the class.
   ii. Teacher will lead a class discussion on why it is all right to express feelings and attitudes. (This part will take one day to complete.)

7. *Audio-visual aids, materials, and resources*
Pictures of people expressing various feelings and attitudes.

8. *Evaluation procedures*

- In the brainstorming exercise, the teacher will look for student ability and participation.
- In the visual aid producing exercise, the teacher will evaluate both the students' ability to understand the feelings or attitude they are representing and their ability to explain the feeling or attitude.
- In the small group activity, the teacher will evaluate how well the students distinguish feelings and attitudes and how well they work in a cooperative way.
- Teacher will evaluate by observation, the respect students display towards each other while displaying and explaining their visual aids.

9. Vocabulary: Words that need to be defined will be identified as the unit progresses.

This is an example of the first three daily lesson plans for the Sample Unit Plan 1, "Feelings and Attitudes". Using the unit as a reference, complete the daily lesson plans for the fourth day and fifth day.

Sample Unit Plan 1

First Day

Objective
Children will be able to distinguish between feelings and identify additional feelings and attitudes to those already listed on the board as a result of class discussion.

Content, method, activities
Content: What are feelings and attitudes?
Method: Transmission.
Activities: Class discussion and brainstorming.

Summary and evaluation
Summarize by pointing to board, and naming and defining each of the feelings and attitudes listed. Leave list on board for next day's lesson.

Second Day

Objective
Children will be able to identify how feelings and attitudes are expressed by showing the correct expression on their face when asked.

Content, method, activities
Content: How do I show feelings and attitudes?
Method: Transmission.
Activities: Class discussion and practice showing expressions of feelings.

Summary and evaluation
Review words describing various feelings and attitudes.

Third Day

Objective
Children will choose and make a visual aid of a feeling or attitude to display to the class.

Content, method, activities
Content: Why do I feel that way?
Method: Problem solving.
Activities: Class discussion and construction of visual aids by children.

Summary and evaluation
Quick review of what causes feelings. Check on construction of visual aids by children.

Fourth Day

Objective

Content, method, activities

Summary and evaluation

Fifth Day

Objective

Content, method, activities

Summary and evaluation

Sample Unit Plan 2

Topic: Homes in Our Neighbourhood, Village, or City

1. *Introductory statement:* This unit is designed for five- to six-year-old students. The unit is based on developmental topics that are usually covered in the primary years.
2. *Duration:* This unit will take five class periods to complete.
3. *Rationale:* This unit can be used with appropriate topics in the five to six age group. The focus at this level is on home and school, including the immediate community - all of which are part of the child's personal experience. The focus is also on "The Place Where We Live: City or Village", which builds on the personal and social experience of children. The following unit plan can be a guide to working on a sense of community at the five to six age level.

   The unit *generalization* is "The study of people, places, and interactions of human environment assist students to create their space and geographic perspective of the world."

   The *concepts* covered in the unit are location, shelter, place, human environment, and interaction.

4. *Topical outline:* Content

- Every living thing (human or animal) needs some shelter.
- The kind of homes people build depends upon where they live.
- Buildings are constructed for different purposes.
- Different types of materials are needed to construct different types of buildings.
- Building materials come from many places.
- People sometimes need special skills to build homes.

5. *Behavioural objectives*
   a. Knowledge
      i. Students will be able to recognize and list on the chalkboard, after class discussion, the factors responsible for the differences in the type of homes people in the neighbourhood or village live in.
   b. Skills
      i. Following a field trip, students will draw a map of their local neighbourhood or village and construct a model of the neighbourhood or village on a sand table.
      ii. Following a field trip, students will be able to locate on a local map, the position of their homes, local hospital or clinic, school, stores, and so on, as observed by the teacher.

c. Attitudes
   i. While working in small groups, students will practise attitudes of cooperation as observed and evaluated by the teacher.

6. *Activities to achieve objectives*

   a. Initiating activities
      i. Class discussion at the beginning of each class period: Why living things need shelter and what kind of shelter birds, animals, and humans need.
      ii. Students will listen to a folk story about shelter and dwellings narrated by a grandparent or elder from the nearby community. (This part will take one class period to complete.)
   b. Developmental activities
      i. Tour of local area to look at different types of homes (human, animals, birds).
      ii. Examine pictures of homes in other parts of the world. Are they different from local homes? And if so, class will discuss why.
      iii. Students will draw or sketch types of homes found in city and village communities. Locate their home on local map.
      iv. Students will tour a construction site to examine materials used and watch performance of specific workers.
      v. Class will collect building materials needed for local home construction. (This part will take three class periods to complete.)
   c. Concluding activities
      i. At the end of the unit, small groups will construct, from local resources, examples of successful communities (farms, villages, or cities – whichever is appropriate to the children's neighbourhood or village) practising its layout on a sand table and then drawing a map of their community to display to the other small groups. (This part will take one class period to complete.)

7. *Audio-visual aids, materials, and resources*

- Pictures of homes in other parts of the world
- Copy of local map
- Folk story related by grandparent or elder
- Sample building materials, for example, thatch, sticks, pieces of tile or brick, plank, roof tiles, pieces of timber, galvanized sheets
- Sand table

8. *Evaluation procedures*

- Teacher will look for and encourage participation in class discussions and attempt to draw responses from most class members.
- Each student will be tested on his or her ability to locate home on local map.
- Teacher will evaluate group performance after reviewing students' work on sand table and reviewing students' preparation of neighbourhood or village map.
- Teacher will note how well students are cooperating, and encourage a cooperative attitude while working in small groups.

9. *Vocabulary:* Words that need to be defined will be identified as the unit progresses, for example, words such as shelter, dwelling, and community.

Look at the example of a set of daily lesson plans for the Sample Unit Plan 2, "Homes in Our Neighbourhood or Village or City" on the next page.

Sample Unit Plan 2

First Day

Objective
Children will be able to recognize and list on the chalkboard, after class discussion, the factors responsible for the differences in the type of homes people in the neighbourhood/village live in.

Content, method, activities
Content: Every living thing needs some shelter.
Method: Transmission.
Activities: Class discussion and story telling.

Summary and evaluation
Summarize the need of shelter by every living thing.
Prepare for second-day field trip.

Second Day

Objective
After a field trip in the local community, students will be able to locate on a local map the position of their homes, local hospital or clinic, school, stores, for example, as observed by the teacher.

Content, method, activities
Content: The kind of homes people build depend upon where they live.
Method: Transmission.
Activities: Field trip, review pictures of different types of homes.

Summary and evaluation: Review field trip

Third Day

Objective
Using observations made on the second-day field trip, students will draw a map of their local neighbourhood/village.

Content, method, activities
Content: Buildings are constructed for different purposes.
Method: Problem solving.
Activities: Drawing local map.
Summary and evaluation
Prepare students for the following day's field trip.

Fourth Day

Objective
After field trip, students will construct a model of neighbourhood/village on sand table.

Content, method, activities
Content: Different types of materials and special skills are needed to build homes and buildings
Method: Problem solving.
Activities: Field trip and collecting building materials.

Summary and evaluation
Review field-trip observations and continue constructing community.

Fifth Day

Objective
Using observations from the previous day's field trip, students will construct a model of neighbourhood/village on a sand table.

Content, method, activities
Content: Building materials come from many places.
Method: Problem solving.
Activities: Building a model village on sand table in small groups and drawing its layout in map to show to other groups.

Summary and evaluation
Review of need for shelter, and preparation for the next unit.

Sample Unit Plan 3

Topic: Mapping Skills

1. *Introductory statement:* This unit will be taught to third-level social studies students, seven- to eight-year-olds, and is part of a developmental social studies curriculum.
2. *Duration:* This unit will take thirteen class periods to complete.
3. *Rationale:* This unit focuses on developing mapping skills. The unit will encourage the exploration of the children's local community and will show the importance of mapping as a means of communication.

   The unit *generalization* is "Location is determined by associating a particular place with other places (near to, or far from)".

   The *concepts* covered in the unit are location, place, region, and mapping.
4. *Topical outline:* Content

- What is a map?
- How to make a map
- Uses of maps
- Classroom maps
- Using scales
- Compass directions
- Neighbourhood maps
- Planning a new community

5. *Behavioural objectives*
   a. Knowledge
      i. After participating in class discussions on what makes a map, the students will identify and explain orally, in small group discussions, all the parts of a map previously discussed.
      ii. After viewing the film *Maps and Their Uses*, the students will identify in a written response six uses of maps with 100 per cent accuracy.

   b. Skills
      i. After discussing, as a class, how to map the classroom, the students will individually construct a map of the classroom with 100 per cent accuracy.
      ii. After making their own classroom map scales, the students will, individually on a teacher-constructed classroom map, use the map scale to determine with 100 per cent accuracy the distance between two given points on the map.
      iii. After discovering and discussing directions (north, south,

east, west) with the class, the students, divided into small groups, will follow directions to specific locations with 100 per cent accuracy.

iv. After construction of a large neighbourhood map as a class, the students will individually use given directions to trace routes from one location to another on the neighbourhood map with 100 per cent accuracy.

v. After planning and constructing a new community as a class, the students will individually make their own maps of a proposed new community with 100 per cent accuracy.

c. Attitudes

i. As a member of a large, task-oriented group for the construction of a neighbourhood map and of the proposed new community, the students will demonstrate self-confidence as they offer suggestions to the group, as observed by the teacher.

ii. After assignment to small task-oriented groups to play games, the students will demonstrate, in their personal relations with others, the attitude of respect as measured by teacher observation.

iii. After working as members of large and small groups for the study of mapping, students will demonstrate their attitudes towards group cooperation on an attitude inventory.

6. *Activities*

a. Initiating activities

i. The students will, at convergent and evaluative higher thinking levels, discuss as a class what they think a map is and what maps can be used for.

ii. View the film *Maps and Their Uses.*

iii. Display and discuss the importance of various types of maps as well as what things are on a map.
Examples of maps include road maps, blueprints, weather maps, airline maps, maps of the Caribbean, and world maps.

iv. Guest speaker: A postman will discuss how important maps are to postmen. They use a neighbourhood map to know where to deliver the mail.
(This introduction to maps will take two class periods.)

b. Developmental activities

i. Mapping our classroom. Have the students pretend they are viewing the classroom from a perch near the ceiling, a bird's eye view. Have them construct a simple map to show what the classroom would look like from the perch. The students decide on the symbols, and the teacher should assist in determining a scale. Further discussion of symbols, scales, and map keys.

ii. Using scales. Provide the students with a teacher-constructed classroom map. Have the students use rulers and interpret the scale to answer questions such as, "About how far is the teacher's table from the bookshelves?"

iii. Directions. Take the students outside on a sunny day. Have the students identify the directions of north, south, east, and west using the shadows cast by the sun. N, S, E, and W should be labelled on the classroom walls and on the classroom map.

iv. Treasure hunt. To practise following directions, play the following game. Divide the students into small groups, and give each group a card. The cards will have directions on them that lead to the "treasure" (for example, "Take five steps north"). The students can then plan their own treasure hunt directions.

v. The school neighbourhood. After becoming acquainted with the parts of a map – scale, key, and directions – attention can be turned to the school neighbourhood.

Have the students imagine they are looking down on the school from an airplane. Stimulate imagination by showing an aerial photograph. On a large piece of paper, a neighbourhood map will be made with the teacher's assistance. The streets should be drawn in and the students should construct models of the school, stores, their homes, and gas stations, for example, and place them in position on the map.

vi. Working with the neighbourhood map. The relation between a map and the real world can be established by playing the following game. On the neighbourhood map, the teacher will name two locations, and the students are to trace the shortest route between them and give directions as they go. A toy car can be used to "drive" to the locations.

vii. Additional practice. For additional practice working with the neighbourhood map, the following activities can be used:

- Have one student describe to another student, with directions, how to get from one place to another.
- Have directions written on cards for an individual to "drive" from one location to another.

(These activities will take nine class periods.)

c. Concluding activities

i. Planning a new community. As a class, the students must decide what a community needs. Things such as airports, buildings, stores, parks, roads, homes, landforms, and so on should be included. They should then use construction paper and pieces that are three-dimensional, like tiny boxes, to lay out what they, as a group, feel would be the best community. Then, individually each student will make a map of the new community. It should be properly labelled, including directions, and have an appropriate key. (These activities will take two class periods to complete.)

7. *Materials and resources*

- Reading materials, audio-visual materials, and others:
  Film: *Maps and Their Uses*
  Maps: various types of maps, such as the road map, tourist maps
  Textbook
- For this unit, the teacher will want to bring in a guest speaker. To do this, the teacher will need the permission of school officials, and to write a letter to the guest speaker.

  No other outside resources or facilities will be needed. However, if the students want to research for further information, the library may have additional information.

8. *Evaluation procedures*

- This unit begins with an introductory film about the uses of maps and is followed by discussions of what makes a map. Following the film will be a guest speaker who will tell about the importance of maps in that person's work. The evaluation of these activities will be done in small group discussions. The teacher still observes and participates in each group to see how the children interpreted the materials presented.

Ways for students to measure their progress:

- The games and activities provide immediate feedback in most instances.
- Through the making of maps and comparing and discussing them, the students will realize that there are many variations of a single map. If the essentials of a map are present, no-one's map will be wrong.
- Students will be working in large and small groups whereby they can perceive each other and judge for themselves how much they contributed to each activity. The teacher will use the forms "Evaluation of Self and Group" from chapter 5 "Applying Methods, Techniques, and Strategies".
- Ways of measuring student growth: In this unit, student growth in understanding, skills, and attitudes will be measured by the teacher's

examination of their completed maps and by their participation in large and small group activities and discussions. Finally, the students will be asked to identify, in a short quiz, the six uses of maps that they had discussed in class.

9. *Vocabulary:* Words that need to be defined will be identified as the unit progresses. For example, words such as map scale, map key, compass directions.

Sample Unit Plan 4

Topic: Caribbean Resources, Conservation, and Industries

1. *Introductory statement:* This unit will be taught to fourth-level students (ages eight to nine), and is part of a developmental social studies curriculum.
2. *Duration:* This unit will take ten class periods to complete.
3. *Rationale:* This unit is part of the study centred on the Caribbean that focuses on resources, conservation, industries, production of goods and services, and on cooperation and interdependence.

   The unit *generalization* is "People have wants and needs that often exceed the resources available to them."

   The *concepts* covered in the unit are needs, wants, goods, services, interdependence, and resources.

4. *Topical outline:* Content

- People depend on resources to satisfy their basic needs and wants.
- Human utilization of natural resources sometimes creates social problems.
- Groups cannot use the resources of the natural environment without changing it.
- People must use and protect their resources wisely.
- Every society has its own process of creating goods and services that will satisfy human needs and wants.
- Groups of people in our country depend upon the work of other groups to satisfy their needs and wants.

5. *Behavioural objectives*
   a. Knowledge
      i. Given a list of the natural resources in the country, students will list, on the chalkboard, these resources grouping them under one of the three headings: natural, renewable, or non-renewable.

ii. Following a class discussion on industry, students will be able to categorize a list of industries into primary, secondary, and tertiary or service, to identify goods and services in the country, and what can be locally produced and what must be imported.

b. Skills

i. Working in small groups, students will collect pictures of one specific industry, and prepare a chart or poster on that industry.

ii. After a class discussion on pollution, students will collect pictures and articles on conservation, and prepare a display of conservation techniques.

c. Attitudes

i. While working in small groups, students will be able to demonstrate attitudes of cooperation as observed by the teacher and recorded on an "Evaluation of Cooperative Attitude towards Small Group Participation" chart. (See chapter 12.)

6. *Activities*

a. Initiating activities

i. Class discussion will be held on identifying the resources of the Caribbean territories, their connection to industry, occupations provided by those and other industries. (This will take two class periods to complete.)

b. Developmental activities

i. Students will collect pictures of the environment, displaying natural resources, industries, and economic activities.

ii. Students will take a field trip to a botanical garden or forest reservation to observe conservation of natural resources. (An alternative field trip could be a tour of a local industry.)

iii. Students will separate into small groups to produce charts or posters of industries.

Each group will research a single industry to find out what resources the industry uses (local or imported), the type of workers employed, and the type of product made. (This will take six class periods to complete.)

c. Concluding activities

i. Each small group will display its charts or posters to the class for class discussion and teacher evaluation. (This will take two class periods to complete.)

7. *Materials and resources*

- Pictures of resources and industries
- Examples of locally produced goods

8. *Evaluation procedures*

- Quality of poster or chart prepared for class display will be judged by teacher.
- Group work will be judged by teacher using observation and by reviewing groups' poster or chart at the end of the unit.
- Students will evaluate their own work by filling out two charts: "Evaluation of Self and Group" (see chapter 5), and "Evaluation of Student's Attitude towards Small Group Participation".

9. *Vocabulary:* Words that need to be defined will be identified as the unit progresses. A list of some possible words might include

- resources industry
- manufacture primary
- trading secondary
- imports tertiary or service
- exports conservation

Summary and Conclusion

As you have read through the sample unit plans in this chapter, did you see in those plans evidence of ideas which were covered in the preceding twelve chapters? Did those unit plans suggest that the social studies lessons were a reinforcement of citizenship education as proposed in chapter 1, "Social Studies Is Citizenship Education"? Do the units match the age level of the students with appropriate content for that age group as suggested by one of the four stages of growth and development in chapter 2, "The Social Studies Curriculum According to Theories of Growth and Development"? Do the unit plans take into consideration the differing percentages of learning and remembering for different activities as found in chapter 3, "How Students Learn Best: Effective Teaching Practices to Promote Learning and Remembering"? Do the methods, techniques, and strategies in the units encourage active learning as recommended in chapter 4, "Methods, Techniques, and Strategies for Teaching Social Studies"? Are appropriate audio-visual aids identified for teaching the units as found in chapter 6, "Audio-Visual Aids for Teaching Social Studies"? Is there evidence that the unit plans take into consideration the taxonomies as in chapter 7, "The Three Taxonomies: Cognitive, Affective, Psychomotor"? Do the unit plans make use of the four different levels of questions as recommended in chapter 8, "Practising the Skill of Asking Questions"? Are the objectives written as behavioural objectives as specified in chapter 9, "Identifying and Writing Complete Behavioural Objectives"? Are the lessons aimed at illustrating how knowledge is created, as shown in chapter 10, "How Facts, Concepts, and Generalizations Become Knowledge"? Have the units been planned to demonstrate a problem-solving method as suggested in chapter 11, "Teaching by the Problem-Solving Method"? Do the units emphasize evaluations in learning, thinking, and performance as illustrated in chapter 12, "Evaluating Growth and Development: Learning, Thinking, and Performance"? And finally, do the plans follow the organization as advised for unit planning and daily lesson planning as found in this chapter, "Planning to Teach Social Studies"?

If you were able to evaluate each of the unit plans based on what you have learned from reading this methods book, then you should feel confident about achieving the purpose of the book. And that purpose was to provide you with the basic knowledge, skills, and attitudes required of a professional teacher in the twenty-first century.

Now, develop a unit plan on a topic in social studies for a selected age group at your school. Subject it to the same critical questions asked above.

▶ *We learn and remember*

10 per cent of what we hear
15 per cent of what we see
20 per cent of what we both see and hear
40 per cent of what we discuss with others
80 per cent of what we experience directly or practise
90 per cent of what we attempt to teach others

Glossary

Abstract: A mental image in the mind only that summarizes an idea or experience. (See *Concrete.*)

Acculturation: The process of cultural change in which more or less continuous contact between two or more culturally distinct groups results in one group taking over elements of the culture of the other group or groups.

Action words: Words found in a taxonomy that specify an observable behaviour.

Authentic evaluation: Judging student's performance based on actual class work and experiential activities, usually placed in a portfolio.

Authentic teaching and learning: Related to the problem-solving process, meaning genuine or real-life problem-solving activities and in-depth investigations.

Adaptation: Adjustment or development of physical structure or behaviour patterns in response to natural or cultural environment.

Affective taxonomy: One of the classifications of educational objectives. The objective in this classification describes changes in interests, attitudes, and values, and the development of appreciation and maturing behaviour.

Anthropology: The social science discipline that is built around studying the culture of various groups of people.

Articulation: A term used in curriculum development referring to continuity and communication across and between lower and upper levels of instruction.

Attitudes: Patterns of thinking that influence the way people react to their natural or cultural environment. Attitudes may be based on emotions or on reason, or both. A term referring to acquired tendencies to respond in certain ways to certain situations, persons, events, or ideas.

Authority: The right to determine or otherwise settle issues or disputes; to control, command, or rule.

Basic needs: What is important for survival; food, clothing, shelter.

Behaviour (innate): Patterns of response resulting from factors built into people from birth.

Behaviour (learned): Patterns of response resulting from experiences and information acquired after birth (socialization).

Beliefs: An acceptance of the truth of something without positive proof.

Case study: A mode of analysis that views any social unit as a whole, such as an individual, family, institution, association or a society. The variables relevant in the given case make it possible to develop an understanding of a class or type of phenomena by the full description and detailed analysis of one or a series of cases belonging to that class.

Change (cultural): Basic alternations in a society's general attitudes or way of life.

Change (social): Alterations in people's day-to-day patterns of living in groups or communities.

Citizenship: Membership in a nation, with attendant rights and responsibilities. In recent years, the meaning of citizenship includes family, community, or any group to which the individual belongs.

Civilization: The total culture or social organization of a specific group of people.

Cognitive-memory questions: Cognitive means knowledge, so cognitive-memory means memorized knowledge. Questions of this type seek one right answer, which usually requires students to answer with factual information or definitions relying on recall or recognition.

Cognitive taxonomy: One of the classifications of educational objectives. The objectives in this classification range from those that emphasize simple recall to actually combining, synthesizing, and developing intellectual abilities.

Collage: A form of picture in which layers of materials form a symbolic picture and deliver a message.

Communication: Exchange of ideas and information between two or more parties.

Community: A social group of any size, whose members live in the same place, and who share political, cultural, or historical heritage.

Competition: Contests between two or more parties to obtain an advantage or a goal.

Compromise: A settlement of differences by mutual concessions; an adjustment of conflicting claims, principles, or positions.

Complete behavioural objectives: Objectives that meet three criteria: conditions for the behaviour, observable behaviour, and acceptable performance.

Concept: An idea or notion represented by a word or term standing for a class or group of things, which may range from simple ideas to complex abstractions.

Concrete: Directly experiencing an event, something actually seen or done.

Conflict: Opposition of individuals and groups, or opposition of emotions within an individual.

Convergent question: These questions require students to establish a relationship between facts and ideas in order to construct an answer.

Cooperation: Activity shared for mutual benefit.

Cooperative learning: Where a group is given a task to do that should include the efforts of all the members in the group. Each student is held accountable for learning the subject matter and contributing to the task.

Creating knowledge: An individual's unique perspective of an experience that brings something (meaning, understanding) into existence.

Critical thinking: A form of problem-solving based on a careful, persistent, and active consideration of any issue, situation, belief, value system or formation of knowledge. It is determined in light of the evidence that supports it and in terms of the conclusions than can be generated from it.

Culture: The learned behaviour of a group of people.

Current issue: This implies a degree of controversy concerning a contemporary problem that may or may not be resolved at a future time.

Custom: Usual and accepted behaviour or practice among a group of people.

Decision making: The process leading up to the act of deciding an issue. The dynamic process of interaction among all participants who determine a particular policy choice. Decision-making studies focus on all factors relevant to a policy choice.

Deductive reasoning: Thinking from the general to the particular (facts).

Democracy: A system of government in which the people freely choose or elect the persons (representatives) to govern them, at stipulated intervals.

Didactic strategy: A teaching strategy that employs a direct explanation of a topic or theme. It is commonly used in lecture, film, or reading where conveying information is the teacher's major objective.

Diorama: A three-dimensional depiction of some scene or event.

Discipline: A recognized body of knowledge with its own methods of enquiry, method of proof, and unique structure.

Discovery: A form of problem solving that involves students in the process of thinking things through and determining things for themselves. Students are encouraged to draw plausible inferences from evidence presented.

Divergent questions: Divergent means to hypothesize or enquire, to encourage a variety of answers, all of which are possible, yet can be supported by evidence.

Ecology: The total pattern of relationships between living things and their environment.

Economic: The social science discipline that concerns itself with the study of production, distribution, and consumption of goods and services.

Electronic world: Technology of computers and software, cellular phones, fax machines.

Emotions: The feelings and attitudes of people.

Enquiry: A form of problem solving as a mode of investigation which rests on a particular activity or strategy that encourages students to manipulate data, raise questions, seek solutions, and thereby determine answers for themselves.

Environment: All the conditions and events that surround and influence living things.

Ethical and aesthetic: The decisions and acceptance within a group about right and wrong and what is good and beautiful.

Ethnic origins: The background handed down through customs, traits, and traditions among groups of people.

Evaluative questions: These questions deal with that area of thinking related to judgement, values, and choices. Evaluative questions tend to force students to organize their thoughts and knowledge to reach their own personal opinion.

Expository: An approach where the teacher dominates in the instructional process.

Fact: Concrete information, has been objectively verified and known as a certainty.

Family: A group consisting of one or more adults and one or more children related by blood or marriage, the adults being responsible for the maintenance and care of the children.

Freedom: Absence of force or compulsion in making a choice or in acting.

Generalization: A broad, overall statement or conclusion drawn from a number of related concepts. It involves a statement of some principle that usually has universal application and is verifiable.

Geography: The social science discipline that deals with the study of the interrelationship of man and his physical environment.

Group: A number of people who interact, communicate and share common interests and goals.

Heredity: Unlearned characteristics passed from parents to children, such as physical traits, innate ability.

History: The social science or humanities discipline concerned with the study, recording, and examination of man's activities in the past.

Hypothesis: A testable assertion, statement, or proposition about the relationships between two or more phenomena in the field of enquiry. It can be proved or disproved through supportive data.

Identity: Awareness of one's own values, attitudes, and capabilities; self-knowledge, individuality.

Individuality: The sum of a person's characteristics and qualities.

Inductive enquiry: A form of problem solving in which the students are taken from the specific to the general. In concept teaching, inductive enquiry occurs when students are asked to observe particular instances or samples and, from the patterns they discover, group, and label the data into categories. After the concepts are developed, students can make generalizations and applications around them.

Inductive reasoning: Thinking from the particular (facts) to the general.

Industrialization: Introduction of a system of production based on large-scale use of non-manually powered machinery; the accompanying, economic, social, and cultural change.

Institutions (social): Structured or organized patterns of behaviour or activities arising from human interaction in groups.

Interaction: Communication, conflict or cooperation between individuals or groups.

Interdependence: Reliance upon the exchange of goods and services among nations or among several members of a group.

Interdisciplinary approach: A teaching strategy employed in a social studies programme, course, or learning opportunity by drawing upon the structure, information, and conclusions of more than one, and often all, of the social science disciplines (history, geography, sociology, economics, anthropology, and political science).

Justice: The ideal of fair treatment for all.

Leadership: Direction of a group of people in the achievement of a purpose.

Learning activities: Activities that students are asked to perform (such as listening, comparing, asking questions, investigating) in order to achieve learning.

Learning centres: Designated areas in the classroom containing a specific number of stations or work areas where resources and learning aids are provided to guide individuals and groups of students in specific learning activities.

Location: The position of an individual or a place.

Maps and globes: Representations of reality: the Earth, universe, or parts of them. Can be used to locate people, landforms, and other features.

Method: A teacher's overall approach to instruction: either the transmission method or the problem-solving method.

Mobile: A three-dimensional poster which moves, causing changing visual effects.

Motivation: That which inspires or impels someone to do something.

Multi-text: Utilization of a variety of textbooks as opposed to a single-text approach.

Mural: Art work that covers a wall, depicting a single topic or theme.

Organization: A group of people committed to accomplishing some goal or work.

Perception: Use of the senses and intelligence to observe and interpret the environment.

Political science: The social science discipline concerned with the question of how people govern themselves and their interaction with their political environment.

Population: The number of people living in a given area.

Post-test: A test or activity that measures students' knowledge about the content and topics after they have been covered.

Pre-test: A test or activity that measures students' knowledge about the content and topics before they are covered.

Priority: Precedence in order of importance.

Problem solving: A teaching method which uses a mode of enquiry allowing students opportunities for finding answers to questions, or solutions to problems.

Progress: Change towards or away from a desired goal or purpose.

Psychology: The social science discipline concerned with the study of behaviour and behavioural change, learning, and mental development.

Psychomotor taxonomy: One of the classifications of educational objectives which emphasize muscular movement, coordination between the mental and physical.

Race: Large groups of people having clearly distinguishable features – physical, cultural – that differentiate them from other groups of people.

Reading comprehension: Gaining information and understanding from what is read in textbooks or other resource materials.

Recitation: The oral delivery of memorized materials by students normally addressed to the teacher.

Reflective enquiry: A form of problem-solving teaching strategy in which the students are engaged in the process of investigating problems or issues of concern, and are encouraged to analyse what is involved in a decision – asking important questions, finding satisfactory answers.

Region (geographical): A part of the world that has at least one feature in common throughout the area.

Reliability: Refers to test measures that are trustworthy, dependable – a test that has achieved its purpose.

Responsibilities: Obligations accompanying membership in a group.

Resources (human): People and the skills they have acquired.

Resources (natural): Things in nature for which man has found a use.

Rights: Prerogatives to which a person is entitled.

Role: The part played by someone in a particular event; patterns of behaviour adopted by individuals in carrying out specialized functions of a group.

Role-playing: A teaching technique that provides a group problem-solving situation in which students explore the problem, the alternatives available to them, and the personal and social consequences of the proposals.

Rule: A guideline for behaviour.

Scope: Refers to the depth of knowledge, skills, and attitudes studied at a given grade level.

Self-esteem: The respect one has for oneself.

Sequence: Refers to the pattern or order in which instructional materials are to be taught in a school curriculum.

Services: Work performed to satisfy needs and wants.

Simulation: A teaching technique in which a simplified model of a social situation is established so that students may work through a specifically devised problem or situation, having at hand the materials and equipment needed.

Skills: Organized ways of dealing effectively with materials, problems, or situations.

Socialization: The process by which social attitudes and roles are taught and learned.

Social participation: Involvement or interaction with others. This requires many skills, such as communication and working with others. This is one of the broad goals of social studies and particularly refers to the application of what is learned in class to issues, concerns, and involvement in the community.

Social science: The body of knowledge that has been researched and developed by the social scientist in his attempt to logically interpret human relationships.

Social studies: The integration of social sciences and humanities concepts for the purpose of practising the citizenship skills of problem solving and decision making on social issues.

Society: A group of people having some common interests, beliefs, and attitudes.

Sociology: The social science discipline that concerns itself with the nature, conditions, and consequences of group interaction.

Specialization: The development of a variety of jobs or roles, each designed to meet specific wants or needs of a community.

SQ3R Reading Strategy: A system of reading lessons that improves comprehension.

Strategy: A sequencing of learning activities.

Taxonomy: A strategy of classifying.

Teaching and learning aids: Audio-visual (media) materials designed for classroom use.

Teaching and learning aids approach: A teaching strategy in which a wide variety of materials is used to stimulate student learning. Materials may range through the entire spectrum of educational technology, including such aids as books, films, transparencies, and simulations.

Teaching technique: An action performed or undertaken by the teacher in order to facilitate student learning. Techniques reflect a given teaching method.

Technology: The system through which people supply their needs and wants.

Three traditions of teaching social studies: Refers to the three historical traditions of teaching citizenship education in a social studies programme: (1) teaching social studies as citizenship transmission, (2) teaching social studies as social science, and (3) teaching social studies as reflective enquiry.

Traditions: Handing down of beliefs, legends, customs from generation to generation.

Unit plan: A unit of instruction that deals with a set of ideas and skills related to a particular aspect of instruction. The unit can be divided into short segments, sequentially arranged to provide for individualized instruction.

Validity: Refers to the extent to which the test measures what it is supposed to measure. Is it precise, well defined, accurate, well written?

Value judgement: Judgements which rate things with respect to their worth. These may be positive, negative, neutral, or prescriptive evaluations.

Values: Principles, standards, and preferences that determine behaviour. The result of judgements made by an individual or the society as a whole which determine the relative importance or worth of a thing, idea, practice, or belief.

Verification/problem solving: Requires students to test their knowledge through such processes as seeing and solving problems, making and applying generalizations, and model building and prediction.

Wants: What is desired by people over and above the basic needs of food, clothing, and shelter for survival.

References

Beddoe, I.B., and K. Seepersad. 1985. "Origins and Development of Social Studies Education in Trinidad and Tobago". *Caribbean Curriculum* 1, no. 1: 69–75.

Bloom, B.S., M.D. Engelhart, E.J. Furst, W.H. Hill and D.R. Krathwohl, eds. 1965. *Taxonomy of Educational Objectives Handbook 1: Cognitive Domain.* New York: David McKay.

Bluergenthal, T., and J. Torney. 1976. *International Human Rights and International Education*. Washington, DC: US National Commission for UNESCO.

Goodridge, R.V. 1976. "The Development of Social Studies Programmes for Caribbean Secondary Schools: Considerations and Perspectives". *Social Studies Education,* no. 7 (June): 46–50.

Griffith, A.D. 1995. "Social Participation as a Major Goal in Social Studies: Towards Authentic Instruction and Learning in Caribbean Schools". *Caribbean Curriculum* 5, no. 2: 47–66.

———. 1990. "Social Studies for Nation-Building: A View from a Developing Society". *Social Studies* 81, no. 4: 161–65.

Krathwohl, D.R., B.S. Bloom and B.B. Masia. 1964. *Taxonomy of Educational Objectives: The Classification of Educational Goals, Handbook 2: Affective Domain.* New York: David McKay.

Morris, P. 1976. "Social Studies in Jamaica". *Social Studies Education,* no. 8 (October): 41–46.

Morris P., M. Morrissey and R. King. 1996. "The Development of Social Studies in the Commonwealth Caribbean". In *Education in the West Indies: Development and Perspectives, 1948–1988,* edited by D. Craig. Kingston: Institute of Social and Economic Research, University of the West Indies.

Piaget, J. 1970. *Science Education and the Psychology of the Child.* London: Longman.

State of California. 1975. *Developing Useful Objectives: California Evaluation Improvement Project.* Sacramento: State Department of Education.